Love
Warriors

The Rise of the
Marriage Equality Movement
and Why It Will Prevail

— • —

DAVINA KOTULSKI PH.D.

TABLE OF CONTENTS

SECTION EIGHT: REPEALING DOMA AND PROP 8

Dedication

To my lawfully wedded wife, Molly McKay-thank you for your love, your support, and for championing our marriage and marriage equality.

To all the volunteers of Marriage Equality USA-thank you for selflessly sharing your stories, your time, your resources. Your dedication is changing the world!

To all my readers-together we can bring more love into the world and uplift humanity.

To Tuck and Patti the original Love Warriors.

Introduction

On June 26, 2003, the United States Supreme Court struck down all the remaining state laws that found homosexuality to be a crime. In the historic *Lawrence v. Texas* decision, Supreme Court Justice, Anthony Kennedy, wrote "Times can blind us to certain truths and later generations can see that laws once thought necessary and proper in fact serve only to oppress. As the Constitution endures, persons in every generation can invoke its principles in their own search for greater freedom."

Most Americans today clearly see that laws that once allowed slavery, denied women the right to vote, upheld the internment of Japanese Americans during World War II, and supported segregation and anti-miscegenation were unjust and wrong. However, during the eras in which these laws were in effect, the majority of American society supported and defended them as necessary, proper, and for the good of the nation.

Today, we are at a pivotal moment with regard to equality for lesbian, gay, bisexual, and transgender people. Once "live and let live" was considered a generous mindset towards gays and lesbians. Our position however has advanced, and we recognize what the President of the United States, Barack Obama, acknowledged at the Human Rights Campaign Dinner on October 10, 2009, that "relationships between two men or two women are just as real and admirable as relationships between a man and a woman." And, I would add, worthy of the same respect, relationship recognition, and equality under the law.

As our vision as a country expands, we can see too how in our generation certain "laws once thought necessary and proper in fact serve only to oppress," and how we have the opportunity to remove the barriers to equality and end unnecessary suffering. The time has come to end discriminatory barriers banning same-sex couples from civil marriage and allow Lesbian, Gay, Bisexual, and Transgender (LGBT) people the opportunity to live full and equal lives.

"By creating a legal – and, subsequently, a social and economic – barrier between one segment of the society and the rest of us, we create all sorts of resentments, hardships and pathologies. Most fundamentally, we propagate an unjust society, which exacts untold costs for generations."

—Former Speaker of the California Assembly and Former Mayor of San Francisco, Willie Brown

LIBERTY AND JUSTICE FOR ALL!

In the United States, there are more than a thousand federal rights and hundreds of state rights that are automatically bestowed with a civil marriage license. Every time a heterosexual couple says "I do" and receives a marriage license from their state, both partners are automatically granted access to the 1,138 federal marriage rights. Their marriage license is also automatically recognized in all 50 states because of the equal protection clause and full faith and credit clause of the U.S. Constitution which grants access to the hundreds of rights that each state provides to married couples. Regardless of where you were married, if you are heterosexual, your marriage license is recognized in all U.S. states, territories and on Indian reservations, and world-wide.

Same-sex couples simply want what your run-of-the-mill marriage-license-carrying heterosexual couple has access to:

- a marriage license
- the hundreds of state rights that come with marriage
- the 1,138 federal rights that come with marriage
- the right to have our marriages recognized in all 50 states and the right to marry in all 50 states
- all the benefits, responsibilities and obligations that come

with marriage
- the same dignity, recognition, and universally understood status for our relationships.

ONLY IMMEDIATE FAMILY ALLOWED!

Presently we live in a society where heterosexual married couples can take their relationship protections for granted, while same-sex couples face uncertainty. In some regions same-sex couples may be granted some rights through alternative-to-marriage relationship status, but denied those same rights in another locale. Marriage means not having to wonder if you are still considered married when you leave Iowa to vacation in Virginia. If there is a medical emergency, wondering whether you'll be denied the right to be with your spouse at the hospital or the right to make medical decisions for them. It means not having to worry that if, God forbid, your loved one dies when you are on vacation, whether you will be denied the right to claim your spouse's body.

But because same-sex couples are denied access to marriage they do have to worry about being denied these rights. Take the real-life story of San Francisco couple Bill Flanigan and Robert Daniel who were traveling from San Francisco to Washington, DC for a family vacation when Robert became suddenly ill with complications from AIDS. He was taken to the DC hospital where Bill was recognized as kin and even spent the night at his bedside. However, as Robert's condition worsened, he was transferred to the Maryland Shock Trauma Center where he arrived unconscious. Bill advised the staff that he had medical power of attorney rights and that the couple was registered as domestic partners in California. The hospital staff told Bill that Maryland did not recognize domestic partnerships and that unless he could produce the advanced medical directive he should go sit down in the waiting room and call Robert's family.

Numerous heterosexual couples have told me that they've never had to produce a marriage license or an advanced health care directive to access an emergency room when their spouse was being admitted. Heterosexuals can simply declare they are a married couple. My friends, Tim and Barb, had a religious marriage ceremony but never filed for a marriage license. They've never been asked for proof of their marriage and they've made numerous trips to the hospital in the forty years they've been together.

Since the advanced medical directive was kept where most of us keep our important documents, in a filing cabinet back home, Bill sat in the waiting room for four hours and watched helplessly as other people were admitted inside as "family" while he was not. He was not even given the opportunity to talk with the doctors about Robert's wishes, nor given an update on Robert's condition. Time was of the essence, so he got on the phone and called Robert's mother, explained the situation, and asked her to come to Maryland immediately. When she arrived, the hospital staff provided her with the information they had denied Bill. Only after she affirmed that Bill was the designated power of attorney for Robert, did they finally allow Bill back to see Robert.

> *"Bill and Bobby were soulmates and one of the best couples I've known. They loved each other, took care of each other, came to family holidays as a couple, and Bill still babysits for my grandson. If that isn't family, then something is very wrong. When someone is dying, hospitals should be bringing families together rather than keeping them apart."*
> —Mrs. Daniel, Robert Daniel's Mother

But it was too late. Robert had already died. He had died alone, while Bill sat in the waiting room, denied the respect shown other family members and denied the simple, yet priceless, act of being able to hold his loved one's hand as he passed. Since Bill was not allowed at his bedside, he was also unable to carry out Robert's last wishes, and to his dismay, Robert had had procedures done that he had expressly not wanted.

This situation was beyond disrespectful, it was cruel. And it was perfectly legal. Bill and Robert's mother sued the hospital, but the court ruled that the hospital staff was only following policy that did not recognize same-sex partners as family, regardless of the fact that they were registered domestic partners in another state.

It is unfair that even when same-sex couples take extra steps to create family protections automatically bestowed to heterosexuals with marriage, they are treated as second-class citizens at the whim of anyone simply following an impersonal policy.

MARRIAGE HAS ITS PRIVILEGES.

"Marriage laws and rules weave a much more delicate and invisible web than most of us know. 'Married' is a shorthand taken seriously by banks, insurers courts, employers schools, hospitals, cemeteries, rental car companies, frequent flyer programs, and more."

—E.J., Graff, author of "What is Marriage For?"

And then there are the everyday realities of not being treated equally. A gay man waiting at the rental car counter notices that he is paying extra to put his "partner" down as a second driver, while the heterosexual man next to him pays nothing extra because his wife has automatic driving privileges under state law. A lesbian couple's joint checking account statement shows two separate charges from their local gym because they don't qualify for the discounted family membership. And the car insurance commercials remind same-sex couples of the money they could be saving if they only had access to the auto insurance marriage discounts in their state.

In this book you will learn more about the thousands of rights, responsibilities, and obligations that come with marriage and understand why same-sex couples and their families need access to civil marriage too. If marriage for same-sex couples feels like too radical a change, or if you're on the fence and unsure which direction to move, I trust that by reading this book you will have a better understanding of the ways in which marital status and the rights of marriage are intertwined in all aspects of our culture. You will learn how denying same-sex couples entry into this institution hurts them and their families in tangible ways.

Whether you have been a passive supporter or an active ally in the marriage equality movement, what I call a "love warrior" for equality, this book will help you take your talking points, your commitment, and your strategy to win marriage equality to the next level. For everyone, this book will give you a greater appreciation and understanding of the institution of marriage, so you will know what you're getting yourself into when you say "I do."

As you read this book, I trust that your heart and mind will be opened to why marriage equality for same-sex couples is a basic issue of fairness, equality, and justice. As Dr. Rev. Martin Luther King, Jr. said, "All life is interrelated. We are caught in an inescapable network of mutuality, tied in a single garment of destiny... strangely enough I can never be what I ought to be until you are what you ought to be. You can never be what you ought to be until I am what I ought to be. This is the way the world is made. I didn't make it that way, but this is the way, the interrelated structure of reality."

A NOTE ON TERMINOLOGY AND DISCRIMINATION

Because laws differ widely on whether or not they recognize a person's transition from male to female or female to male, winning marriage equality for same-sex couples would allow transgender and intersexed people to marry whomever they chose, regardless of their own or their partner's gender identity or birth sex. Therefore, even though the terms, *gay marriage, same-sex marriage, gay, gay couples,* and *same-sex couples* are employed, they are meant to be inclusive of marriage in which one or both partners are bisexual, transsexual or intersexed.

Additionally, while the term "gay" implies someone who only romantically loves and is attracted to members of his/her sex, in this context, it is meant to include bisexual men and women in same-sex relationships and marriages.

When discussing the discrimination that Lesbian, Gay, Bisexual, Transgender and Intersexed people face today I will make references to patterns of discrimination and propaganda used to justify discrimination against other populations who are/ were discriminated against because their race, religion, ethnicity, etc. It is not my intent to compare groups' levels of discrimination or in any way say the suffering of gay people is more, less, or equal to that of any racial or ethnic group. Or, to say that homophobia and heterosexism are the direct equivalent to racism.

My perspective is similar to Martin Luther King, Jr's that "injustice anywhere is a threat to justice everywhere," and discrimination must not go unchecked in any aspect of life. We should continue to work to create a world where all people are treated equally regardless of race, religion, sex, gender, ethnicity, ability, sexual orientation, gender expression, etc. For those who would wish to argue the impact and level of discrimination faced by gay people is either less or more compared to other groups, I remind you that while you are busy debating, discrimination is going unchallenged. Let's get busy.

> "*There is not any room in American society for discrimination based on sexual orientation. We're one people; we're one family, the American family... discrimination is discrimination and we have to speak up and speak out against discrimination...Martin Luther King Jr. use to say 'races don't fall in love and get married; individuals fall in love and get married.' So if two men or two women fall in love and get married it's their business... Love is love. It is better to love than to hate, it is better to be together than to be divided.*"
>
> —Congressman John Lewis[1]

---

1 Interview with Gay Agenda

SECTION ONE:
LAW AND HISTORY

CHAPTER ONE:
CIVIL MARRIAGE AND RELIGIOUS FREEDOM

"The separation of church and state is one of the founding principles of our democracy. However, I have always believed that our public space is large enough to accommodate and respect religious freedoms while ensuring civil equality under the law for all citizens. This bill successfully balances these requirements."

–Washington D.C. Councilmember, David Catania, speaking about the "Religious Freedom and Civil Marriage Equality Amendment Act of 2009" enacted into law by the Washington D.C. Council on December 18, 2009

Aside from homophobia, one of the biggest challenges to getting marriage equality in the United States is the confusion between religious and civil marriage. Understanding the distinction between the civil contract, (the marriage license issued and regulated by the government), versus respecting the various religious rites, (beliefs and traditions that are incorporated into many people's marriage ceremonies) is critical to finding our way through this seemingly intractable conundrum.

SEPARATION OF CHURCH AND STATE

America is a democracy, not a theocracy. The founding fathers of the United States drafted into the First Amendment of the Constitution the guarantee that its citizens would have the right to worship as they choose unfettered by government influence, and conversely, that government would not endorse or sanction one religious view over others. Additionally, the First Amendment ensures that religious organizations will always have the right to marry only the people that their religion chooses to recognize.

For example, the Catholic Church is not required to marry people who were previously married and divorced because it is inconsistent with the Catholic Church's position and beliefs about marriage. However, it would be impermissible governmental discrimination for a marriage clerk, who is a practicing Catholic, to refuse to issue you a marriage license because it was your second go at it and offended her personal beliefs. Or, if the United States government refused to recognize your second marriage (or for some, your "third-time's-a-charm" marriage) calling it "adultery" because some religions see marriage as a binding covenant with God that can't be broken.

It would be equally unconstitutional for the government to force the Catholic Church to perform that second or third marriage of yours, just like the government cannot force an Orthodox Rabbi to marry non-Orthodox Jews or a Mormon Minister to marry non-Mormons within, or outside of, their temples. This would be unheard of, as would be the state or federal government forcing any religious organization to marry same-sex couples.

DON'T BELIEVE THE HYPE

Recently, many anti-gay leaders have misinformed Americans to believe that same-sex marriage will take away their religious freedoms and they've used this fear to take away rights from gay people. These leaders benefit from, and encourage, confusion between religious and civil marriage because, in many cases, it has resulted in the government codifying their particular viewpoint and religious beliefs into law applicable to all citizens.

Don't believe the hype. Allowing same-sex couples the right to civil marriage has no bearing on religious marriage. Religions that choose not to recognize and perform holy unions for same-sex couples (such as the Catholic Church, the Mormon Church, and Orthodox Jewish Synagogues) will still have the religious freedom to choose to perform marriages for heterosexuals only and continue to view homosexuality a sin.

Just as despite strong governmental protections against gender discrimination in the secular world, religions are still free to prohibit women to serve as clergy, and many still do. This has not caused massive civil unrest. A Catholic Church sits across the street from a Unitarian Universalist Church which is a few blocks down from an Orthodox Jewish Synagogue and American life goes on. And in a growing number, some of those religions, already recognize and bless same-sex marriages (such as the Unitarian Universalist Churches, Metropolitan Community Churches, the Reform Jewish Traditions) exercising their religious freedom to marry same-sex couples and declare gay and lesbian people as whole, complete, and perfect in the eyes of God.

The confusion between religious marriage and civil marriage is aided by laws in every state that allow religious leaders to also serve as informal deputies of the state, permitting them to perform and sign marriage licenses, and yet also allowing religious leaders the right to refuse to perform and sign marriage licenses for couples that are inconsistent with that leader's particular religious beliefs. However, it is important to keep in mind that there is no requirement for people to believe in God to get married. Avowed atheists, or even Satanists for that matter, so long as they are heterosexual, can get married today at their local marriage counter.

Because of the ongoing confusion over civil marriage legislators seeking to secure the right of same-sex couples to obtain a civil marriage license have found it necessary to also reiterate the right of religious leaders to refuse to marry same-sex couples. This is not a new right that is created by the legislation, but rather a re-statement of the religious freedom provisions that are already embedded and in effect in every State and Federal Constitution.

The "Religious Freedom and Civil Marriage Equality Amendment Act of 2009," enacted into law by the Washington D.C. Council for the purpose of giving same-sex couples marriage rights while reaffirming the separation of church and state and ensuring that religious institutions understand that they are exempt from blessing same-sex unions if they so desire. The "Religious Freedom and Civil Marriage Equality Amendment Act of 2009," restates the religious freedom in the First Amendment to the U.S. Constitution in the marriage equality legislation to address the widespread confusion between religious and civil marriage. The bill states:

- Marriage is the legally recognized union of two people. Any person who otherwise meets the eligibility requirements . . . may marry any other eligible person regardless of gender. Each party to a marriage shall be designated "bride," "groom," or "spouse."
- No priest, minister, imam, or rabbi of any religious denomination and no official of any nonprofit religious organization authorized to solemnize marriages, as defined in this section, shall be required to solemnize any marriage in violation of his or her right to the free exercise of religion guaranteed by the First Amendment to the United States Constitution.
- Each religious organization, association, or society has exclusive control over its own religious doctrine, teachings, and beliefs regarding who may marry within that particular religious tradition's faith, as guaranteed by the First Amendment to the United States Constitution.
- Notwithstanding any other provision of law, a religious organization . . . shall not be required to provide services, accommodations, facilities or goods for a purpose related

to the solemnization or celebration of a marriage, or the promotion of marriage, that is in violation of the entity's religious beliefs, unless the entity makes such services, accommodations, or goods available for purchase, rental, or use to members of the general public.

Similar to the D.C. bill, almost all marriage equality legislation has included the terms "Civil Marriage" and "Religious Freedom" to reaffirm First Amendment religious protections enjoyed by churches and religious organizations and to make clear that extending civil marriage to same-sex couples will not require any religious leader to perform or solemnize a marriage that is in violation of their religious beliefs. It also allows churches and religious organizations to refuse to offer their facilities, goods, or services for the solemnization or promotion of a marriage that is not recognized by their religious doctrine—and there is no jeopardy to their tax-exempt status for refusing to perform any such civil marriage. The language deepens the distinction in state law between religious and civil marriage, defining the latter as a civil contract that requires a state-issued marriage license.

THE REAL SLIPPERY SLOPE: OVERSTEPPING RELIGIOUS FREEDOM

The First Amendment Constitutional right of freedom of religion protects us from having other people's religious beliefs forced on us or dictating how our government runs. However, the issue of marriage equality for same-sex couples has drawn fundamentalists out of the woodwork who believe that their religious beliefs should take precedence over other people's civil rights. There are even some fundamentalist religious conservatives who advocate that all of our current laws *should* be consistent with biblical laws.

Is it only a matter of time before religious zealots start advocating the following biblical mandates for marriage?[2]

"Marriage shall be considered valid only if the wife is a virgin. If the wife is not a virgin, she shall be executed."

Deut. 22, 13-31

"Marriage of a believer and a non-believer shall be forbidden."

Gen 24:3; Num 25 1-9; Ezra 9:12; Neh. 10:30

"Since marriage is for life, neither this Constitution nor the constitution of any state, not any state or federal law, shall be construed to permit divorce."

Deut 22: 19; Mark 10:9

"If a married man dies without children, his brother shall marry the widow. If he refuses to marry his brother's widow or deliberately does not give her children, he shall pay a fine of one shoe and be otherwise punished in a manner to be determined by the law."

Gen. 38 6-10; Deut. 25 5-10

While applying these Biblical passages seems absurd to us today, there are those who espouse other selected passages from the Bible, in order to advocate for a more intolerant society and to take away currently protected constitutional rights for same-sex couples. Religious conservatives are using gay marriage to motivate their base and raise funds to enforce their religious <u>doctrine on state and federal governments</u>, (i.e. posting the Ten

2   *From Oakland PFLAG Newsletter Sept/October 2003.*

Commandments in public parks). They are also finding ways to overstep their "religious freedom" to take away other people's right to be free from their religious beliefs (i.e. taking away the right of a woman to choose to end her pregnancy even in the case of rape or incest).

Stopping the "homosexual agenda" continues to be a great fundraiser pitch and has helped finance the implementation of the radical right's agenda. **According to an article in the** *Salt Lake City Tribune*, **Mormons in Utah sent nearly $2.6 million to California's Yes on Proposition 8 campaign which took away the State Supreme Court-declared constitutional right of same-sex couples to marry in California. Allowing Mormons to freely practice their religious beliefs in their own personal lives is vastly different than allowing Mormons to impose their religious doctrine on all Americans.**

TEST YOUR KNOWLEDGE ON THE SEPARATION OF CHURCH AND STATE WITH REGARD TO MARRIAGE

I've provided a quiz below to help you understand the distinctions between civil and religious marriage with regard to the separation of church and state. Let's see if you can apply the U.S. Constitutional Guarantee of Freedom of Religion in the following scenarios.

1. A Hassidic Rabbi can refuse to marry a Jewish man and his chosen love—a devout Christian woman? True or False
2. The County Clerk can refuse to marry a Jewish man and his chosen love—a devout Christian woman? True or False
3. The state must accept the marriage license for Sally and Steve from the United Church of Christ minister who solemnized their vows and signed their marriage license? True or False
4. The state must accept the marriage license for Sally and Sarah from the United Church of Christ minister who

solemnized their vows and signed their marriage license? True, False, or True *only* in states that recognize marriages between same-sex couples.

5. The Catholic Church can refuse to marry a previously divorced woman and a never-married man? True or False

6. The state can refuse a marriage license to a previously divorced Catholic woman and a never-married man? True or False

7. The Catholic Church can refuse to marry two men because their faith does not recognize same-sex marriages, even if both men are Catholic and live in Massachusetts? True or False or True only in states that recognize marriages between same-sex couples.

8. The Unitarian Universalist Church can't *force* the state to give two men marriage licenses even though their church recognizes marriages between people of the same-sex and performs same-sex weddings? True, False, or True only in states that recognize marriages between same-sex couples.

9. A lesbian minister or rabbi can sign Steve and Sally's marriage license as a marriage officiant? True, False, or True in states that recognize marriages between same-sex couples

10. That same lesbian minister or rabbi can't marry her chosen partner, even if her church or synagogue recognizes same-sex marriages. True, False, or True *only* in a state that does *not* recognize marriages between same-sex couples.

You can find the answers at the end of the chapter.

The History of Religious Intolerance and Civil Marriage Barriers

Laws governing the issuance of marriage licenses have historically been used as a way to limit a person's ability to marry the person they love. According to Stephanie Koontz, author of

Marriage, A History: How Love Conquered Marriage, legal marriage ceremonies were introduced in Europe in the sixteenth century to pass on property and to keep adult children from marrying into families that their parents disapproved of. In the United States, the first colonies restricted and controlled the provision of marriage licenses, but the courts traditionally still recognized cohabitation for inheritance rights until the mid-nineteenth century when marriage licenses were required by the government for the provision of benefits, in part, as a means to discourage and prevent interracial marriages and miscegenation ("children of mixed races").

Koontz noted that by the 1920s, thirty-eight states had laws on the books preventing whites from marrying non-whites, which is an astonishing mirror of today's *31[3] states that have amended their constitutions with language expressly denying the right of same-sex couples to marry* and the ten others that have laws restricting marriage to "one man and one woman." Historically, there is a connection between marriage discrimination and a larger agenda of denying a segment of people the same individual rights, freedoms, and common humanity enjoyed by others. In 1935, *"the Law for the Protection of German Blood and Honor,"* an anti-miscegenation law, was passed in Germany by the Nazi's to deny Jews the right to marry non-Jews. During Apartheid, marriages between person of different races was banned under the "Prohibition of Mixed Marriages Act of 1949" and the "Immorality Act of 1950" made sexual relations with a person of a different race a criminal offense in South Africa.

3   Unlike other states, Hawaii's legislature has the right to overturn the constitutional ban denying same-sex couples the right to marry. In most of the other cases, the only way to overturn these bans is by majority vote.

GUILTY OF LOVE IN THE FIRST DEGREE

"Discrimination cannot stand—not on account of color or gender; how you worship or who you love. Prejudice has no place in the United States of America."

—Barack Obama, President of the United States, at the 2009 NAACP Centennial Celebration.

In 1958, Richard Loving and his wife, Mildred Loving, were arrested in their bedroom and taken to jail, their crime—interracial marriage. She was African-American and he was white. The couple had married in their neighboring state, Maryland, and were found guilty of violating Virginia's "Racial Integrity Act of 1924." They were told that they had to leave Virginia and not return for twenty-five years, or serve a year in prison for being married to each other.

"God's will" was used to justify this discriminatory law. The Virginia Judge assigned to their case wrote in his legal opinion that "Almighty God created the races white, black, yellow, malay, and red, and He placed them on separate continents. And but for the interference with His arrangement there would be no such cause for such marriages. The fact that He separated the races shows that He did not intend for the races to mix."[4]

Mildred Loving and her husband hired the American Civil Liberties Union (ACLU) who took the case to the United States Supreme Court. In 1967, the United States Supreme Court, finally ruled that, "Marriage is one of the basic civil rights of man... The Fourteenth Amendment requires that the freedom of choice to marry not be restricted by invidious racial discrimination. Under our Constitution, the freedom to marry, or not marry, a person of another race resides with the individual and cannot be infringed by the State," and with this ruling, the court

---

4   *Leon Bazil as quoted in the Virginia trial court case of Mildred and Richard Loving*

struck down the ban against interracial marriage in the seventeen remaining Southern states.[5]

However, the sad truth is that in 1968, a full year after the United States Supreme Court struck down this ban against interracial marriage, only 20%[6] of Americans approved of marriages between whites and non-whites according to a 1968 Gallup Poll. The poll also found that the United States was the lowest of all of the thirteen countries surveyed. Sweden had the highest support for interracial marriage at 67%, followed by France 62%, Finland 58%, Netherlands 51%, Greece 50%, Switzerland 50%, Austria 39%, Canada 36%, West Germany 35%, Norway 35%, Uruguay 30%. The second lowest country was Great Britain with only 29% of its citizens approving of interracial marriage.

It wasn't until, almost thirty years later, in 1997 that a Gallup Poll found that a majority (64%) of Americans finally approved of interracial marriage. If the Lovings had to wait for the majority of Americans to approve of their marriage it would have taken almost thirty years until they would have had their rights.

The most recent poll on interracial marriage conducted in June 2007 found that 77% of Americans approved of marriages between whites and blacks. Older people still disapproved of interracial marriage with greater frequency than younger people. (As I will discuss in the chapter entitled *How to Win Marriage Equality*, this is true for marriage equality with LGBT people. A majority of younger people in the U.S. already approve of marriage equality for same-sex couples).

Many comparisons between the laws against interracial marriage and gay marriage have been made as the debate around same-sex couples marrying grows. Kevin Fong, an Asian American attorney who co-authored an amicus brief in support of marriage equality filed on behalf of the Asian American community, drew

5   In South Carolina and Alabama these unenforceable bans nonetheless remained on the books until they were finally removed 1998 and 2000 respectively.
6   Gallup Polls on Interracial Marriage- http://www.gallup.com/poll/28417/Most-Americans-Approve-Interracial-Marriages.aspx

parallels between the anti-miscegenation laws of the past and the current marriage discrimination against same-sex couples. He says that "Constitutional issues are much easier to see with 20/20 historical hindsight." Additionally, Fong states that "examining how Asian Pacific Americans were previously restricted from the right to marry will allow Americans to consider their position and obligation to protect the fundamental Constitutional principles at stake as we again consider exclusionary marriage laws aimed at gays and lesbians today."

Plaintiff Mildred Loving also noted the similarity between laws banning interracial couples from marrying and laws banning same-sex couples from marrying. In 2007, on the 40th anniversary of the *Loving v. Virginia* Supreme Court Ruling, she issued a public statement supporting marriage equality for same-sex couples:

"Surrounded as I am now by wonderful children and grandchildren, not a day goes by that I don't think of Richard and our love, our right to marry, and how much it meant to me to have that freedom to marry the person precious to me, even if others thought he was the 'wrong kind of person' for me to marry. I believe all Americans, no matter their race, no matter their sex, no matter their sexual orientation, should have that same freedom to marry. **Government has no business imposing some people's religious beliefs over others, especially if it denies people's civil rights**. I am still not a political person, but I am proud that Richard's and my name is on a court case that can help reinforce the love, the commitment, the fairness, and the family that so many people, black or white, young or old, gay or straight seek in life. I support the freedom to marry for all. That's what Loving, and loving, are all about."

ANSWERS

1. True   2. False
3. True
4. True in states that recognize marriages between same-sex couples.
5. True   6. False
7. True   8. True
9. True
10. True *only* in a state that does *not* recognize marriages between same-sex couples.

Chapter Two:
The Long Road to Marriage
Equality for All!

"We hold these truths to be self-evident, that all men are created equal, that they are endowed by their Creator with certain unalienable Rights, that among these are Life, Liberty and the pursuit of Happiness."

—The Declaration of Independence July 4, 1776.

The Massachusetts's Supreme Court Decision

Marriage equality for same-sex couples became a legal reality in the United States on May 17, 2004, which happened to be the 50th anniversary of the United States' Supreme Court decision in Brown v. Board of Education that declared "separate is not equal."

Brown v. Board of Education was a turning point in American history with regard to previous disparate educational treatment of black and white citizens. This ruling said that having two different systems, for two different groups of citizens— be it schools or water fountains—for no other purpose than to keep those groups separated, created an inherent inequality. Dr. Martin Luther King Jr., expounded on the harmful psychological effects of separate and unequal in his April 16, 1963 *Letter From Birmingham City Jail*, when he said that the creation of two separate systems leads one group to view itself "with a false sense of superiority" and the other group with a "false sense of inferiority." King also added that "any law that uplifts the human personality is just. Any law that degrades the human personality is unjust."

On November 18, 2003, the Massachusetts Supreme Judicial Court applied the logic of Brown v. Board of Education to their ruling allowing same-sex couples to marry. They concluded that "the Massachusetts Constitution affirms the dignity and equality of all individuals. It forbids the creation of second-class citizens." The court found that the government simply lacked any rational basis for denying same-sex couples marriage licenses and issued a 180-day stay on the decision "to permit the Legislature to take such action as it may deem appropriate in light of this opinion."

However, Massachusetts Republican Governor Mitt Romney and the attorney general proposed a civil union status instead of letting same-sex couples marry. The Massachusetts Supreme Court clarified that the only way to ensure equality was for same-sex couples to be able to marry. They wrote, "The dissimilitude between the term 'civil marriage' and 'civil union' is not innocuous. It is a considered choice of language that reflects a demonstrable assigning of same-sex couples to a second-class status."

The Massachusetts Supreme Court echoed the United States Supreme Court's Brown v. Board of Education ruling in their judgment. And, whether by intention or not, by setting the date for the marriages to begin on Brown v. Board of Education's historic anniversary, they extended this same principle to a new generation in regards to sexual orientation. A new chapter in equality was written and Massachusetts earned its place in U.S. history as the first state to remove the prohibition against same-sex couples marrying.

INTEGRATING MARRIAGE

The 1957 integration of black students into Little Rock, Arkansas's all-white Central High School required the presence of the National Guard as did the integration of same-sex couples into Cambridge, Massachusetts's County Recorder's Office, at midnight on May 16, 2004. The guards lined the outside steps of Cambridge City Hall forming a human barricade to protect the couples trying to get into the building from groups of angry anti-gay protestors who held signs that read "God Hates Fags," "Fags Wed" with a cartoon picture of two pigs, and "Dykes Wed" with a cartoon picture of two dogs.

My wife and I were in Massachusetts on a book tour for my first book, *Why You Should Give A Damn About Gay Marriage,* and we watched history in the making. Fortunately, the guardsmen never had to intervene. Unlike in Little Rock, Arkansas, there were more supporters of equality, than opponents. In fact, that night felt similar to the night that Barack Obama was elected the 44th president of the United States. A significant barrier had been broken and it was celebratory. Exuberant people cheered and threw rice at the couples coming out of City Hall who proudly held their applications for a marriage license (Massachusetts has a three day waiting period). Gay, straight, black, white, young and old, all stood outside Cambridge City Hall in happy celebration for the couples who finally had the constitutional right to marry in a state known for having the oldest Constitution in the nation. Equality was ushered in with flowers, champagne, and wedding cake.

THE CALIFORNIA MARRIAGE EQUALITY GOLD RUSH OF 2004 AND 2008

Only a few months earlier, a newly elected San Francisco mayor, Gavin Newsom, made history by changing the marriage license applications in San Francisco from "bride and groom" to "applicant one and applicant two." For approximately one month, from February 12, 2004-March 11, 2004, same-sex couples from around the world rushed to San Francisco to exchange vows. Couples who had been together for over fifty years, including gay rights pioneers Del Martin and Phyllis Lyon, as well as marriage equality activist Marvin Burrows and his partner of 51 years, Bill Swenor, finally had the right to marry.

Molly and I, who had been going to San Francisco City Hall and other county clerk's office's since 2001, had planned what was to be our fourth annual "marriage license counter action and rally" that day. We were prepared for the pain of being turned away, so we were amazed and thrilled when we approached the counter and were actually given a marriage license by beaming clerks who had sadly told us "we can't" for the previous three years. We were happily married on the steps of San Francisco City Hall, the seventeenth of the four thousand same-sex couples who were married there in 2004.

Gavin Newsom's courageous stand for the equal rights of same-sex couples to marry, backed by the enthusiastic support of the men and women at the San Francisco City Attorney's Office, County Clerk Assessor's Office, and Board of Supervisors,[7] inspired several other elected officials across the country to follow suit. Jason West, the Mayor of New Paltz, New York, city officials at the clerk's office in Asbury Park, New Jersey, Sandoval County Clerk Victoria Dunlap in New Mexico, and Diane Linn, Multnomah County Commission Chairwoman along with three other commissioners in Portland, Oregon all followed Mayor Newsom's lead.

But this wedded bliss was short-lived. Six months after we said "I do," the California Supreme Court invalidated all of the marriage licenses concluding that a mayor does not have the right to change state marriage laws and would need to file a proper lawsuit for the courts to consider changing the laws. All of the marriage licenses were voided and several lawsuits[8]

---

7   The deepest gratitude to Dennis Herrera, Terry Stewart, Mabel Tang, Nancy Alfaro, and Minna Tao for supporting Gavin Newsom in this historic first.
8   Tyler v. County of LA on behalf of Robin Tyler and Diane Olson and Reverend Troy Perry founder of the Metropolitan Community Church and his long-term partner, Phillip DeBliek; Woo v Lockyer on behalf of several same-sex couples.

were filed challenging the constitutionality of denying same-sex couples the right to marry.

Then after four long years, the California State Supreme Court ruled that it was indeed unconstitutional to deny same-sex couples the right to marry and declared that, beginning June 16, 2008, same-sex couples were eligible to receive marriage licenses.[9] The marriage equality rush was back on again. Unfortunately, as same-sex couples across the state were saying "I do," anti-gay groups, with huge donations from the Mormon and Catholic Church, were organizing to pass a constitutional amendment to take away gay people's long awaited marriage rights.

Same-sex couples had less than five months to plan their wedding, get married, and fight a ballot initiative that would strip them of their marriage rights. Our weddings were rushed and our wedded bliss was short-lived. On November, 4, 2008, California voters went to the polls, and on the next day, our right to marry was taken away from us. California was no longer the second marriage equality state.

> " *A guarantee of equality that is subject to exceptions made by a majority is no guarantee at all.* "
> —Therese M. Stewart Chief Deputy City Attorney from the oral argument held in the California Supreme Court in the Proposition 8 Cases (Strauss v. Horton and related cases) on March 5, 2009

Connecticut Welcomes You!

On November 12, 2008, responding to a court ruling that civil unions were a separate and lesser status than marriage,

Connecticut replaced California as the second state granting marriage licenses to same-sex couples. Since Connecticut had no residency requirements, same-sex couples from across the country were finally able to tie the knot New England-style.[10]

EQUALITY IN THE HEARTLAND

Over a three month period in 2005-2006, six same-sex couples attempted to get a marriage license from the County Recorder's Office in Polk County, Iowa. After being denied marriage licenses, the couples brought a lawsuit against the Polk County Record, Timothy Brien, stating that they were denied marriage rights under Iowa's equal protection clause.

On April 3rd, 2009, the Iowa Supreme Court handed down its unanimous 7:0 decision in support of marriage equality (Varnum v. Brien). The Court ruled that "the exclusion of gay and lesbian people from the institution of civil marriage does not substantially further any important governmental objective," and that "the legislature has excluded a historically disfavored class of persons from a supremely important civil institution without a constitutionally sufficient justification." As for why they ruled for marriage and not civil unions, the court stated that "a new distinction based on sexual orientation would be equally suspect and difficult to square with the fundamental principles of equal protection embodied in our constitution." Within three weeks, same sex couples began exchanging vows in Iowa, the heartland of America, confirming that true American family values means valuing *all* families.

Some may wonder how Iowa, a mid-western state, could be the third state in the nation to grant same-sex couples marriage

---

10 *At the time same-sex couples were granted the right to marry in Massachusetts, there was still a law on the books from 1913 that denied a marriage license to non-resident couples if their marriage would not be recognized in their home state. This was originally designed to prevent out-of-state interracial couples from marrying and returning to their home states and almost 80 years later was revived by then Governor Mitt Romney to prevent out-of-state same-sex couples from marrying as well.*

equality. Historically, Iowans are fair-minded people and Iowa has a long record of civil rights breakthroughs. In 1868, Iowa became the first state in the nation to desegregate its public schools, eighty-six years before *Brown v. Board of Education* ruling. And, in 1869 the Iowa Supreme Court struck down a ban preventing women from practicing law which made it the first state in the nation to allow women to take the bar exam and practice law.[11]

Setbacks in Maine

On May 6, 2009, the Maine Legislature and Governor signed a marriage equality bill that was slated to take effect September 2009. However, an anti-gay marriage referendum, initiated and financed by the same people who put forward Proposition 8, passed with the support of 52.8% of the Maine electorate on November 3, 2009.

Marriage equality in the United States

As of July 1, 2010, five states had full marriage equality: Massachusetts (May 2004), Connecticut (November 2008), Iowa (April 2009), Vermont (September 2009), and New Hampshire (January 2010). Same-sex marriage is also recognized and performed in the District of Columbia (March 2010) and when one partner is a member of the Coquille tribe when the marriage is performed on the Coquille Indian Reservation in Oregon (May 2009).

There are also 18,000 same-sex couples who were legally married by the state of California before Proposition 8 passed and took away the right of same-sex couples to marry. Same-sex marriages are also recognized in California (performed prior

---

11 See "One Iowa Presents Iowa's Noble Courage in Civil Rights," publication for more information on Iowa's civil rights milestones.

to November 4, 2008)[12] and in the states of New York, Rhode Island, and Maryland, although same-sex marriages can not be legally performed in those states at this time.

MARRIAGE EQUALITY AROUND THE WORLD

Same-sex marriage is legal in ten countries and growing: The Netherlands (April 2001), Belgium (January 2003), Canada (June 2005), Spain (June 2005), South Africa (November 2006), Norway (January 2009), Sweden (April 2009), Portugal and Iceland (June 2010) and Argentina (July 2010). Same-sex marriage is also legal in Mexico City (December 2009) and Israel recognizes same-sex marriages performed in other countries. Many regions also offer "marriage-lite" alternatives which will be discussed in the next chapter.

Important Dates in the United States related to Marriage Equality

February 12, 2004-San Francisco Mayor Gavin Newsom starts issuing marriage licenses to same-sex couples.

May 17, 2004- Massachusetts is the first state to allow same-sex couples access to civil marriage.

May 16, 2008- California State Supreme Court rules that same-sex couples have a constitutional right to marry.

June 16, 2008 Same-sex couples begin marrying in California.

November 4, 2008-In a 52.3% to 47.7% vote, California voters outlaw same-sex marriage.

November 12, 2008-Same-sex couples being marrying in Connecticut.

April 3, 2009- Iowa State Supreme Court rules that same-sex couples have a constitutional right to marry in Iowa.

---

12 Until Prop 8 is overturned, California family law only recognizes marriages of same-sex couples performed out-of-state prior to November 5, 2008. Same-sex couples married in other states after that date, are entitled to all the same rights and responsibilities that spouses receive, but without the designation of marriage.

April 29, 2009-Same-sex couples begin marrying in Iowa.

May 6, 2009-Maine legislature and Governor approve bill to extend the right to marry to same-sex couples

September 1, 2009-Same-sex couples begin marrying in Vermont.

November 3, 2009- In a 52.8% to 47.2% vote, Maine voters outlaw same-sex marriage.

January 1, 2010-Same-sex couples begin marrying in New Hampshire.

March 3, 2010-Same-sex couples begin marrying in Washington, DC.

August 4, 2010-Federal judge rules Prop 8 is unconstitutional.

CHAPTER THREE:
FOOL'S GOLD: DOMESTIC PARTNERSHIPS, CIVIL UNIONS AND RECIPROCAL BENEFICIARIES

"Words matter. Names matter. We know that from cases like Sweatt v. Painter and United States v. Virginia. In those cases, the Supreme Court held that the injustice of excluding blacks and women from institutions of higher learning that were highly regarded and rich in traditions and prestige could not be remedied by creating new and separate institutions that were lacking those qualities."

—Therese M. Stewart Chief Deputy City Attorney from the oral argument March 4, 2008 held in the California Supreme Court in *In re Marriage Cases.*

SECOND-CLASS STATUS

In an attempt to provide same-sex couples with some of the legal relationship protections that heterosexuals have, while still excluding them from marriage, several cities, states, and other countries have created new relationship categories like civil unions and domestic partnerships. These new status categories do not carry the tradition or recognition of marriage. Not only are they not equal with regard to rights and recognition, they stigmatize the individuals in them who know that they are being denied something better.

Domestic partnerships and civil unions send the message that a same-sex couple's relationship, commitment, and love for each other are less worthy than a heterosexual couple's and affirm a false inferiority. It is similar to how segregation laws, put in place by a white voting majority, sent the message that white people were superior to black people, and justified the unequal treatment of blacks. This might seem like progress for same-sex couples, but civil unions are more like a road block to equality, rather than an alternative route. Domestic partnerships and civil unions are the metaphorical equivalent of segregation-era "colored" restaurant sections and movie entrances that allowed access where it was initially denied. They create the impression of equality, but "marriage-lite alternatives" are a lesser status with fewer rights and protections and everyone knows it.

Additionally, like the term cohabitation, there's nothing romantic about the notion of or the words—domestic partnerships, reciprocal beneficiaries, or civil unions. These words lack feeling and true equality, so they ring hollow.

> "*No one writes love songs about domestic partnerships!*"
> —*Molly McKay, J.D., wife of the author and Media Director of Marriage Equality USA*

DOMESTIC PARTNER: A FANCY WORD FOR ROOMMATE?

> Child: "Mommy, where did domestic partnerships come from?"
>
> Mother: "From Berkeley."

The concept of domestic partnership first emerged in 1979 when the city of Berkeley, California granted its city employees' same-sex partners local city benefits that heterosexuals already had access to under marriage. LGBT people and straight allies were seeking to recognize long-term committed same-sex relationships when they created the term "domestic partner." They wanted something less sexual than "lover," more committed than "friend," more intimate than "roommate," and less traditional than "spouse," so they came up with the term "domestic partner."

While initially, domestic partner may have seemed like a winner compared to the other archaic terms "special friend" "companion" or "roommate," if we really compare them, domestic partner is vague and less defined than "special friend" and at least the "mate" in roommate could imply some sort of intimate relationship. But clearly, none of these terms carries the respect and dignity that describes a relationship that is more involved than cohabitation. Furthermore, the term "domestic partner" completely lacks heart. Domestic partner may work well as a designation for businesses or government agencies to decide who should be an eligible health care beneficiary (something unnecessary in countries with universal health care), but only marriage carries the weight, both emotionally and socially, to describe the level of intimacy and connection of a lifetime commitment between two people.

Unlike marriage, there is no universal understanding of a domestic partnership. Domestic partnerships are a confusing house of mirrors compared to the clarity of marriage. The definition of a domestic partnership can vary from city to city. Cleveland, for example has a non-binding domestic partnership registry that does not require couples to live in the city, and allows, but does not require, employers, hospitals and other organizations to give rights and privileges to same-sex couples that are normally given to married couples. While Miami's domestic partnership registry, on the other hand requires that the couple reside in Miami or one member of the couple be employed by the city and domestic partnership benefits are available to same and opposite-sex couples.

The definition of domestic partnerships can also differ from state to state. For example, domestic partnerships in Oregon are only between members of the same-sex and grant some, but not all, of the state rights entitled to married couples. While in Washington and California, same-sex couples and opposite-sex couples with one member who is 62 or older can register for domestic partnership benefits and are entitled to all of the state rights that married couples have access to. Domestic partnership registries can also differ with regard to the number or type of rights that come with a domestic partnership and the jurisdiction in which the domestic partnership is recognized. For example, a person may have to register as a domestic partner in the city they live in to get domestic partner benefits from their partner who works for the city, then register again with the state to the get the state benefits, and have to register a third time with their employer to be able to give their partner their work-related domestic partnership benefits, such as discounted airfare. And, after all that, they better not move, lest they risk losing it all or having to register again for another city/state/company DP registry. And this gets expensive, compared to the cost of a single marriage license!

Domestic partner benefits can also differ from employer to employer. Kaiser Permanent for example offers health benefits to domestic partners of its employees. The Department of Justice, a federal agency, does not.

Note that New York City requires a higher level of commitment for a domestic partnership certificate than for a marriage license. Domestic partners must have a "close and committed personal relationship, live together, and have been living together on a continuous basis," and share an address before entering into a domestic partnership. The only requirements for getting a marriage license are that both of you are over 18, or have parental approval, show up in person, and wait 24 hours from the time you get the license to the time you have the marriage ceremony. To add insult to injury, if you sign up for the domestic partnership registry in New York City, you only have access to rights within that city and no access to any of the state marriage rights.[13] Further, a city domestic partnership will not be recognized in other states that have a domestic partner registry (i.e. California, Maine, Maryland, Nevada, Oregon, Rhode Island, Washington, Wisconsin).

To make things even more complicated, some states recognize other states domestic partnership registries and others don't. For example, if you complete the Washington State domestic partnership registry, you will only have guaranteed rights within Washington State but questionable rights in other regions.

Some states allow all opposite-sex and same-sex couples to register as domestic partners while others have age requirements for heterosexual couples. For example, straight couples can now register as domestic partners in Nevada, but their domestic partnership rights may not be recognized in any other state that defines domestic partnerships differently, like in California and Washington where only heterosexual couples with one partner over the age of 62 is eligible to register as legal domestic partners.

Important Domestic Partnership Trivia

- The concept originated in Berkeley, California in August 1979 and was enacted in December 1984 giving city employees benefits to unmarried couples of any gender.
- Domestic partnership legislation was introduced in San Francisco in 1982, but vetoed by then Mayor Diane Fienstein. It was finally enacted in 1989.
- West Hollywood was the first to create a city-wide domestic partnership registry in 1985.
- California Governor Gray Davis signed a domestic partner bill in 1999 making California the first state to legally recognize same-sex couples by providing one right—the

---

13 Go to http://www.cityclerk.nyc.gov/html/marriage/marriage_bureau.shtml to view the different requirements for domestic partnership and marriage and the disparity in rights.

right to visit your partner in the hospital. Since then, more rights have been added.

ALOHA TO YOU AND YOUR RECIPROCAL BENEFICIARY!

In 1993, the Hawaii Supreme Court declared that it was unconstitutional to deny same-sex couples the right to marry, but the court failed to immediately require that clerks provide licenses to same-sex couples. This gave the Mormon and Catholic Church, who adamantly opposed marriage equality for same-sex couples, ample time to effectively lobby the state legislature to insert the following language into the Bill of Rights in Hawaii's State Constitution: *"The legislature shall have the power to reserve marriage to opposite-sex couples,"* short-circuiting the court's ruling and taking away same-sex couples right to marry.

As a concession for taking away LGBT people's constitutional rights, the legislature created another category called "reciprocal beneficiaries," which sounds like a bartering service and comes with a tiny percentage of state marriage rights. The reciprocal beneficiary law allows you to designate one person of your choice (e.g. a grandchild, niece/nephew, friend, or same-sex partner) to be the recipient of your health insurance and to have access to other benefits traditionally afforded to spouses only. So, if you are raising your granddaughter and want to put her on your health insurance you would complete a form making her your reciprocal beneficiary.

Reciprocal beneficiaries are a perfectly reasonable alternative for non-traditional extended families, but they fail to convey the dignity, respect, and special recognition of the relationship between two people that marriage does.

CREATING A MONSTER: THE BIRTH OF CIVIL UNIONS

In 2000, the Vermont Supreme Court, like the Hawaii Supreme Court in 1993, determined that marriage discrimination was unconstitutional, but authorized the state legislature to fix the problem as they thought appropriate. Vermont politicians minted a new institution—the "civil union." The civil union is a secular union between two people of the same-sex with all of the state rights afforded married couples, so, it is a step up for same-sex couples. However, a civil union does not come with a marriage license or any of the 1,138 federal rights, and is not recognized in states that do not have civil unions. The Vermont legislature could have just educated the public about the difference between civil and religious marriage and tried calling it a "civil marriage" and allowed couples access to a marriage license. It would have saved a lot of time and money and prevented the mayhem that followed. But alas, the wheels of justice turned slow and took another strange turn on the road to equality.

Nine years later, the Vermont State Legislature, like Massachusetts, concluded that civil unions are inferior and create a second-class status for same-sex couples. New legislation was passed to allow same-sex couples to marry and Vermont no longer issues civil unions.

Unfortunately during that nine year period Connecticut, New Hampshire and New Jersey followed in Vermont's footsteps in their pursuit of a middle ground that would appeal to appeal to both left and right, and instituted their own "civil unions." However, they quickly found these substitutes unjust.

In October 2008, after four years of offering civil unions, rather than marriage equality to same-sex couples, the Connecticut Court concluded in *Kerrigan & Mock v. Connecticut Department of Public Health*, that only marriage equality was truly equal. "Although marriage and civil unions do embody the same legal rights under our law, they are by no means 'equal'…the former is an institution of transcendent historical, cultural and social significance, whereas the latter most surely is not." They went on to say that, "gay persons are entitled to marry the otherwise qualified same-sex partner of their choice," and that "to decide otherwise would require us to apply one set of constitutional principles to gay persons and another to all others." Connecticut began allowing same-sex couples to marry in November 2008. They will no longer issue civil unions after October 1, 2010 and all previous civil unions will become legal marriages on that date.

On January 1, 2010 New Hampshire eliminated civil unions and began offering same-sex couples the right to marry. The state upgraded all existing civil unions to be thereafter recognized as marriages.

A New Jersey Civil Union Review Commission also concluded that civil unions are not equal to marriage and fail to provide couples with the same rights and benefits that marriage provides. The Commission called civil unions a "failed social experiment." Unfortunately, in January 2010, the New Jersey legislature voted down a bill that would have allowed same-sex couples the right to marry. So, civil unions still remain in effect, but only in New Jersey. I am hopeful that one day civil unions will go the way of "colored only" drinking fountains.

MARRIAGE ALTERNATIVES

The laws relating to marriage for same-sex couples are changing quickly. Below is a list of states with marriage-lite alternatives.

Civil unions-New Jersey

Domestic Partnerships- California, Maine, Maryland, Nevada, Oregon, Rhode Island, Washington, Wisconsin.

Reciprocal Beneficiaries-in Hawaii and something to that effect in Colorado.

MARRIAGE-LITE ALTERNATIVES NOT ACCEPTED AROUND THE WORLD AND NOT ACCEPTABLE AROUND THE WORLD

Borrowing from the perceived successes for relationship recognition for same-sex couples in California, Denmark enacted a new status for same-sex couples on October 1, 1989 called *registered partnerships* and became *the first country* in the world to offer legal recognition to gays and lesbians.

Several other countries have employed second-class measures for same-sex couples by creating "registered partnerships," "civil partnerships," "civil unions," "civil pact of solidarity" also known as PAC, and the least creative of all "unregistered cohabitation," which is the domestic partnership equivalent to "common-law marriage."

All of these terms sound ridiculous. They are like cubic zirconia compared to diamonds. Gay people want the diamond standard of marriage, not some cheap knock off. I think it's pretty clear that no one aspires to have a "civil pact of solidarity" with the man or woman they are in love with.

Countries with "marriage-lite" alternatives include: Andorra, Australia, Austria, Czech Republic, Denmark, Finland, France, Germany, Greenland, Hungary, Iceland, Luxembourg, New Zealand, Slovenia, Switzerland, United Kingdom, Uruguay, and New Zealand. Some parts of Mexico and Venezuela recognize same-sex unions and the list continues to grow.

While these countries offer some rights to loving, committed same-sex relationships, "marriage-lite" alternatives are not honored and recognized from country to country the way marriage is. And just as LGBT Americans are not content with "marriage-lite" alternatives, neither are gay men and lesbians in other countries. They too seek full equality under the law and access to the respect and dignity that marriage equality provides.

STEPPING UP TO MARRIAGE

While same-sex couples have had access to registered part-nerships in Norway since 1993 and Sweden since 1995, both countries have determined that registered partnerships were outdated and abolished them. As of 2009, marriage is gender neutral in both Sweden and Norway where same-sex couples are able to obtain marriage licenses.

Marriage equality advocates from Australia feel that civil unions are half-measures too. Equal Love Australia state that "Some people believe same-sex couples should ask for civil un-ions instead of same-sex marriage, but the Equal Love Australia campaign firmly believes that there is no substitute for equal-ity in marriage. If Australia establishes a national civil union scheme instead of removing marriage discrimination, we will be entrenching the second-class status of same-sex couples, opening them up to greater discrimination, and defying a global trend towards full legal and social equality."[14]

THE LANGUAGE OF LOVE

Marriage is not just a word. It's a word embedded in a whole cultural system that we are at once asked to participate in, yet be excluded from enjoying ourselves. Marriage equality is about people, regardless of sexual orientation, having access to the same rights, responsibilities, protections, and obligations as every oth-er married couple. It's about being able to partake in one of the most important adult rituals and legally, socially, emotionally, and for many spiritually, binding yourself to the one you love.

HOWDY PARTNER!

There's a vast emotional expanse between talking about your partner and talking about your *wife, husband,* or *spouse*—roles

---

14 *For more information about Equal Love Australia and to check out their highly effec-tive marriage equality public service announcements, go to www.equallove.info*

that are recognized in almost every culture. Before Molly and I were married, when I introduced her as my partner more than one person thought we were in business together or that I was one of the attorneys at her law firm.

There's no such confusion with the terms husband and wife. They are clear, emotion-laden, significance-bearing terms—honorific titles even—that have until recently been reserved only for heterosexuals. That's why many straight people, and some lesbian feminists, often look aghast when I introduce Molly as my wife or she introduces me as hers. A few people, only minutes after I've introduced her as my wife—and she is my lawfully wedded wife—have down-graded her by referring to her as my "partner," "girlfriend," and even my "friend!" I'm giving y'all one last warning, this is my final polite correction of this faux pas.

When heterosexuals start dating, people watch and wait. Will they graduate from *boyfriend* and *girlfriend* to *husband* and *wife?*—terms that even strangers understand which explains the level of importance and commitment to one another. With marriage, the couple is now elevated in the eyes of their families and society. They are welcomed into a shared network of family relatedness: *husband, son-in law, brother-in-law, uncle*, etc. and connected to a larger clan. Marriage is an adult rite of passage, and a wedding is one of the most cherished moments in one's life.

Gay people should have access to that experience too. All people need to grow up knowing that one day they can access that rite of passage that recognizes the transition from being only responsible for ourselves to taking on the legal and emotional responsibility of caring for our beloved. We need the state's protections and family support to care for each other and to help make our relationships vibrant, healthy, and long lasting. Enough with the myth that gay relationships are all about sex! Our relationships are built on the same ideals of romantic love and committing to building a life together as everyone else.

In the past when friends or family have tried to acknowledge our relationships they searched for the right words. We were asked about our *friend* or our *roommate,* maybe now *girlfriend* or *boyfriend.* But, hey, a *girlfriend* is what you have in high school, or someone you have an affair with, or hook up with after a divorce. A *girlfriend* is *not* someone you've been with for 30 years. As marriage equality continues to take hold, many family members and friends find that being able to finally access the language of marriage is easier than trying to find the en vogue or politically correct term of the moment for their "gay" friends and use the same term for all.

Our families need to be able to integrate our mates into their lives and into the extended family too, and the easiest way to solve that challenge is by giving LGBT citizens equal access to legal marriage so that the relationship and kinship connections are crystal clear. Molly recently went to her family union and after anxiously staring at the poster of the extended family tree, she saw her name with a line connected to my name and it said "spouse." She felt so welcomed and affirmed by her entire family who repeatedly asked where I was. She explained that I was in New York with my mother (her mother-in-law) helping my brother (her brother-in-law) to take care of his children (our niece and nephew), while his wife (our sister-in-law) was in the hospital giving birth to third child (our nephew). See how easy marriage makes things. Put another way "My wife and mother-in-law are in New York helping my brother-in-law with our niece and nephew while my sister-in-law is getting ready to give birth to our nephew. Otherwise she'd be here at our family reunion."

"Commitment ceremonies" and partnerships may initially be less threatening, but there is no cultural prescription for a commitment ceremony. On the other hand, everyone understands the concept and tradition of a wedding and a marriage and their meaning.

"You may now kiss your reciprocal beneficiary!" sounds nice—well, at least interesting—while "You may now kiss your bride (groom, spouse)!" sounds a lot better. Consider "I now pronounce you domestic partners!" versus "I now pronounce you spouses for life."

Chapter Four:
Marriage Rights Your Average Incarcerated Heterosexual Serial Killer Has Access to That Your Average Upstanding Gay Citizen Does Not!

Question: What do a serial rapist, a murderer, a child pornographer, a lifer, and an armed bank robber share in common?

Answer: As long as they are heterosexual, they can all get married in prison, never even have to live with their spouses, and their spouses can still have access to all the federal and state rights of marriage.

Death row inmate, Scott Lee Peterson who killed his pregnant wife and unborn baby has the legal right to marry, as does the "Night Stalker," serial killer Richard Ramirez, who is known to have raped and killed fourteen people. However, Tammy Baldwin, a Democratic member of the United States House of Representatives, and Lt. Daniel Choi, a West Point Graduate and Iraq War Combat Veteran do not have the right to marry the person of their choice.

The U.S. Supreme Court long ago determined that the right to marry the person of one's choice was a fundamental civil right, even afforded incarcerated men and women while still in prison. This includes inmates on death row (Turner v. Safley, 1987).

The U.S. Supreme Court's June 1, 1987 ruling on Turner v. Safley determined that "... inmate marriages, like others, are expressions of emotional support and public commitment. These elements are an important and significant aspect of the marital relationship. In addition, many religions recognize marriage as having spiritual significance; for some inmates and their spouses, therefore, the commitment of marriage may be an exercise of religious faith as well as an expression of personal dedication… Finally, marital status often is a precondition to the receipt of government benefits (e. g., Social Security benefits), property rights (e. g., tenancy by the entirety, inheritance rights), and other, less tangible benefits (e. g., legitimation of children born out of wedlock)."

Therefore, the government is generally not permitted to set up roadblocks or otherwise second-guess whether marriage is a good idea for any particular couple. There is no limit to the number of marriages one may enter into in one's lifetime. There are no laws requiring people to marry for a specific reason (such as love or procreation), nor are there any rules against people marrying solely to upset one's parents, or for money, publicity, or fame. You can even marry your cousin in twenty-six states.

The United States Supreme Court declared in the Lawrence v. Texas (2003), decision that "Moral disapproval of a group does not justify discrimination." Yet, loving, committed same-sex couples, a third of them raising children together, are being turned away at the marriage license counter and being denied marriage rights because religious groups argue that homosexuality is a sin and have raised money hand over fist, to re-write our state constitutions to read like their Bibles.

THE SO-CALLED "DEFENSE" OF MARRIAGE ACT OF 1996

On September 21, 1996, President Clinton, up for a tough re-election fight, signed Public Law No. 104-199, 110 Statute 2419 that expressly denied recognition of same-sex marriages.

This law also called the "Defense of Marriage Act," or DOMA[15] for short, states that the federal government, will only recognize "a legal union between one man and one woman as husband and wife," and defines spouse as only "a person of the opposite sex who is a husband or a wife." DOMA states that these definitions apply "[i]n determining the meaning of any Act of Congress, or of any ruling, regulation, or interpretation of the various administrative bureaus and agencies of the United States." 1 U.S.C. § 7.

Thirteen years later, in July 2009, former President Clinton stated that he now supports the right of marriage for same-sex couples and feels that it is time to repeal this law. Additionally, Bob Barr, who authored the DOMA, also believes it should be repealed.

FEDERAL MARRIAGE RIGHTS

In 1997, following the passage of the DOMA, the United States General Accounting Office (GAO) identified 1,049 federal rights that came with marriage. In January 2004, the GAO recounted and released an updated report noting that the number of statutory provisions involving marital status had increased by 89, raising the number of federal rights that come with marriage to 1,138. The list of federal marriage rights is so extensive that I would not be able to list each of those rights without adding an additional 75 pages to this book. If you'd like to read the comprehensive GAO reports go to www.marriageequality. org and type in "GAO" and you'll find the initial 1,049 rights documented in 1996. For the most current GAO report on the 1,138 rights provided by marriage go to http://www.gao.gov/ new.items/d04353r.pdf

The GAO *Defense of Marriage Act: Update to Prior Report* defines 13 categories in which marital status is a factor. Below are the definitions from Appendix 4 of their report.

---

15 I prefer to call it the "Denial of Marriage Act" or the Denial of Gay Marriage Act (DOGMA).

1. **Social Security and Related Programs, Housing, and Food Stamps**

Includes the major federal health and welfare programs, Social Security retirement and disability benefits, food stamps, welfare, and Medicare and Medicaid.

2. **Veterans' Benefits**

Includes pensions, indemnity compensation for service-connected deaths, medical care, nursing home care, right to burial in veterans' cemeteries, educational assistance, and housing. Husbands or wives of veterans have many rights and privileges by virtue of the marital relationship. There are approximately 93 provisions related to marriage and veteran's benefits.

3. **Taxation**

There are 179 marriage provisions associated with taxation. While the distinction between married and unmarried status is pervasive in federal tax law, terms such as "husband," "wife," or "married" are not defined. However, marital status figures in federal tax law in provisions as basic as those giving married taxpayers the option to file joint or separate income tax returns. It is also seen in the related provisions prescribing different tax consequences, depending on whether a taxpayer is married filing jointly, married filing separately, unmarried but the head of a household, or unmarried and not the head of a household.

4. **Federal Civilian and Military Service Benefits**

Includes statutory provisions dealing with current and retired federal officers and employees, members of the Armed Forces, elected officials, and judges, in which marital status is a factor. Typically these provisions address the various health, leave, retirement, survivor, and insurance benefits provided by the United States to those in federal service and their families.

There are approximately 275 provisions related to marriage and federal civilian and military service benefits.

5. Employment Benefits and Related Laws

Marital status comes into play in many different ways in federal laws relating to employment in the private sector. Most provisions appear in Title 29 of the United States Code, Labor. However, others are in Title 30, Mineral Lands and Mining; Title 33, Navigation and Navigable Waters; and Title 45, Railroads. This category includes laws that address the rights of employees under employer-sponsored employee benefit plans; that provide for continuation of employer-sponsored health benefits after events like the death or divorce of the employee; and that give employees the right to unpaid leave in order to care for a seriously ill spouse. In addition, Congress has extended special benefits in connection with certain occupations, like mining and public safety.

6. Immigration, Naturalization, and Aliens

This category includes federal statutory provisions governing the conditions under which non-citizens may enter and remain in the United States, be deported, or become citizens. Most are found in Title 8, Aliens and Nationality. The law gives special consideration to spouses of immigrant and nonimmigrant aliens in a wide variety of circumstances. Under immigration law, aliens may receive special status by virtue of their employment, and that treatment may extend to their spouses. Also, spouses of aliens granted asylum can be given the same status if they accompany or join their spouses.

7. Indians

The indigenous peoples of the United States have long had a special legal relationship with the federal government through treaties and laws that are classified to Title 25, Indians. Various laws set out the rights to tribal property of "white" men marrying

"Indian" women, or of "Indian" women marrying "white" men. The law also outlines the descent and distribution rights for Indians' property. In addition, there are laws pertaining to health care eligibility for Indians and spouses and reimbursement of travel expenses of spouses and candidates seeking positions in the Indian Health Service.

8. Trade, Commerce, and Intellectual Property

This category includes provisions concerning foreign or domestic business and commerce, in the following titles of the United States Code: Bankruptcy, Title 11; Banks and Banking, Title 12; Commerce and Trade, Title 15; Copyrights, Title 17; and Customs Duties, Title 19. This category also includes the National Housing Act (rights of mortgage borrowers); the Consumer Credit Protection Act (governs wage garnishment); and the Copyright Act (spousal copyright renewal and termination rights).

9. Financial Disclosure and Conflict of Interest

Federal law imposes obligations on members of Congress, employees or officers of the federal government, and members of the boards of directors of some government-related or government chartered entities, to prevent actual or apparent conflicts of interest. These individuals are required to disclose publicly certain gifts, interests, and transactions. Many of these requirements, which are found in 16 different titles of the United States Code, apply also to the individual's spouse.

10. Crimes and Family Violence

This category includes laws that implicate marriage in connection with criminal justice or family violence. The nature of these provisions varies greatly. Some deal with spouses as victims of crimes, others with spouses as perpetrators. These laws are found primarily in Title 18, Crimes and Criminal Procedure, but some statutory provisions, dealing with crime prevention and family violence, are in Title 42, Public Health and Welfare.

11. Loans, Guarantees, and Payments in Agriculture

Under many federal loan programs, a spouse's income, business interests, or assets are taken into account for purposes of determining a person's eligibility to participate in the program. In other instances, marital status is a factor in determining the amount of federal assistance to which a person is entitled or the repayment schedule. This category includes education loan programs, housing loan programs for veterans, and provisions governing agricultural price supports and loan programs that are affected by the spousal relationship.

12. Federal Natural Resources and Related Laws

Federal law gives special rights to spouses in connection with a variety of transactions involving federal lands and other federal property. These transactions include purchase and sale of land by the federal government and lease by the government of water and mineral rights.

13. Miscellaneous Laws

This category comprises federal statutory provisions that do not fit readily in any of the other 12 categories. Federal provisions that prohibit discrimination on the basis of marital status are included in this category. This category also includes various patriotic societies chartered in federal law, such as the Veterans of Foreign Wars or the Gold Star Wives.

> *"The distinction between married and unmarried status is pervasive in federal tax law; this is one of the largest categories with 179 provisions."*
> GAO report January, 1997.

Now that you are clear how involved the federal government is in the marriage business, I hope you won't fall for that "marriage is a state's right issue" nonsense that politicians use to get themselves off the hook. (Slavery was also seen as a state's rights issue when it was politically expedient.) Since seventy-five percent of the rights that come with marriage (including the right to have your marriage recognized in all 50 states under the full faith and credit clause), are federal rights, it is clear that marriage equality is a national issue that requires a national response to correct this injustice. We need President Barack Obama to repeal DOMA and to abolish the laws that keep same-sex marriages from being recognized in all 50 states.

STATE MARRIAGE RIGHTS

That said, let me show you how intertwined the state government also is in marriage. Every state has its own rules and regulations on eligibility to obtain a marriage license. For example, with parental notice, you can marry at age 14 in Alabama and Texas, and age 15 in Utah, while many other states require applicants to be 18. There is no waiting period for applying for a marriage license in Wyoming, but in Oregon and Massachusetts you must wait three days and Massachusetts's officials require that you have a medical exam to rule out syphilis and other venereal diseases. In Minnesota you can save money on your wedding costs by reducing your marriage license fee if you complete an "approved marriage education course" and in twenty-six states you can marry your first cousin though in twenty-four states you can't.

A marriage license entitles a couple to hundreds of state marriage rights. Below is a table of rights and responsibilities that come with marriage in the state of California adapted from a 2003 publication created by attorney Jon Davidson at Lambda Legal. Each state has its own Family Code and laws for what rights and responsibilities come with civil marriage in addition to the 1,138 federal marriage rights. (This is the last chart I promise).

Before you read it, let me begin by saying, "the contract of marriage is most solemn and is not to be entered into lightly, but thoughtfully and seriously, and with a deep realization of its obligations and responsibilities."[16] This is the small print you sign on to when you sign that marriage license.

CALIFORNIA MARRIAGE RIGHTS AND DUTIES

Rights and duties to one another

- Rights and duties of support during the partnership
- Fiduciary duty between partners
- Right not to be excluded from partner's dwelling
- Right to damages for attempted murder
- Rights and duties of support after termination of the partnership
- Restriction on altering relationship by contract, except as to property

PROPERTY RIGHTS AND OBLIGATIONS

- Joint ownership of property acquired during the partnership, with rights of survivorship
- Equal management and control of property acquired during the partnership
- Joint obligation for debts incurred during the partnership
- Protection against assignment of partner's wages
- Homestead protection against creditors of surviving partner after death of declared owner
- Attachment of jointly owned property by creditors
- Protection under rent control laws
- Property interests governed by federal law (such as patents and copyrights)
- State constitutional guarantees for protection of separate property

---

16 Taken from Santa Cruz County wedding ceremony script.

RIGHT TO ACT ON BEHALF OF AND RECEIVE INFORMATION REGARDING ONE'S PARTNER/SPOUSE
- Right to use any necessary force to protect partner from wrongful injury
- Ability to request and obtain absentee ballot for partner
- Ability to appear on behalf of partner in small claims court
- Ability to defend partner's rights in certain civil actions
- Ability to obtain notice that partner is being involuntarily held in mental institution
- Ability to obtain notice that partner who is a parolee or probationer has certain medical conditions

RIGHTS IN JUDICIAL AND OTHER OFFICIAL PROCEEDINGS
- Privilege for confidential communications among partners
- Privilege not to be forced to testify against partner
- Right to sue for loss of consortium
- Right to sue for violation of right of publicity of deceased partner
- Right to sue person who provided illegal drugs to partner
- Right to recover damages against employer liable for partner's wrongful death

PROTECTION OF THE PARTIES' CHILDREN
- Presumption of parenthood regarding child born during the partnership or through alternative insemination
- Judicial determination of custody and support of children born during the partnership
- Ability to authorize medical treatment of partner's children

DEATH-RELATED MATTERS
- Right to control disposition of remains, authorize autopsy, make anatomical gifts, and authorize exhumation
- Right to be buried in joint or family cemetery plot
- Identification of partner on death certificate

- Provisions for handling inheritance after simultaneous death of partners
- Protection of survivor's interest in joint property following partner's death
- Protection against disinheritance by partner
- Ability to avoid probate of jointly owned property
- Ability of surviving partner to collect compensation provided to victims of violent crime
- Availability of presumptions protecting interests of surviving partner under workers' compensation

TAXES

- Ability to file joint state income tax returns
- Ability to obtain tax treatment that takes relationship into account
- Exemption from transfer tax on deed or other writings transferring, dividing or allocating joint property among partners pursuant to termination of the relationship
- Exemption from reassessment under Prop. 13 of jointly held property between partners, upon separation or termination of the relationship or after death
- Exemption from property tax on the homes of survivors of veterans who died on active duty
- Partial exemption from property tax provided survivors of certain veterans
- Unlimited exemptions from federal gift and estate taxes on transfers to partner

LICENSES, PERMITS, AND FRANCHISES

- Right of franchisee to designate surviving partner to operate franchise
- Joint interest in fishing permits
- Ability to inherit partner's commercial fishing license

- Ability to inherit license to run driving school
- Ability to obtain transfer of deceased partner's special license plates
- Ability of veteran's surviving partner to succeed on pending application for farm or home purchase
- Partial exemption from license fee on mobile home or trailer coach owned by and constituting principal place of residence of surviving partner of veteran

EMPLOYMENT RIGHTS AND BENEFITS
- Right to take extended unpaid leave to care for a partner
- State government hiring preference for surviving partners of veterans and partners of disabled veterans

NON-TAX FINANCIAL MATTERS
- Consideration of partner's income and need for support in determining student financial aid
- Exemption of current or former partners from requirements upon transfers of real property
- Prohibition on acceleration of mortgage on transfer to partner
- Coverage of partner as an insured under auto insurance policies
- Tuition fee exemption for surviving partners of veterans
- Education assistance for surviving partners of victims of September 11
- Eligibility for Medi-Cal payments if partner is in a nursing facility

MISCELLANEOUS PROVISIONS
- Access to married student housing
- Authority to use car rented by partner if licensed and of sufficient age
- Ability to obtain overnight visitation with partners who are in prison

- Recognition of relationship under the California Political Reform Act and Prop.34

SPECIAL BENEFITS PROVIDED TO PUBLIC EMPLOYEES AND THEIR FAMILIES

- Certain employees' entitlement to leave of absence after death of partner
- Protection of partner's interest in public employee's retirement benefits and pension
- Right to continued health coverage and benefits after death of public employee partner
- Right of surviving partner of a deceased legislator to collect benefits
- Right to be buried in state burial grounds if partner is a legislator
- Death benefits for surviving partners of firefighters and police
- Scholarship for surviving partners of firefighters and peace officers
- Prohibition on certain crimes against, and disclosure of residences or phone numbers of, partners of certain public officials and employees

CONFLICTS OF INTEREST AND REQUIRED DISCLOSURES

- Exclusion of gifts from partners from limitations on judges' receipt of gifts
- Coverage of partners in laws governing conflicts of interest by certain government officials based on personal relationships with parties
- Exclusion of interest in the income of one's partner from certain conflict of interest laws
- Coverage or relationship under conflict of interest rules governing Coastal Commission members and employees

DISCRIMINATION PROTECTIONS

- Coverage under state laws prohibiting discrimination based on being or not being in the legal relationship
- Coverage under federal laws prohibiting discrimination based on being or not being in the legal relationship

ENTRY INTO THE INSTITUTION OF MARRIAGE

- Right to marry legally in California
- Issuance of licenses by county clerks
- Submission of certificates of registry to county clerks containing vital statistics
- Solemnization by government or religious officials

TERMINATION OF THE LEGAL RELATIONSHIP

- Rights and obligations relating to, and assistance in resolving disputes regarding, division of property, support, and other matters when the partners have children or significant property or debts or have been long-term registered partners
- Requirement to file court proceedings in all cases where the relationship is being terminated

You'll notice that unlike Miranda rights, which can be read to you in less than a minute before you are arrested, it would take hours to read you the 1,138 federal and hundreds of state marriage rights. Now you get why justices of the peace and clergy shorten the list to your standard vows: "In sickness and health, for better or worse, 'til death do you part," etc. They assume that what when you say "I do," you have a vague idea about what you're signing on for. Fred Hertz,[17] a family attorney, says that "Marriage is the only contract people don't review before they sign."

---

17 *Attorneys Fred Hertz and Emily Doskow co-authored a book called* Making It Legal: A Guide to Same-Sex Marriage, Domestic Partnership & Civil Unions *to help same-sex couples decide in states where both marriage and alternatives to marriage are available which would be best for their unique financial situation.*

And this list does not reflect all of the marriage rights afforded in other states because each state is unique. While heterosexual couples enjoy contiguous rights under the full faith and credit clause, meaning that they are granted the marriage rights of each state, because of DOMA, married same-sex couples are only guaranteed state marriage rights:

a) in the state they were married in,

b) in a state that allows same-sex couples to marry, or

c) in a state that expressly recognizes same-sex marriages.

For example, a same-sex couple married in Iowa would only have their marriage recognized in states that allow same-sex couples to marry, and in the District of Columbia, and in Maryland, New York, and Rhode Island even though same-sex couples cannot marry there. Their marriage would be recognized in California as a marriage if the marriage occurred before November 8, 2008. Same-sex marriages performed in other states after November 8, 2008 would only be recognized as domestic partnerships in California. Additionally, their marriages may also be recognized as civil unions in states with civil unions; domestic partnerships in states with domestic partnership rights; and reciprocal beneficiaries in states with reciprocal beneficiaries. And because CUs, DPs, and RBs differ with the amount and kind of rights granted, same-sex couples can't even consistently count on what rights they will have in states with marriage-lite alternatives. Also because the rights of same-sex couples to marry, form civil unions, or register in domestic partnerships continues something people can vote on a same-sex couples' relationship rights can easily be stripped away by a vote of the people or their representatives.

CHAPTER FIVE:
"GET A LAWYER" OR OTHER STUPID THINGS YOU CAN SAY TO GAY PEOPLE.

"*Homosexual activists say they need legal status so they can visit their partners in hospitals, etc. But hospitals leave visitation up to the patient except in very rare instances. This 'issue' is a smokescreen to cover the fact that, using legal instruments such as power of attorney, drafting a will, etc., homosexuals can share property, designate heirs, dictate hospital visitors and give authority for medical decisions. What they should not obtain is identical recognition and support for a relationship that is not equally essential to society's survival.*"

—Bob Knight, member of the Family Research Council

Some people just can't stop perpetuating myths. You know like the number of spiders a person will swallow in their lifetime, or that eating Pop Rocks and drinking Coke will explode your stomach. One bizarre myth put forward by anti-gay people is the claim that same-sex couples can just hire an attorney and POOF get all the rights that come with marriage. If that were the case why wouldn't gay people just do that and move on?

It's not possible. You can't hire an attorney and draw up a contract to become someone's health care beneficiary, pension or Social Security recipient, or to file joint state and federal income taxes. Even if super-lawyer Johnnie Cochran were still alive, he couldn't draw up paperwork that would give a couple the 1,138 federal marriage rights. Why? Because the federal rights and protections that come with marriage can only be given by a

Presidential Executive Order, the United States Supreme Court, or Congress.

The same is true for state marriage rights. They have to come through legislation, litigation, or a vote of the people.[18] Same-sex couples, like heterosexual couples, need a *marriage license* to be able to access marriage rights. To do that, we have to repeal the discriminatory Federal DOMA and all the state laws and state constitutional amendments, that not only ban same-sex couples from marrying in their state, but allow states to refuse to recognize legal same-sex marriages performed in other states.

It's wrong that when same-sex couples and their children cross the border into another state they suddenly become *single* and *legal strangers* to their spouse. Non-biological parents also run the risk of losing parental rights in states that don't recognize same-sex couples' marriages or adoption rights for gays and lesbians.

So, gay people, don't forget that three-inch stack of paperwork, including your Power of Attorney, will, health directive, domestic partnership registration form, civil union form, marriage license, and your second-parent adoption paperwork when you travel across the "home of the free."

THE GAY EXCEPTION!

After scanning those tedious lists of rights and responsibilities, you might be thinking that marriage is probably the last thing anybody should want to do. Marriage is a lot of responsibility. It is a serious commitment, and people need to consider carefully whether they are ready to be financially and emotionally intertwined. But how can anyone think it fair for an entire group of people to be denied these rights and responsibilities? Gay people serve as your doctors, lawyers, judges, teachers, and psychologists but we aren't entitled to a leave of absence after

---

18 As we saw in California and Maine even when same-sex couples are granted rights by the courts or the legislature, voters have stripped same-sex couples of those rights.

the death of a life partner, like straight people are. How can we create one set of rules for one couple, and a different set of rules for another —straight firefighters' survivors deserve benefits, but gay firefighters' survivor's don't?

SPOUSES-YOU HAVE THE RIGHT TO REMAIN SILENT!

The right of marital privilege prevents married individuals from having to testify against their spouses. One cannot be forced to reveal details of private intimate spousal conversations or be required to turn over letters between them–no matter how key that evidence is to a lawsuit, either criminal or civil.

In 2003, Rosie O'Donnell was involved in a legal battle with magazine publisher Gruner and Jahr. At the time she was unable to marry her now-wife, Kelli. So, Kelli was forced to testify as to the content of her and Rosie's conversations, and even turn over their personal e-mails. In response to the publisher's attorney's questions, Kelli prefaced her replies with an indirect protest: "In the privacy of our home, between the two us, just as any spouse would go home and talk to their other half about a bad day at work—yeah, we had that conversation." Rosie voiced her frustration with this injustice saying: "Kelli and I are not allowed any kind of title that gives us the validation of who we are, a family. Any and all correspondence that Kelli and I had was allowed to be entered into evidence. While any and all correspondence our married CEO had with his wife was not required to be disclosed."

WHAT BROWN WON'T DO FOR YOU

Daniel and Frank had been together for 27 years when Frank's employer, United Airlines, closed its San Francisco office and relocated its employees to Chicago. Daniel, who had worked for United Parcel Service for 20 years, requested a transfer to UPS's Chicago office. But, according to Lambda Legal, "although UPS has a policy that allows employees to transfer to other offices to follow a spouse,

UPS refused to allow Daniel to transfer because he and Frank are not legally married." Despite the fact that the two live in a state with domestic partnership benefits, because they have no access to a civil marriage license, Daniel and Frank have had to live apart from each other, at great emotional and financial cost.

AND THE LIST GOES ON...

Each of the thousands of marriage rights is meaningful. Couples who are denied access to these rights can suffer devastating consequences. No one wants their gay friends, family members and co-workers to be harmed by these types of injustices.

I, for one, never considered needing the "loss of consortium" and had no idea what it was until a cab sped through a red light and struck my friend Donna while she was commuting to work on her motorcycle. Donna managed to survive the accident with broken ribs, two broken legs, and a broken arm. Donna's partner, Lori, was pregnant at the time and experiencing extreme morning sickness. Lori had basically been dependent on Donna for physical, emotional, and financial support. Suddenly, Donna was unable to provide for the couple. When Donna was finally able to return home after eight weeks in the hospital, Lori had to take care of her.

Graced with the love and support of their local Episcopal Church, Lori and Donna made it through the most difficult time in their lives. Members of the parish provided a never-ending supply of hot dishes and supportive visits. When Donna was finally well again, and the pregnancy was going more smoothly, Lori contacted an attorney. She was ready to deal with the civil aspect of the suit against the careless cabby who almost killed her wife. To her dismay, she learned that "loss of consortium" damages are only payable to the spouse of an injured party whose injuries render him or her unable to provide emotional, physical, financial, or even sexual support. Lori was not a spouse.

It may sound petty, but the psychic damages and hardship Donna and Lori faced were no less serious than if they had been a heterosexual couple in the same situation. If Donna had been a man, Lori would have received compensation for her suffering. I can just hear the plaintiff's attorney for the heterosexual married couple espousing the added tragedy that the husband was unable to care for his pregnant wife and his injuries added additional stress to her pregnancy, increasing the risk to her and the baby.

WRONGFUL DEATH

Sharon Smith, was a Vice President for Charles Schwab, when her partner of seven years, Diane Whipple was tragically killed in the hallway of the couple's apartment building by their neighbors' dogs, known throughout the building to be dangerous. The dogs were owned by Paul Cornfed Schnieder, an identified white supremacist friend of the neighbors' who were caring for the dogs since he is serving a life sentence in a California prison. The neighbors' knew their dogs were dangerous. One had even bit Diane once before in the elevator and the neighbors had responded by making condescending gay jokes to her. While the dogs were attacking Diane, the neighbor, Marjorie Knoller, apparently did little to help her. When Diane was taken to San Francisco General Hospital's trauma ward, the doctors said it was one of the worst attack cases they had ever seen.

Sharon wanted to sue her neighbors for Diane's wrongful death, meaning that they had full knowledge that the dogs were dangerous. Proving wrongful death was not going to be a challenge, but because Sharon and Diane were not legally married, she was shocked and outraged to learn had she no legal right to sue in the first place.

The brutality of Diane's preventable death, coupled with the lack of remorse by Marjorie Knoller and Knoller's husband, propelled Sharon Smith the center of the national dialogue on same-sex couple's rights.

An accidental activist, Sharon committed herself to justice for Diane and to increase public awareness of the insults same-sex couples face by not being able to marry. Sharon's situation touched the judge hearing her plea and he changed the course of history by agreeing that Sharon should be able to sue for wrongful death just like any other spouse.

Sharon's story also moved the California legislature, encouraging Governor Davis to pass AB 25, a domestic partnership bill that gave registered domestic partners in California the right to sue for wrongful death and 13 other important rights. Why did a young woman have to die so tragically to get lawmakers and justices to sit up and take notice? How many men and women will face similar hardships because until our nation grants same-sex couples the right to marry in all 50 states?

ONE RIGHT AT A TIME?

On June 15, 2009, the Obama Administration granted same-sex couples the right use their married name, their spouse's surname, on their passports. This is a no-brainer for heterosexual couples. You get married and frequently the woman changes or hyphenates her name with her husband's and fills out paperwork for her name change and that's the name she uses to apply for a passport. Well, same-sex couples in Massachusetts had to file a lawsuit and wait five years to have the same right begrudgingly given to them in June 2009. Does everything have to be a lawsuit and a struggle? Wouldn't it just be easier to treat our families equally and give us access to the same rights all at once? **If we were granted one right ever year it would take 1,138 years to get federal marriage rights and another 300-600 years for the state rights.** Equal marriage would immediately remedy every inequality for same-sex couples.

Section Two:
Money

Chapter Six:
Equal Pay For Equal Work

———————————•———————————

Denying LGBT people the right to marry, denies them access to the employment benefits that their heterosexual co-workers enjoy. Marriage allows employees access to employee-benefits (i.e. family medical and sick leave, bereavement leave of a spouse, health insurance benefits, life insurance, adoption assistance, disability-related benefits and relocation assistance and support to one spouse when the other spouse is relocated for work).

But because of the DOMA and a federal statute known as the **Employee Retirement Income Security Act of 1974 (ERISA)**, the federal government and national companies deny benefits to married or domestic partnered same-sex couples even in states that allow and recognize same-sex marriage.

Frank and Joe's Story

Frank and Joe Capley-Alfano are a married same-sex couple and the first same-sex couple recognized within the Free Masons, reportedly "the oldest and largest world wide fraternity dedicated to the Brotherhood of Man."[19] Frank is an elevator mechanic and gets his health insurance benefits from the National Elevator Industry Health Benefits Plan (NEIHBP) through the *International Union of Elevator Constructors (IUEC) Local 8*. Because of DOMA, IUEC does not have to provide a member's same-sex spouse the health care benefits it provides to opposite-sex spouses.

Joe has a degenerative physical condition that requires medical treatment or he will lose the ability to walk. He is already

—————————————————————————

19 *According to the Free Mason Website* www.freemasonry.org

unable to work as a construction worker, his former trade, and is only able to work part-time. Because he is part-time, he is unable to get health insurance. He could get health insurance through his husband and be able to get the operation if he needs if DOMA were repealed, or if the elevator union simply chose to recognize state sanctioned same-sex marriages, civil unions, and domestic partnerships. However, because of the fall back on the federal DOMA and lack of regard for the suffering of their union brother, Joe was denied spousal health benefits since the couple first filed their request in October 2004.

If the couple were Canadians, Joe would have already had his surgery. Some friends suggested they move to Canada. "Why should I have to move to Canada?" Frank asks, "I'm an American and what's happening is unfair. It's un-American. All the guys at my work can put their spouses on their health insurance, but I can't because my union won't recognize my legal marriage to Joe." Joe agrees, "How can it be fair that we are legally married and still denied the rights of marriage by our own country?"

Frank and Joe petitioned the International Union of Elevator Constructors (IUEC) for five years hoping for a policy change before Joe permanently disabled. In late 2009, Marriage Equality USA and several other organizations worked to gain support from local officials and lobbying groups for the couple's situation and Local 8 of the IUEC changed its policy and agreed to provide health benefits to same-sex couples who are married, but not same-sex couples in domestic partnerships, civil unions, or reciprocal beneficiaries.

While Frank and Joe are clearly elated that after five years of waiting Joe will have his operation, the couple is deeply disappointed with the union's choice not to recognize same-sex couples who have made legal commitments to one another to the extent that their state provides. To get benefits couples who live in states with domestic partnerships, civil unions, reciprocal beneficiaries, or those that offer no legal recognition for same-sex couples must travel to another state where same-sex couples can legally marry or to Canada to obtain a marriage license. This creates an unwarranted financial hardship for employees with same-sex partners over those with opposite-sex partners. Frank and Joe are now speaking out on behalf of another member of the IUEC, who has been in a registered domestic partnership for four years, but missed the four and a half month window to marry, and has had to work two jobs to be able to provide her domestic partner and their child with health care.

Frank and Joe hope that by sharing their story, others will be inspired to speak up for their own and fellow union member's needs and challenge unfair union policies that hurt same-sex couples and their families. "These things take time," Frank says, "but if we hadn't filed this first complaint back in 2004, who knows how long this would have taken." The couple encourages other people to advocate for their rights. "It's been a very emotional journey," says Joe, "it's hard to stand up in front of people and ask for their help, sometimes I would break down, but no one is going to do this for us. We've got to stand up for the rights of our families."

TAXES AND WORK-RELATED DOMESTIC PARTNER BENEFITS

LGBT Americans pay extra taxes to the Social Security Administration. A January 2007 Human Rights Campaign Report noted that 53 percent of Fortune 500 companies (265) provide domestic partnership benefits and many other businesses provide health insurance for the same-sex spouses and partners of LGBT employees. The U.S. government, however, considers those health insurance benefits as a "special benefit" and taxes it as if it were additional income. Heterosexual married couples are not taxed on this benefit. While my wife's law firm and the state of California recognize our marriage, we are taxed thousands of dollars more than our married heterosexual counterparts for the "special benefit" of my health insurance under the family plan! This means that *LGBT Americans are paying extra taxes to the Social Security Administration* and then are also being denied survivor's benefits that are given to heterosexuals!

EMPLOYMENT BENEFITS—NOW YOU HAVE THEM NOW YOU DON'T

And unlike marriage benefits that you only lose when you divorce, LGBT Americans can lose previously held domestic partnership benefits. When Exxon merged with Mobile, instead of extending domestic partnership benefits to Exxon employees, the newly merged company chose to eliminate domestic partnerships altogether. The company reduced their costs by taking away benefits from gay employees. Can you imagine if straight employees were told that they would no longer have spousal health care benefits after the merger? The union, not to mention the angry spouses, would have wiped up the floor with those execs.

EMPLOYMENT BENEFITS FOR FEDERAL EMPLOYEES

The U.S. Government is the largest employer in the U.S. The Williams Institute estimates that there are approximately 30,000 federal employees in same-sex relationships, yet because of DOMA the Federal Government does not provide health insurance benefits to same-sex couples and a host of other employment related benefits that heterosexual spouses are provided. The U.S. Government is lagging behind 2/3 of the Fortune 500 companies and the 4,500 other companies that do.

I was one of those 30,000 federal employees for almost thirteen years, yet I could not provide Molly with health insurance. I worked for the Bureau of Prisons as a psychologist and had I been killed on the job, she would have been denied the survivor's and pension benefits that my heterosexual co-worker's spouses would have received. I also earned a pension while I worked there, and if I were to die today the government would get to keep it, not Molly.

THE DOMESTIC PARTNERSHIP BENEFITS AND OBLIGATIONS ACT (DPBO)

"It's time for the federal government to follow the lead of 11 state governments, over 150 local governments, and more than five thousand private-sector employers and recognize that providing benefits to domestic partners is not just the fair thing to do, it's good business. Corporations are not required to do this in most places. They do it because it helps attract high quality employees."

—Rep. Barney Frank, Massachusetts

PUTTING OUR HOUSE IN ORDER

On June 17, 2009, President Obama signed a memorandum reiterating the few rights that federal employee's same-sex partners have had access to since the Clinton Administration, but were not publicized and frequently denied LGBT employees during the anti-gay Bush administration. Office of Personal Management Director, John Berry, who is an openly gay man called Obama's June 17, 2009 memo "an attempt to get our federal house in order" and said that "federal employees will no longer have to rely on whether or not their supervisor is enlightened or not."

One year later, in June 2010, President Obama signed another memorandum that explicitly acknowledged that when federal appointments were made and employees were required to move for their jobs, relocation benefits that were previously only afforded heterosexual spouses would now be afforded to same-sex domestic partners. The memo stated that federal employees could take leave to care for their same-sex domestic partners and spouses and their children. The memo also extended child-care services and subsidies to federal workers with same-sex partners and granted uniform access for same-sex partners and spouses to federal credit unions and other memberships spouses of heterosexual federal workers have had access to.[20]

I honor President Obama's intention to affirm his support of equality, an about face from the previous President, but for this to be a true step forward, LGBT federal workers need to have access to all the same rights and benefits that their heterosexual co-workers have; most importantly health care and pension benefits. Additionally, it is still unclear if Obama's memos will be as easily washed away as Clinton's executive orders and proclamations were when the next president takes office. Do these memos expire like Cinderella's coach at midnight the night of the next presidential inauguration? LGBT people deserve lasting reliable policy changes.

DOMESTIC PARTNERSHIP AND BENEFITS OBLIGATION ACT (DPBO

Even though it creates a separate and unequal system within the federal workplace, the Domestic Partnership and Benefits Obligation Act (DPBO) would at least begin to provide LGBT federal workers benefits and protections they and their families are currently denied.

The Domestic Partnership and Benefits Obligation Act, reintroduced in May 2009 as HR 2517[21] into the House of Representatives by Tammy Baldwin (D-Wisc.) and Ileana Ros-Lehtinen (R-Fla.) and as SB 1102 in the Senate by Joseph

---

20 My wife, Molly, has been a joint member of my federal credit union for almost a decade. However, membership for same-sex partners or spouses of federal workers was not uniformly available at all credit unions.
21 The bill was first introduced in 2002 by Senator Mark Dayton, (D-Minn) in the Senate and by Congressman Barney Frank (D-Mass) in the house.

Lieberman (I-Conn,) and Susan Collins (R-Maine), would provide the same-sex spouse/partner of a federal employee the same benefits as a heterosexual spouse of a federal employee. Benefits would include: health care; family, medical, and emergency leave; retirement and disability benefits; life and long-term care insurance; compensation for work-related injuries or death; travel, transportation, and related relocation benefits. Additionally, the DPBO would hold the same-sex spouse/partner of a federal employee to the same regulations as heterosexual spouses of federal employees with regard to anti-nepotism rules and financial disclosure laws. However, it would do nothing for the private sector.

Both bills have bi-partisan support and at the symbolic June 2009 memo signing, President Obama stated that he believed Congress should pass the DPBO. He said "Extending equal benefits to the same-sex partners of federal employees is the right thing to do. It is also sound economic policy. Many top employees in the private sector already offer benefits to the same-sex partners of their employees; these companies recognize that offering partner benefits helps them compete for and retain the brightest and most talented employees. The federal government is at a disadvantage on that score now, and change is long overdue."

GAY SPOUSES DEMOTED UNDER FEDERAL DPBO ACT

There are some drawbacks to the DPBO Act. Under DPBO, heterosexual spouses of federal employees would be recognized as spouses, but same-sex spouses would not. Same-sex spouses will be demoted to "domestic partners." Additionally, unlike heterosexuals who are not required to provide proof of marriage, LGBT federal employees would be required to submit an affidavit of eligibility for benefits to the Office of Personnel Management. This is definitely a separate and unequal bill that holds same-sex couples to a more rigorous standard than heterosexual couples.

The affidavit submitted must certify that the federal employee and their "domestic partner" meet the following criteria:

1. Are each other's sole domestic partner and intend to remain so indefinitely.
2. Have a common residence and intend to continue the arrangement.
3. Are at least 18 years of age and mentally competent to consent to contract.
4. Share responsibility for a significant measure of each other's common welfare and financial obligations.
5. Are not married to or domestic partners with anyone else.
6. Are same-sex domestic partners, and not related in a way that, if the two were of opposite sex, would prohibit legal marriage in the State in which they reside
7. Understand that willfull falsification of information within the affadavit may lead to disciplinary action and the recovery of the cost of benefits received related to such falsification and may constitute a criminal violation.

Heterosexual federal employees don't need to sign an affidavit stating that they intend to remain together "indefinitely" for their spouse to be entitled to family health care benefits. This hardly seems fair. What if there is a separation? Will they be taken to court for breaking their intentions? What if they separate from their domestic partner and later want to have another domestic partner? Will they be denied that right? Heterosexuals are able to marry multiple times over the course of their employment and provide each consequent spouse benefits.

> *Sidebar: Heterosexual married employees are not required to submit an affidavit or even their marriage license to get benefits.*

Despite, its serious flaws, the DPBO would provide benefits to LGBT federal employees in all government agencies, except the agencies connected to the Department of Defense and the U.S. Military. Agencies that would provide benefits, for example, include: U.S. Post Office, Department of Justice, Internal Revenue System, Homeland Security, Environment Protection Agency, Department of Health and Human Services, and the U.S. Forestry Service to name a few.

Even though the federal government is the largest employer in the country, providing these benefits would increase the cost of the federal benefits program by *less than .5 percent* according to the Congressional Budget Office (CBO). Congressman Barney Frank thinks the DPBO is a good investment. "At a time when there is a substantial salary gap between government and private-sector employers with similar jobs, it simply makes sense to add a low cost benefit to help attract more qualified people to the federal government, and make it easier to retain them once they start work." He also adds that, "There is simply no good reason to discriminate among employees in committed relationships: equal work should mean equal pay–and benefits."

While DPBO would provide gay federal employees some rights, nothing short of full marriage equality will create full equality under for LGBT employees, except for those who work for religious organizations. Religious organizations are exempt under Title VII and will always be able to hire or fire people based on their sexual orientation, gender, or race if they so choose.

TAKE ACTION NOW

You can take action now by writing a sending a letter to your elected officials in support of the DPBO.

Sample Letter to Senators to Support Domestic Partnership Benefits for Federal Employees

The Honorable (Senator)
Address
Senate Office Building
Washington, DC Zip

RE: SUPPORT Domestic Partnership Benefits and Obligations Act (DPBO) (S-1252 and HR 2426)

Dear Senator (Name):

Please support the **Domestic Partnership Benefits and Obligations Act (DPBO) (S-1252 and HR 2426)**, so that lesbian, gay, bisexual, and transgender federal employees can provide the basic relationship protections of health care and pension benefits to their same-sex partners.

As you know, many federal employees work in dangerous settings to ensure that all Americans obtain the benefits and protections of our government. However, currently LGBT people considering civil service must choose between their country and providing basic protections to their loved ones (partners and children). No one should be asked to make this choice. Failing to provide health care and pension benefits to same-sex partners is denying patriotic LGBT people the opportunity to serve their country. Unlike their heterosexual co-workers who are able to marry, LGBT people who choose federal employment over corporate or non-profit work leave their families uncovered by health insurance or they are forced to pay higher health care costs.

Many Fortune 500 companies truly committed to a diverse work force, like Ford Motor Company and Charles Schwab, see the importance of providing domestic partnership benefits as part of retaining good employees. Because LGBT people make up only

10% of the population, providing domestic partnership benefits to federal employees would be fiscally insignificant.

I urge you to consider the value of LGBT employees and to treat their families fairly by supporting the Federal Domestic Partnership Bill that would allow federal employees access to domestic partnership benefits.

Thank you for honoring diversity and supporting all families.

Sincerely,

Chapter Seven:
Social Security, Seniors,
and Retirement

"Most of us don't like to talk about death or even think about it. But wouldn't you feel better knowing that, if you were no longer living, Social Security would help take care of your family? Of course, you would."

—Social Security Web Page Ad

The Social Security Rip-off

I know I'd feel more comfortable knowing that if I die, my wife would have access to the fund I've been contributing to *all* my working life. I'd want her to be able to live as comfortably as possible in the same home and within the same means as she did during my lifetime. But for LGBT people, Social Security as a part of the retirement equation is not an option because DOMA denies same-sex partners Social Security survivor benefits. This is especially unfair to gay seniors who are already denied other survivor benefits available to their heterosexual counterparts. Even in states where gay Americans are legally married, they are denied Social Security survivor benefits.

Marvin's Story

Marvin and Bill were teenagers when they met and fell in love in Flint, Michigan in the 1950s. They came out to their families and eventually moved to California. Bill worked in the trades and Marvin worked for Lavender Seniors and Meals on Wheels helping elders in need. In February 2004, when the city of San Francisco was allowing gay couples to marry, Marvin and Bill happily tied the knot after being together for 50 years.

Nine months later, Bill died suddenly. And with the loss of the love of his life, Marvin also discovered that he was losing his health insurance, something that would not have happened if their marriage had not been invalidated by the California Supreme Court. But because they were only domestic partners and not legally married, he could no longer access health insurance through Bill's employer, and was denied Bill's pension and Social Security.

Marvin was in dire straights. The financial losses were devastating. Marvin could no longer pay the rent on the apartment he'd lived in with Bill for over thirty years. And if all those things combined weren't bad enough, he realized that his own Social Security payment would only cover his health insurance costs with nothing left over for food and housing. Within a week of losing the love of his life for over fifty years, Marvin was losing everything and facing homelessness, simply because he and Bill were unable to legally marry and have their marriage recognized at the state and federal level.

Under Bill's union, only surviving spouses continue to receive health insurance benefits. Domestic partners of union members lost their benefits once their domestic partner died. Additionally, spouses are entitled to survivor's pension benefits, but domestic partners are not. Despite the fact that Marvin and Bill were together for 50 years, Marvin could not claim Bill's Social Security survivor's benefit because of DOMA. However, if Bill had been married five different times to five different women for 10 years each and none of these women had remarried, all five of them would be entitled to collect Bill's full Social Security benefits.

I met Marvin in 2003, two years before Bill died, at a conference organized by the National Gay and Lesbian Taskforce (NGLTF) called Creating Change. We were both attending a roundtable discussion on marriage equality. We were all working for equal marriage rights and it was so exciting when all of us were able to be married in San Francisco thanks to Gavin Newsom. None of us could have ever predicted the great tragedy that was looming on Marvin's horizon. When I wrote *Why You Should Give A Damn About Gay Marriage*, I included a chapter on LGBT seniors and Social Security, but I had no idea that I would soon witness first hand a friend's sheer helplessness because of these callous homophobic laws. Despite the fact that Marvin and Bill were registered California domestic partners, the undertaker at the first mortuary Marvin called refused to recognize him as Bill's family. Marvin had to move Bill's body to another crematorium. Can you imagine this happening to a heterosexual spouse?

After Bill's funeral, another gay widower, Frank Howell, took Marvin in as a roommate. It was a shocking wake up call at how vulnerable our gay seniors are. But it takes courage and dedication to stay with the same man for 51 years, especially during a time when society was working to tear them apart, and Marvin was not about to stay silent about this injustice. After Bill's death, he petitioned the union for Bill's pension. Because of Marvin's advocacy, several years after Bill's death, the union changed the law and now treats survivors of same-sex domestic partners the same as married survivors. They also retroactively awarded Marvin, Bill's pension. But why should anyone have to go through all of that just to get the same rights as their heterosexual counterparts?

SOCIAL SECURITY SURVIVOR'S BENEFITS

Some of the Social Security taxes you pay go towards survivors insurance. In fact, the value of the survivors insurance you have under Social Security is probably more than the value of your individual life insurance."

—SSA Publication

Do gay Americans have less of a work ethic or put less time into their chosen fields of employment than straight colleagues? Do gay Americans work any less hard to earn those pensions? Do gay Americans not fork over an equal share of their salaries?

The National Gay and Lesbian Task Force wishes to eliminate the discrepancies in treatment of gay and straight seniors. In their publication "Key Policy Recommendations for GLBT Elders" they state that "Social Security pays survivor benefits to widows and widowers, but not to the surviving same-sex partner of someone who dies." According to the Taskforce, collectively "this costs GLBT elders $124 million a year in unaccessed benefits. Medicaid regulations protect the assets and homes of married spouses when the other spouse enters a nursing home or long-term care facility; no such protections are offered to same-sex partners. Tax laws and other regulations of 401k's and pensions discriminate against same-sex partners, costing the surviving partner tens of thousands of dollars a year, and possibly over $1 million during the course of a lifetime." They argue that the hardship a gay senior faces is "particularly striking when one takes into consideration that, even with full access to benefits, eleven percent of all elders live below the poverty level and another six percent are classified as near-poor. And same-sex partners are often denied even the most basic rights of hospital visitation or the right to live or die in the same nursing home."

Let's crunch numbers just to show you how big the Social Security loss is for gay Americans. Feel free to try this at home. Go to www.ssa.gov.[22]

EXAMPLE 1

A surviving partner or state-recognized spouse of an LGBT American born January 1, 1960 who made *$25,000* the last year

---

22 *http://www.socialsecurity.gov/planners/benefitcalculators.htm*

of their life and died in September 2009 based on an "assumed earnings growth rate for past earnings" would be denied *$943 a month* at normal retirement age, which is usually 67. A child that the deceased was caring for, but was unable to secure legal relationship status with and therefore not recognized by the federal government, would be denied *$707 a month* in survivor's benefits.

EXAMPLE 2

If you were a surviving partner or state-recognized spouse of an LGBT American born January 1, 1960, who made on average *$50,000* the last year of their life and died in September 2009 based on an "assumed earnings growth rate for past earnings" would be denied *$1,455 a month* at normal retirement age. The child that you and the deceased were caring for, but that the deceased could not secure legal relationship status with and therefore is not recognized by the federal government, would be denied *$1,091 a month* in survivor's benefits.

EXAMPLE 3

If you were a surviving partner or state-recognized spouse of an LGBT American born January 1, 1960, who made *$75,000* the last year of their life and died in September 2009 based on an "assumed earnings growth rate for past earnings" would be denied *$1,913 a month* at normal retirement age. The child that you and the deceased were caring for, but that the deceased could not secure legal relationship status with and therefore is not recognized by the federal government, would be denied *$1,435 a month* in survivor's benefits.

As you can see, this is a significant amount of money denied gay seniors, made more egregious by the fact that gay people pay more money into Social Security than our straight colleagues because under DOMA our family health benefits are axed as extra income, unlike heterosexual married couples.

Joyce Pierson, self-proclaimed "lesbian over 60," and head of the Elder Law Project for the National Center for Lesbian Rights believes that marriage equality would give gay seniors equal survivor's benefits and eliminate unfair fiscal and emotional treatment. She says, "Our income lowers as we age and Social Security is our major form of retirement. However, LGBT people are not eligible to receive benefits because we don't fit the marriage framework. Pensions don't recognize same-sex couples. We can't get health insurance either. I know of 401Ks that deny same-sex partners. Marriage secures that spouses receive benefits that right now LGBT people can't get. And domestic partners are so tenuous."

RETIREMENT HOMES

Let's face it: One day we are all going to be old and gray, some of us old and gay! Eventually most of us will need some assistance with our everyday activities and may need to relocate to a retirement or assisted living home. Many of these retirement communities are run by religious organizations that have rules about unmarried people living together. They can refuse to recognize same-sex couples and force cohabiting heterosexual sinners—whoops, seniors—to marry or "get out."

WHO ARE THE REAL SINNERS?

At age 89, my straight grandmother-in-law, Juanita, started dating again after the death of her second husband. It wasn't more than a month of seeing her new boyfriend's car parked in her driveway that the "morality police" came knocking on her door. She was told that she either had to marry her new beau or she would have to leave the retirement community where she had lived for more than ten years. She had served this community by teaching fitness classes, winning the green-thumb award for her gardening around the facility, and by being a great friend to the people who lived there.

It was a tough choice, but Juanita wasn't going to be forced into a third marriage and have to give up her survivor's pension if things didn't work out. And she also wasn't going to give up her new boyfriend either. So, at age 89, Grandma Juanita packed up her stuff and moved to a private house.

At least Grandma Juanita could have married her boyfriend if she had wanted to and moved him in to her apartment. However, same-sex partners can't conform to most retirement home's definition of "family," and are separated unjustly from their loved ones and long-term partners. Even in states where gay and lesbian seniors are legally married, retirement homes that are owned and operated as faith-based, religious organizations are exempted from recognizing same-sex marriages. This is their constitutional right.

DOLORES AND FRAN'S STORY

Imagine what it's like for Dolores and Fran. They've been together for 45 years. They own a home together. They've raised Dolores' children from a previous marriage, and have taken care of each other through thick and thin. Now Dolores's health is declining and her medical needs and personal assistance are more than what Fran can handle on her own.

The two begin looking into retirement communities. Repeatedly, the message they are given is that two single ladies are not eligible to share a one-bedroom apartment. They can move in to the retirement community, but they will have to maintain separate residences, or at least rent a two-bedroom, which they can't afford and don't need. Despite, the myth of gay affluence, on average, lesbian couples have lower family incomes than heterosexuals and gay male couples. Maintaining separate residences is costly and unfair. It's also as ridiculous as squeezing into the twin bed at the hotel room, or pretending to have another bedroom to fool the company. Should gay seniors in retirement homes have to sneak down the hall to their spouse's/ partner's residence?

> " *Senior same-sex couples are more likely to be poorer than their opposite-sex married peers. The national average for couples 65 and above living below federal poverty line in the United States is— 4.6 % for opposite-sex couples, 4.9 % for male couples, and 9.1% for female couples.* "
>
> —Williams Institute Report, March 2009.

HOMOPHOBIA IN NURSING HOMES AND HOSPITALS

What's worse is that the care Dolores will receive may be influenced by the homophobia of the care providers. According to Terry Kaelber, Executive Director for Senior Action in a Gay Environment, (SAGE), "a woman was left unbathed because an aide refused to 'wash the lesbian.'" Kaleber says gay seniors are more likely to live alone in old age and "less likely to have ties to a biological family or a religious institution." And as of 2003, according to the Lesbian and Gay Retirement Communities Website, there were only six LGBT retirement communities in the United States and none of them offer skilled care. This means LGBT seniors are more likely to need to rely on existing retirement and care services than their heterosexual counterparts. Yet, because they are gay, they are less likely to be welcome to use these services. According to the National Gay and Lesbian Task Force (NGLTF), a 1994 study found that almost 50% of Area Agencies on Aging (AAA's) would not want LGBT people at their centers. NGLTF notes that AAAs "provide the bulk of federally supported social services."

"Many seniors feel the need to hide pictures and other signs of their gay identities or their care will be compromised," notes Kaelber. And these seniors are not paranoid. An article from the Minnesota Board on Aging cited a study that found that "two thirds of doctors and medical students reported knowing of biased care giving by medical professionals; half reported witnessing it, and nearly 90 percent said they've heard disparaging remarks about GLBT patients."

According, to Stephen Karpiak, Ph.D. Executive Director of the Pride Senior Network, "The elderly lesbian and gay community experiences a lot of frustration when they have to go to the hospital, or if they get a new nurse or physician. Having to continually explain who you are and what your relationship is to the person you are there with is demeaning. Instead of dealing with that, they often just stay away from care."

Should LGBT people have to hide their sexual orientation or limit contact with their loved ones to ensure that they are not provided sub-standard medical care? And what about transgender and intersex people who cannot hide their bodies from medical staff? Is it fair that they should be treated poorly by the medical and retirement communities?

When Robert Eades, a female to male transexual living in Georgia was diagnosed with ovarian cancer, he was denied medical care by twenty different doctors who did not want to treat a transgender person. By the time Robert finally received medical care, more than a year later—the cancer had metastasized to his internal organs. He died shortly after receiving treatment from the Medical College of Georgia. See the documentary *Southern Comfort* for Robert's full story.

We must end the homophobia and transphobia that permeates the medical profession and retirement communities. We must ensure that our LGBT seniors do not have to go back into the closet to get good health care or to have a safe environment to live in. We must change discriminatory policies that deny LGBT seniors access to health insurance, pension benefits, social security survivor's benefits, and other societal protections to ensure the dignity and welfare of aging lavender seniors. Access to full marriage equality would be a huge leap forward in addressing their needs.

Chapter Eight:
Death and Taxes

Till Death Do Us Part With Our Rights

Most of us think bad things will never happen to us. But, unfortunately, people die unexpectedly in car accidents and drop over dead from brain aneurysms or heart attacks all the time. Do you have a will, power of attorney, or an advanced health care directive? When would be a good time to draw up a will? How about now?

Here is a list of important legal documents to create:

1. Will
2. Living Trusts, including an AB Trust
3. Health Care Directive:
4. Living Will
5. Health Care Power of Attorney
6. Financial Powers of Attorney
7. Final arrangements document
8. Important documents for executors

Many rights are automatically granted through marriage, but all people, regardless of legal marital status, would be wise to make their wishes explicit. Same-sex couples, even more than straight couples, need to do as much as they can to protect themselves and their loved ones. By making out your will and following the laws of your state, you will increase the likelihood that your last wishes will be granted for your survivors. But I can't emphasize this enough, please make sure that you carefully read what is required for these documents to be valid.

In a tragic turn of events, Sam, an Oklahoma rancher, lost his partner of 22 years, Earl. Same was the beneficiary of Earl's property in the will, but lost the inheritance gifted to him because the will was notarized by a notary and Oklahoma law requires signatures of two witnesses. This simple mistake allowed Earl's estranged cousins to contest and invalidate the will. Because Sam was not recognized as Earl's legal next of kin, the cousins took possession of the farm and sent Sam packing from the home they shared over their lifetime together. (Sam's story is documented in the film "Tying the Knot").

The death of a spouse is one of the most devastating life experiences anyone will ever face, and lack of social and legal recognition of the reality of that lifetime partnership on top of that is humiliating, cruel, and undeniably heart-breaking! As if losing the love of your life isn't bad enough, as we saw in Marvin's story, with the death of the beloved comes more uncertainties and lack of protections for same-sex couples.

In addition to the denial of Social Security, pension benefits, and in some cases insurance and workers compensation benefits, same-sex couples are also not allowed to own a home together the way that straight married couples are. For example, when a same-sex partner dies, the house is reassessed for taxes at current market levels. This means that if the prices have gone up, the survivor may not be able to afford to pay the tax increase and could be forced to move.

However, the most despicable situation, as noted above, is if relatives of your loved one come scavenging around to take possession of your shared property. Yes, *your* property, which they can claim as their own if you don't have a will stating that you are to receive your shared television set, sofa, antique dishware, Monet painting, or whatever, and receipts to prove that you purchased them. I wish I were kidding. But relatives looking for a freebie may decide to rummage through your home and take their pick of what they believe they are entitled to. This is even more likely to happen if the deceased was closeted about the nature of the relationship.[23]

BURIAL AND FUNERAL ARRANGEMENTS

Who is authorized to make funeral and burial arrangements? The family, the so-called *next of kin*. But the surviving partner of a same-sex relationship is often not recognized as family. Surviving same-sex partners in most states are considered legal strangers with no more right over their loved one's body than the next door neighbor.

What are the practical implications of being a legal stranger? You cannot view the body. You cannot direct whether your beloved will be buried, cremated, or donated to science. You cannot arrange the funeral. In fact, if the family wants to get nasty, they may fly his or her body to another state, and not even tell you when or where the funeral is scheduled, or, where your beloved is buried.

> **"***We have seen many cases where the surviving partner thinks they have the right to make decisions for their partner, but they don't. We have seen the family of the partner who has passed elbow the surviving partner away. It's heartbreaking for us!***"**
>
> —Alison Rodman, Chapel of the Chimes

In almost every state, burial rights and funeral arrangements go to the spouse first, then to the "next of kin," a term that does not include same-sex partners. That's right. In most states, even if you are in a relationship with a same-sex partner for 50

---

23 The movie *If These Walls Could Talk 2* has an excellent dramatization of what happens to be the survivor from a closeted long-term lesbians couples when her long-term partner suddenly dies.

years, if he or she dies, your partner's family members (i.e. niece, nephew, brother/sister, or even third cousin) will be the ones to decide where your loved one will spend eternity. Not you. This is the true viciousness of the law and why LGBT need marriage to grant same-sex couples the rights and respect they deserve.

FIREFIGHTERS, POLICE OFFICERS, CORRECTIONAL WORKERS—OH, MY!

Every day state-employed, uniformed men and women put their lives on the line to protect us from criminals, terrorists, and natural disasters. In return for their heroic acts these individuals are granted certain benefits, so that—should they be injured or killed in the line of duty—their loved ones will continue to be sustained.

That is, unless they're gay, as Detective Lieutenant Laurel Hester found. According to the website devoted to the documentary film *Freeheld*, "Detective Lieutenant Laurel Hester spent 25 years investigating tough cases in Ocean County, New Jersey, protecting the rights of victims and putting her life on the line. She had no reason to expect that in the last year of her life, after she was diagnosed with terminal cancer, that her final battle for justice would be for the woman she loved."

Before her death, Lt. Hester petitioned the New Jersey Board of Freeholders for survivor's benefits for her domestic partner, Staci. Under the policy, only married survivors of public servants were eligible for death benefits. Since New Jersey did not allow same-sex couples to marry, same-sex survivors, like Staci, were denied monthly annuities which could help pay their mortgage or the surviving children's medical bills. Lt. Hester did not want Staci to have to sell their home after her death and she knew if Staci received her pension, as a heterosexual spouse would, Staci would be able to afford to pay the mortgage alone and remain in the couple's home after she was gone. Lt. Hester knew that because same-sex survivors are denied the benefits heterosexual widows and widowers get, they are often presented with income loss and unfair taxation that leads to their having to give up their homes after the death of an unrecognized spouse.

After initially rejecting Lt. Hester's petition, the New Jersey Board of Freeholders agreed to extend pension benefits to registered domestic partners. Lt. Hester died three weeks later at age 49.

Officer Lois Marrero's surviving partner, Mickie Mashburn, was not as fortunate. Marrero and Mashburn were both police officers in Tampa, Florida. Lois was killed while responding to a robbery.

"There was a time in my life when I thought human rights work did not impact me. But in 2001, I lost my partner of 10 years, Lois Marrero, a fellow police officer who was shot and killed in the line of duty. Despite being married in a church and affirming our lifelong commitment, I was denied the pension benefits due a surviving spouse because our relationship isn't recognized by Florida law. Having my life with Lois denied in such a public way has been painful and demeaning."

—Officer Mickie Mashburn.

Lois had worked as a police officer for 19 years and was nearing retirement. The Police Chief recognized Mickie as the widow of the slain officer at the funeral, providing her with the flag from Lois's coffin, something done for all spouses of slain officers. But he stopped with this symbolic gesture and denied Mickie the more tangible right to Lois's pension. Because they were not legally married, Mickie was denied survivor benefits to Lois's pension and Social Security.

Same-sex survivors of firefighters and law enforcement agents are denied access to scholarship benefits and are often denied the community recognition that surviving spouses get. Why should gay people have to choose between being good citizens who serve the public, and being good spouses who provide for and protect their families? Don't the two go hand in hand? Those who make these kinds of personal sacrifices—and the partners who support them—should be honored and recognized for it.

9/11 SAME-SEX SURVIVORS

The World Trade Center catastrophe provided a microcosm for the legal inequities between similarly situated surviving partners of married and unmarried couples. Newlywed spouses received hundreds of thousands of dollars in state and federal aid without question. Long-term committed same-sex couples were denied any death benefits. And, really, for the first time, the nation turned its attention to this unfairness and in several surprising cases, remedied the problem...but only for this national tragedy.

Larry Courtney lost his partner of 14 years, Gene Clark, when a plane hit the South Tower of the World Trade Center. Larry immediately had to move out of the apartment he could no longer afford alone. Because Larry and Gene were not legal spouses, Larry was not eligible to receive the $20,000 in worker's compensation that a widower from an on-the-job death would normally be entitled to under New York law. Nor was he entitled to Social Security spousal survivor benefits.

Because Gene died without a will, Gene's estranged father stood to inherit all of Gene's assets. Moreover, due to Gene's father's lack of cooperation, Larry was unable to be appointed administrator of Gene's estate. Larry, with the help of Lambda Legal, was able to help apply political pressure such that the New York legislature granted workers' compensation to domestic partners–but only for 9/11 survivors.

Peggy Neff lost her partner of 17 years, Sheila Hines, in the Pentagon attack of 9/11. Sheila was also the primary breadwinner and thought the couple had taken every legal precaution they could to protect each other. Peggy was threatened with the loss of their house if she did not receive proceeds from the Victims Compensation Fund. She applied for disaster relief and received a letter from the Pentagon, sending their condolences for the loss of her "friend," but indicating that she did not meet the definition of family established for the funds. After several hearings on the issue, the federal government relented and provided Peggy compensation for Sheila's death, marking the first time the federal government has ever recognized a same-sex partner with the kind of support and protection it provides to married couples.

These were small victories sparked by a national tragedy and prominent roles played by gay heroes such as Mark Bingham and Father Mychal Judge, but until DOMA is repealed, the general discriminatory rules still apply to all future national disasters.

CHAPTER NINE:
THE GAY TAX PENALTY

· ────────────── ·

"We pay our bills, we pay our taxes, yet you deny us marriage access!"

—Marriage Equality California Chant heard at the April 15, 2002 Tax Day Protest.

In October 2009, the *New York Times* published an article entitled "The High Price of Being A Gay Couple." According to authors, Tara Siegel Bernard and Ron Lieber, an average same-sex couple's "lifetime cost of being gay was $467,562," which they attributed to disparate realities between heterosexual and same-sex couples with regard to social security benefits, health insurance, tax preparation and taxation, ability to claim head of household, estate planning, and many more financial factors. Attorney and author, Frederick Hertz contrasts the experience of heterosexual married couples and same-sex couples suggesting that being a married heterosexual is like being able to always ride in the carpool lane while being in a same-sex relationship means you always have to "Stop. Wait. Pay a toll." Bernard and Lieber also found that in the best case scenario, "health coverage costs the gay couple $28,595 more" than their married heterosexual counterparts.

MARRIED, STILL FILING SINGLE

There are 179 marriage provisions associated with federal taxation. Because of DOMA, gay Americans cannot file joint federal taxes with their same-sex partners. Even in states where same-sex couples are legally married, the federal government does not recognize our marriages and forces us to complete four tax forms:

a) Two federal tax forms filing "single"
b) One "dummy" federal form with combined income for your married state form.
c) One state tax form filing "married"

This is costly and disrespectful. It requires tax preparers to do more work for same-sex couples than straight couples, and LGBT people have to pay more money to tax preparers to complete the additional complicated calculations. It also means married same-sex couples are treated differently under the law than heterosexual married couples.

Gay survivor's pay inheritance taxes on our spouse's/partner's estate when they die, but heterosexual survivors are exempt from this. We pay death taxes in the 24 states that have death taxes because we are "legal strangers" to our spouses/ life partners. We can't file as head of household. We can't claim our non-biological children, unless we have gone through a lengthy second-parent adoption. We get taxed extra on our health insurance benefits for our domestic partners, while married heterosexuals don't. And on and on!

The IRS expects adults in long-term committed relationships to check "single" when they fill out their taxes and denies them the right to file jointly. And for folks who are legally married, they are expected to check "single," or risk incarceration and tax evasion if they check "married." Meanwhile, heterosexual married couples can decide whether it is most advantageous to file *singly or jointly.*

INHERITANCE TAX

When a person dies, the federal government places a tax on all property and assets owned by the deceased. That tax can be as high as 50% of the total value of the assets. A number of states also have a separate state death tax on top of the federal government tax that must also be paid before the beneficiaries of the will get anything. However, the government authorizes a "marital deduction," exempting all property left to a surviving spouse from taxation. But again since same-sex couples can only own homes and property as joint tenants, the house is reassessed and they are taxed on the new value of the home. The total value of all property held in joint tenancy is included in a taxable estate, minus the portion the surviving joint tenant can prove s/he contributed. Every surviving same-sex joint tenant risks losing their home to estate taxes, whereas every surviving widow/widower can rest assured that they will not lose any of their property at the death of their spouse, *and* their taxes are even *deferred until they die.*

THE TAX EQUITY FOR HEALTH PLAN BENEFICIARIES ACT OF 2009 HR 2625, SB 1153

This bill would amend the IRS code of 1986 to stop taxing employees for the benefit of providing health care to their same-sex spouses and partners. According to the Human Rights Campaign, employers would no longer have to "calculate the portion of their healthcare contribution attributable to a non-spouse, non-dependent beneficiary and to create and maintain a separate system for the income tax withholding and payroll tax obligations for employees using such coverage."

The bill would help elminate one unfair tax burden from same-sex couples, but why go about this piecemeal, adding a crumb or maybe a slice here, when we can eliminate this injustice immediately by repealing DOMA and granting same-sex couples access to full marriage quality.

CHAPTER TEN:
THE MONEY YOU COULD BE SAVING
IF YOU SWITCHED TO MARRIAGE EQUALITY

MARRIAGE EQUALITY SAVES MONEY!

A 2004 United States Congressional Budget Office report (www.cbo.gov) found that allowing same-sex couples to marry in all 50 states and *recognizing same-sex marriages would save the government one billion dollars annually*. One billion dollars is a lot of money! Should I say that again?

> *Recognizing same-sex marriages would save the United States Government ONE BILLION DOLLARS A YEAR!*

And if that that wasn't reason enough in these tough economic times to make even the most conservative person a rainbow-flag-waving-supporter of marriage equality, UCLA's Williams Institute did a series of studies assessing the economic impact of allowing same-sex couples to marry on various states[24] and found that marriage equality generates significant amounts of savings for state governments as well.

According to the Williams Institute's reports, same-sex marriage saves state governments money on state means-tested public benefits programs, like Medi-Cal.

They found that because a single person's benefits are based on their income alone and a married person's income is based on the couple's combined household income, fewer people would

---

24 (http://www.law.ucla.edu/williamsinstitute.com)

be eligible for state benefits (like welfare, student loans, assisted housing), saving the state significant amounts of money.

MARRIAGE EQUALITY IS GOOD FOR BUSINESS

Additionally, allowing same-sex couples to marry increases that state's revenue by bringing money to the state through state sales taxes as couples spend money on weddings and pay marriage license fees.

> "*In total, we estimate that marriage equality has lead to a positive impact to the Massachusetts economy of approximately $111 million over the last four and a half years.*"
>
> —Williams Institute Report, May 2009

WASHINGTON, D.C.

An April 2009, Williams Institute report entitled "The Economic Impact of Extending Marriage to Same-Sex Couples in the District of Columbia," proposed that the "direct spending from same-sex couples on weddings and tourism will generate almost $5.4 million in new revenues." They estimated that the weddings of same-sex couples living in D.C. and outside of D.C. would "generate over $4.8 million in sales tax revenues and hotel tax revenues" and that "the weddings from local and non-resident couples will generate approximately $650,000 in marriage license fees for D.C."

Allowing Same-Sex Couples to Marry in Maine would have boosted the state budget by $7.9 million a year.

MAINE

In April 2009, the Williams Institute released a publication entitled, "The Impact on Maine's Budget of Allowing Same-Sex

Couples to Marry." The study found that same-sex couples marrying in Maine would "boost the state budget by $7.9 million per year" and "that allowing same-sex couples to marry will result in a net gain of approximately $7.9 million each year for the State…" as a result of "savings in expenditures on state means-tested public benefits programs and an increase in revenue from state sales and income taxes and marriage license fees." The authors indicated that Maine has approximately 4,644 same-sex couples and they estimated that half or "2,316 couples, would choose to marry during the first three years after marriage was opened to same-sex couples," based on findings of marriage patterns for same-sex couples in other states with marriage or marriage "lite" alternatives. Too bad the majority of Maine voters chose to lose money by voting for discrimination. Now all those betrothed same-sex couples will spend their gay dollars and honeymoons in neighboring New Hampshire.

IOWA

Keeping marriage for same-sex couples in Iowa will result in a net gain of approximately $5.3 million each year for the State of Iowa (Williams Institute Report, April 2008).

VERMONT

Keeping marriage for same-sex couples in Vermont would "generate $31 million in new spending over the next three years. This new spending will generate 700 new jobs and an additional $3.3 million in state tax revenues." –Williams Institute Report, March 2009.

MARYLAND

Extending marriage rights to same-sex couples would result in a net gain of approximately $3.2 million each year in Maryland. (Williams Institute Report, November 2007).

New Mexico

Allowing same-sex couples to marry in New Mexico would result in a net gain of $1.5 million to $2 million dollars annually. (Williams Institute Report, March 2006).

It costs money to discriminate!

Discrimination is not only ugly for those who are discriminated against, but continued discrimination against same-sex couples is costing straight Americans money too.

Gay People Are Good For Business!

No, seriously, I'm not just saying that, it's true. Richard Florida's Book *The Rise of the Creative Class*, (Basic Books, 2002), found that regions that value diversity, art, and LGBT people are more attractive to younger, more highly-educated workers who move to these regions, thus creating an environment that breeds creativity and innovation. This is much needed in a global economy. Less-tolerant regions are not attractive to the creative class, and thus, new ideas and energies don't flow to these conservative, stagnant areas, so economic growth is stifled. Florida suggests that towns that wish to flourish should support art and promote respect for racial and cultural diversity, including LGBT people.

Not that we should only be motivated to do good for others because it saves us money. We should eliminate discrimination and usher in equality and respect for diversity because it is the right thing to do and will make the world a better place for all.

SECTION THREE:
HEALTH AND FAMILY

CHAPTER ELEVEN:
MARRIAGE EQUALITY IS
GOOD FOR YOUR HEALTH!

"Now that we are legally married, family and friends finally understand the true depth and commitment of our relationship and we can relax knowing that there are laws in place to protect us and to allow us to make decisions for each other. This has enhanced our well-being considerably."

—Dave & Jeff Janis-Kitzmiller

MARRIAGE IT'S GOOD FOR YOUR HEALTH!

Psychological research has long shown that marriage has numerous health benefits and that married people are healthier than the non-married. In 1990, Catherine Ross and her colleagues at the University of Iowa reviewed a decade of psychological research on the impact of marriage on people's overall health and found significant benefits associated with marriage. Marriage is associated with better physical health, psychological well-being, and lower mortality rates because in general, married people engage in less risky behaviors than single people. Married people eat more healthfully and are less likely to smoke, drink excessively, and drive recklessly, while single people's riskier behavior leads to an "increase in the likelihood of accidents and injuries."[25]

Additionally, married people are more likely to go the doctor when they are sick and to schedule check ups and other

---

25 Ross, C.E., Mirowsky, J. & Goldsteen, K. (1990). *The impact of family on health: the decade in review. Journal of Marriage and the Family, 52, 1059-1078.*

screenings which may be influenced by the fact that more married people have access to health insurance than single people.

Dr. John Gottman, the foremost researcher on marriage and marital satisfaction, has found that people who are in happy marriages tend to be more "health conscious," "live longer," and show "a greater proliferation of white blood cells."[26]

THE PSYCHOLOGICAL BENEFITS OF MARRIAGE

In her review of the research, Ross noted that non-married people reported "higher levels of depression, anxiety, and other forms of psychological distress." "Living with someone rather than alone," was one reason offered to explain the differences in well-being between the married and the non-married. However, when this factor was controlled for, they still found that "the unmarried, living alone or with others, are significantly more distressed than the married," and the "presence or absence of another adult in the household does not explain the patterns of marriage and well-being." They conclude that "marital happiness is still the largest contributor to overall happiness." Even in a recent study[27] showing that though "the [health-benefits] gap between married and never-married is closing, especially for men," researcher Hui Liu stated that "married people are still healthier than unmarried people."

The Health and Marriage Equality in Massachusetts Survey, published by the State Department of Public Health in May 2009, confirms that marriage has perceived wellness benefits for married same-sex couples as well. According to an executive summary of the survey published by the Williams Institute (May 2009), seventy-two per cent (72 %) of individuals in same-sex marriages reported "feeling more committed" to their spouse

---

26 *The Seven Principles for Making Marriage Work, John Gottman, Ph.D. and Nan Silver. 1999. Three Rivers Press, New York: New York.*
27 *Liu, H. & Umberson, D. (2009). The Times Are A Changin': Marital Status and Health Differentials from 1972 to 2003, Journal of Health and Social Behavior, September Issue*

and "70% felt more accepted by their communities." Individuals also reported other important benefits from marriage, including:

(1) feeling that they have to worry less about legal problems (48%),
(2) being able to give their same-sex spouse health insurance (30%),
(3) coming out to co-workers (82%),
(4) coming out to healthcare providers (82%),
(5) feeling that their children are "happier and better off as a result of their marriage" (93%).

Especially notable was the finding that 62% of individuals reported that being married increased their family's acceptance of their same-sex spouse.

Unfortunately, same-sex couples only have access to marriage in 10% of the United States. Lack of recognition of same-sex relationship rights is still the norm. Dr. Sheryl Dagang, a lesbian and clinical psychologist, says that "LGBT people, live, work, love, survive and thrive in a world that continually informs us of our 'less-than' status." She says, LGBT people are "bombarded with messages from television, movies, radio and other media, as well as spiritual communities and friends and family, that we do not deserve equal rights or even equal protection."

That was certainly the case for Patrick Atkins and his partner, Brett Conrad, when Patrick suffered from an aneurysm and a stroke while traveling to Georgia on business. Despite the fact that the couple had been together for 25 years, Brad was unable to make medical decisions for Patrick because there was no advanced health care directive or medical power of attorney (something automatically granted to heterosexual spouses). And worse still, was the fact that Patrick's mother had invoked her legal right to deny Brad, hospital visitation and later visitation to the nursing home that Patrick was moved to.

A similar real-life horror story happened to Lisa Pond and her partner of eighteen years, Janice Langbehn while the couple was on vacation with their three kids. The family was boarding an R Family Cruise in Florida, when Lisa had an aneurysm and was taken to a Miami hospital. Janice and the children were denied access to her hospital bed. The hospital did not recognize their family and refused to recognize Janice as someone who could give and receive medical information, something automatically granted spouses. Eight hours later, Janice and the children were allowed to see Lisa, after she was dead. Janice was also denied a copy of Lisa's death certificate. Without the death certificate, Janice cannot get life insurance benefits for the children. She and the children have been denied Lisa's Social Security survivor's benefits. Janice is suing the hospital with help from Lambda Legal.

Even when couples have marriage-lite alternatives the laws are stacked against them. As was the case for Crispin Hollings whose legal domestic partner, Eric Rofes, a writer, professor, and advocate for gay men's health issues, died from a heart attack while on a summer sabbatical in Massachusetts in 2006. Even though Massachusetts recognized marriages between same-sex couples in 2006, they didn't recognize Eric's registered domestic partnership of sixteen years to Crispin Hollings. Hollings reported that he had several challenges getting Eric's body back to California.

The hardships caused by relationship inequality impacts LGBT people's mental health as well. According to a study by researchers Gil Herdt and Robert Kertzner published in the March 2006 edition of *Sexuality Research and Social Policy: Journal of the National Sexuality Research Center*, marriage discrimination creates 'minority stress' which is "significantly higher levels of stress disorders caused by acts of discrimination." They argue that allowing same-sex couples to marry would reduce psychological distress in LGBT people and lead to an increase in mental health and wellness.

Herdt and Kertzner are not the only researchers that postulate that marriage equality has positive health benefits for LGBT people. HIV researchers are discovering that marriage denial can lead to high risk sexual behavior and increased HIV infection rates for gay men. Emory University conducted a study entitled "HIV and Tolerance" and found that states that have marriage bans have a higher rate of unprotected sex and HIV infections which they attribute to homophobic attitudes. Hugo Mialon, Assistant Professor at Emory University, says that "bans on gay marriage codify intolerance, causing more gay people to shift to underground sexual behaviors that carry more risk."

Additionally, on November 18, 2008, the American Psychological Association issued a press release citing several studies[28] that noted that LGBT people living in states that passed voter approved constitutional marriage bans had higher levels of psychological distress. It was specifically reported that "amendments that restrict civil marriage rights of same-sex couples—such as Proposition 8 that recently passed in California—have led to higher levels of stress among lesbian, gay, bisexual and transgender adults, as well as among their families of origin." Sharon Scales Rostosky, Ph.D. who led a quantitative on-line study of 1,552 participants from all 50 states, and including the District of Columbia, reported that the "stress is not due to other pre-existing conditions or factors; it is a direct result of the negative images and messages associated with the ballot campaign and the passage of the amendment."

---

28 *"Marriage Amendments and Psychological Distress in Lesbian, Gay and Bisexual (LGB) Adults," Sharon Scales Rostosky, Ph.D., and Ellen D.B. Riggle, Ph.D., University of Kentucky; Sharon G. Horne, Ph.D., University of Memphis; and Angela D. Miller, Ph.D., University of Kansas; Journal of Counseling Psychology, Vol. 56, No. 1.*

GAY SPOUSE, STRAIGHT MARRIAGE

Homophobia and marriage discrimination are also unhealthy because they lead many gay and bisexual men and women to marry a member of the opposite sex. Religious teachings that homosexuality is a choice and can be changed is often at the root of what propels a gay person into a straight marriage and leading a double or repressed life.

Both were true for Reverend Troy Perry, Founder of the Metropolitan Community Church, one of the first open and affirming gay churches. Perry says he had his first sexual experience when he was nine years old with another boy his age. But he says, growing up Pentecostal, he knew that "what I was doing the church would feel was wrong. My family moved to Alabama and I married my pastor's daughter, after telling him about these feelings I was having. He said 'All you need is to marry a good woman and that will take care of that problem.'" But that's not true at all.

These "mixed-orientation marriages" as they are called by the Straight Spouse Network,[29] describes a marriage in which one person is attracted to members of the opposite sex and the other person is attracted to members of the same-sex. By denying gay people equal rights and shaming them for who they are, many try and "change" and hide who they are by entering into heterosexual marriages.

This social pressure hurts innocent straight men and women who discover that they've been duped into marrying gay people. Some of the more well-publicized examples of this are novel writer, Terry McMillan's marriage to her gay husband and former politician Jim McGreevy coming out to his wife and New Jersey about his homosexuality. The movie *Brokeback Mountain* also

---

29 *The Straight Spouse Network (SSN) is an international organization that provides support to heterosexual spouses/partners, current or former, of gay, lesbian, bisexual, or transgender mates and mixed-orientation couples for constructively resolving coming-out problems.*

portrayed this reality and the harm it causes to both the gay and straight spouse. It is harmful and fruitless to try and change one's sexual orientation, illustrated by the frequent *scandals* of conservative ministers or politicians who rail against gay people getting married and then are caught cheating on their own wives with men (Ted Haggard, Senator Larry Craig).

My friend and fellow marriage equality advocate, Alison Little shared the personal impact of her parent's mixed-orientation, "My father has been in the closet most of his life. Being married to my mother for thirty years did not make my father straight. It made him a gay man living a lie. When I think of all the pain and isolation that both of my parents have experienced in this union, I want to create in a society where people can be themselves."

Even when there is no extramarital sex, the straight spouse is often in the dark as to why their spouse is disenchanted with them and disinterested in sex. And when they find out about their spouse's sexual orientation, they experience betrayal and the death of their own dreams and happily-ever-after.

As David Boies, one of the straight attorneys challenging Proposition 8, told reporters, "It is impossible to see how [gays and lesbians who marry straight partners] could be thought to be as likely to lead a stable, loving relationship as a marriage to the person they do love."

In sum, marriage has health and wellness benefits that do not come from simply living with someone. Marriage commitment provides stability to men and women, gay and straight, and provides primary and secondary health benefits, including reduced risk taking behavior and substance abuse and an increase in longevity. While marital happiness, rather than simply being partnered, is the greatest factor associated with overall happiness and well-being, marriage discrimination is harmful to the health and well-being of those discriminated against and their families.

Marriage discrimination leads to an increase in stress and stress-related disorders, as well as high risk and down low kinds of behaviors. Marriage access would provide same-sex couples and their families with numerous health and wellness benefits and alleviate unnecessary suffering.

CHAPTER TWELVE:
MARRIAGE DISCRIMINATION HURTS CHILDREN

The American Academy of Pediatrics, the American Psychological Association, and the American Medical Association support the rights of gays and lesbians to be parents, endorse legal protections for same-sex parents and their children, and confirm from thirty years of social science research that children raised by gay and lesbian parents are just as likely to be raised in healthy environments and to be as well-adjusted as children raised by heterosexual parents. In fact, one longitudinal study found that children raised by two mothers "scored higher than kids in straight families on some psychological measures of self-esteem and confidence, did better academically and were less likely to have behavioral problems, such as rule-breaking and aggression."[30]

Yet despite solid evidence, the perpetuation of the myth that children raised by same-sex parents are somehow harmed has led many fair-minded people to reject marriage equality for same-sex couples. It is this rejection of equal marriage protections for same-sex couples that has actually caused real harm to real children.

The denial of equal marriage rights creates a second-class status for children of LGBT parents because they do not have the same rights and protections that children of heterosexual parents have. The children of same-sex parents are often denied the safety and security of two legally recognized parents that can care for them and who are responsible for them. These children have the right to have parents who are legally married and to have access to the same governmental benefits that children of heterosexuals have.

Here's what one young boy had to say about why he wanted his two moms to be able to legally marry. "Having marriage

---

30 Gartrell, N. Bos, H. *The USA National Longitudinal Lesbian Family Study: psychological adjustment of the 17-year-old adolescents. Pediatrics.* 2010;126(1):28–36

makes families happy. We love each other and marriage makes relationships even stronger. When we have that, we can achieve more and feel even better about ourselves. We need to help people see that we need the same rights. I love being a part of my family, we're great. We have a lot of fun and do the same things that other families do, like go to baseball games. So, we should get the same stuff. Marriage means having the same rights as everyone else."—Sam, 10 years old.[31]

> *"The day after we lost Prop 8, my six-year old asked me, with tears running down his face, if we were still a family."*
>
> —Parent Contra Costa County, California.

Children of LGBT parents also experience the negative psychological and physical effects of minority stress. Because their parents and their families do not have the same rights and benefits as other families and because their family's legal recognition has been under attack for over a decade by courts and voters seeking to take away their parents' right to marry and adopt, these children experience heaps of stressors that kids of heterosexual parents never have to think about. This stress can negatively effect a child's learning abilities, self-esteem, sense of well-being, and put them at risk for various health related concerns as well as other ways of coping that could be detrimental to their health, (e.g. drinking, smoking, drug use).

This is also true for LGBT youth who are growing up in a world that tells them their love is disgusting, and despises them for being true to their heart. This would be devastating

---

31 From *Prop 8 Hurt My Family, Ask Me How: A compilation of findings from community forums and on-line surveys*, Pamela Brown, Policy Director Marriage Equality USA, January 2009. www.marriageequality.org.

to anyone, but especially to a young person who is isolated and may not have the support and resources that adults are able to seek out. Coming out in a society that strips LGBT people of their rights and denies them freedoms guaranteed others can be terrifying. Because of this, many LGBT youth attempt suicide. Others turn to substance abuse to numb the pain of rejection or drop out of school to shield themselves from the bullying and physical violence they are exposed to because of intolerance.

BULLYING AND INTOLERANCE AT SCHOOL

Bullying gay kids at school has existed for years, highlighted by childhood games called "smear the queer." According to findings from the 2007 National School Climate Survey report by the Gay, Lesbian, Straight Education Network (GLSEN) 91% of LGBT middle school students said they experienced harassment at school because of their sexual orientation. Fifty-nine per cent reported physical harassment, 39% reported physical assault compared to 20% of LGBT high school students. Eighty-two per cent of LGBT middle-school children heard names like "faggot" and "dyke," and 63% reported that they heard staff make homophobic remarks.

Being the target of school bullying can greatly impact a student's grades. Half of the LGBT middle school students surveyed reported that they had missed at least one day of school in the past month because they felt unsafe. The report showed that LGBT students who missed school because they were afraid of being hurt had lower GPAs than other LGBT students (2.4 to 2.9). More than half (57%) of the students who experienced harassment never reported it because they feared the teachers wouldn't help them or reporting it would only make things worse.

Constitutional amendment initiatives to take away marriage rights from same-sex couples may also encourage bullying against LGBT youth and against children of same-sex parents.

According to a Marriage Equality USA report[32] on the impact of California's Proposition 8 compiled from verbal reports at town halls held across California and from an on-line survey of 3,100 respondents, "forty-five percent of respondents under age 18 reported personally experiencing homophobia, hate speech or threats of violence during the proposition 8 campaign. Children of same-sex and transgender parents, LGBT youth, and straight youth who were open about their support for marriage equality also experienced increased bullying at school.

"Students at my high school often harassed me for being No on 8. I would hear people saying, 'She must be gay,' and taunting me. A group of rambunctious boys made a point of following me as long as possible through the hallways while they yelled 'Yes on 8' and called me derogatory names."

—Straight teenager, San Diego County, California.

"I'm only 16 years old and straight. While supporting No on 8 outside my high school, many people gave me the finger."

—Anonymous, Orange County, California

"During the Prop 8 campaign, someone on campus hung a noose with a confederate flag warning students that if they were black, queer or hippie that they were not welcome. It was very disturbing."

—Anonymous, San Luis Obispo County, California

---

32 *From Prop 8 Hurt My Family, Ask Me How: A compilation of findings from community forums and on-line surveys, Pamela Brown, Policy Director Marriage Equality USA, January 2009. www.marriageequality.org.*

LGBT parents reported an increase of fear in their children as a result of being directly exposed to vitriolic hate speech during the campaign. The quotes below are just a few examples of the things that children heard at rallies during the campaign to take away their parents' marriages.

"During a rally, my son and I were called ugly names. He is eleven and I don't know how calling him a faggot is acceptable."

—Parent, Santa Barbara County, California

"Several groups of 'Yes on 8' people repetitively came up to me and proceeded to scream obscenities and terrorize the children. One person even got in my face and stated 'if it was up to me, I'd kill all the fags.' This scared the children so much, we had to leave."

—Parent, San Bernadino County, California

"My seven year old son asked, 'If the Yes on 8 people win, will you and Mama have to break up?"

—Parent, Contra Costa County, California

"My children don't understand why people want to take away their parent's right to be married."

—Parent, Riverside County, California

MARRIAGE EQUALITY IS GOOD FOR CHILDREN

According to The Health and Marriage Equality in Massachusetts Survey (May 2009), 93% of same-sex couples raising children in Massachusetts reported that their children are happier and better off as a result of their marriage.

As mentioned already, marriage discrimination hurts children in numerous ways. Anti-gay marriage amendments expose children of LGBT parents to discrimination, bullying, negative messages about their families, and sometimes physical violence. Denying children of LGBT parents the right to have married parents and treating these children as second-class citizens increases their psychological distress and sense of insecurity. Children of LGBT parents do not have access to survivor benefits from non-biological parents the way that children whose parents are married do, regardless of a biological link. Because of marriage discrimination many children of LGBT parents do not have the same family law and custody protections that children of heterosexual parents do. These kids can be emotionally and financially abandoned by a non-biological parent who uses the homophobic laws to get out of their parental responsibility, or by a biological parent who uses homophobic law to deny parentage rights of a second, non-biological parent who has played a significant role in the intention of bringing a child into their lives with their same-sex partner either through adoption or insemination, and have been a part of that child's life since their introduction into their family, as was the case below.

MOMMY DEAREST

Sharon S. and her partner, Annette, were already raising one child, when they planned a second child together. Annette inseminated Sharon and together the couple cared for their second child together until their separation. After the separation, Sharon became a born-again Christian and renounced that she was a lesbian. She sought out the legal assistance of anti-gay groups who argued that her ex-partner did not have parental rights to their newborn because a) the child was not hers biologically, and b) the child had not yet been officially adopted by her ex before the break up. The California courts ruled in Sharon's favor.

If the couple had married, the point would have been moot because marriage entitles both the biological and non-biological parent legal parentage. However, in states that don't allow same-sex couples to marry, non-biological parents must adopt their child after the child's birth. The process is expensive, lengthy, and involves a home visit. Even after all that, the parent is only officially a stepparent.

According to April Fernando, Ph.D., a child psychologist and non-biological mother herself, the legal process of securing parental rights for a non-biological same-sex parent is excruciatingly painful for the entire family and can create a tentative quality to the relationship between child and parent. "It's been a real education and until I had the paper that said that I was my son's parent, there was something a little touch and go about our relationship, because the legal aspects of being a parent are so important even though we may not know them all on a conscious level."

Dr. Fernando also indicated that even with their wills, power of attorney, wishes communicated to family members, and a legal decree stating that she would be able to make medical decisions for their unborn child if anything happened to her partner during the pregnancy, the entire process made the couple feel "less than." Dr. Fernando remarked, "They evaluate whether or not you are 'fit to be parent.' I think everyone should have to through a test to ensure you are a good parent, not just me because I'm gay."

CHILDREN OF COLOR ARE HARMED BY MARRIAGE DISCRIMINATION

Christine Chavez-Delgado, Former Political Director, United Farm Workers of American Union and Granddaughter of Civil Rights Leader Cesar Chavez is an advocate for gay Latino families. She says, "There are more Latino same-sex couples in California than in any other state. More than 40 percent of same-sex couples in California identify as Latino and close to half of them are raising children. And as we see the Latino population continuing to grow, we could see in the next 5-10 years Latino same-sex couples as the largest population of LGBT families in California that will be negatively affected by marriage discrimination." She asks fellow Latinos to "remember that the rights of the few should not be trumped by the will of the many."

According to a William's Institute Report entitled *California's Latino/Latina Population* (October 2008), 25% of Californians in same-sex couples are Latino/a and over 24,948 children in California are being raised in LGBT Latino households. Forty-three percent of Latino male couples are raising children and 50% of Latina female couples are raising children compared to 72% of heterosexual Latino couples. Yet, these couples don't have the same rights as heterosexual Latino couples, like head of household tax breaks. Same-sex couples are also less likely to own their homes compared to heterosexual Latino couples. Only 36% of Latino same-sex couples with children own their homes compared to 57% of heterosexual couples. This may be related to the additional taxes that same-sex couples have to pay and other costs from lack of marital employments benefits that heterosexual Latinos are granted through marriage.

According to a report by the National Gay and Lesbian Task Force Policy Institute and the National Black Justice Coalition, Black lesbian couples are also raising children at approximately the same rate as their heterosexual counterparts (61% of black lesbians compared to 69% of black heterosexuals). And almost half of all black gay male couples are also raising children (46%). But black same-sex couples lack the legal protections and tax breaks because they are not able to legally marry and protect their families.

GROWING UP GAY, LESBIAN, BISEXUAL, TRANSGENDER, EMBRACING THE DREAM.

"I want a family. I want a husband. I have dreams of my wedding."

— Gay Latino and Native American Male, under 18, from San Luis Obispo County, California

"I have had many people that are very dear to me turn me away because of who I love and support. This really gets me and I really wish for marriage equality one day."

— White lesbian, under 18, from Maryland.

"I'm young and therefore am not getting married in the near future. However I plan to. I just don't know if it will be with a boy or a girl. It scares me to know that my choice could be taken away from me, and I could be denied the right to marry a girl. It has made me very cautious of the government, more so than I have already been."

—Latino, Bisexual Female, under 18 (no location provided)

Can you imagine growing up in a world that values falling in love, getting married and having children, but being told that dream did not apply to you? Well, that's what it's like for LGBT youth. They live in a society that tells them that they will not be able to fall in love and marry. They hear repeatedly from some churches and society that they are not good enough to be married and that their love is wrong. Telling these kids that they cannot have the dream of love and marriage valued by most cultures causes them emotional pain and suffering. They want to live in a world where they can celebrate love and be treated equally.

Many LGBT young people across California were emotionally wounded by the passage of Proposition 8 because they experienced that a right previously given to gay people was taken away by a slim majority of voters. One young white lesbian from San Diego County wrote, "I am saddened by the passage of Prop 8. My future hung in the balance of this decision, and now I cannot marry the person I love, or feel secure in my relationship with her. It has increased the amount of attacks on the LGBT community. I feel less safe walking down the street than I did before."

Another teenage girl from San Luis Obispo County, California wrote: "I got so upset I cried four times at school in one day... it's just sickening that my future happiness is a simple little conversation for someone, and they think it's perfectly fine to force their religious morals on everyone else."

For some young people the passage of Proposition 8 in California signaled to them that moving to another state or country with marriage equality would be a better choice than remaining in a location that treated them as second-class citizens.

" Although I'm completely out and know that there is a strong support system for me, my closeted friends were deeply disturbed by the Prop 8 passing. It made them lose hope and pushed them further into the closet. It personally made me lose faith in my fellow Californians. It dulled my previously burning desire to stay in California for the rest of my life. I was in a depression for a few weeks after at the thought of finding a man I love and not being able to marry. "

— White gay male youth, Los Angeles County

Relocation to an area that does allow same-sex marriage also hurts family members of LGBT people who want to be close to their siblings, children, cousins, and so forth, but also want their family members to be treated equally and have the freedom to marry.

> *" My twin sister is a lesbian and this ignorant amendment has ruined her plan to be with the one she loves in her future. Now, she plans to move out of the United States and go where it is legal to marry the same sex, in order to have equal rights. This is not right. "*
>
> —White, heterosexual female youth, Missouri

As so aptly described, these young people's futures hang in the balance. As society continues to debate and have popularity contests about whether or not same-sex marriage should be legal, these young people are living in a world that treats them as second-class citizens and casts a long shadow over their future dreams and hopes. While I have still yet to see how marriage equality damages society, the causalities of denying marriage equality are quite plain.

THE IMPACT OF MARRIAGE EQUALITY ON PARENTS OF LGBT PEOPLE

> *" My only wish for my son, Jason, is that he continues to experience a rich life of love, happiness, joy, and fulfillment, both creatively and personally. "*
>
> —Barbara Streisand Advocate, Aug 17, 1999

Marriage equality also has a positive impact on parents of LGBT children who want their children to live happily-ever-after lives too, free of harassment and discrimination. Sam Thoron, former National President of Parents, Families and Friends of Lesbians and Gays (PFLAG), an organization whose mission is to "promote the health and well-being of gay, lesbian, bisexual and transgender persons, their families and friends," wants equal marriage rights for his daughter, Liz. Sam and his wife, Julia, are working for marriage equality because Sam says, "We are deeply committed to the principle that our daughter, Liz, deserves to be treated with the same respect and dignity as her two straight brothers." He joined the board of Marriage Equality USA, a national grassroots organization committed to ensuring equality for all couples, regardless of sexual orientation and gender, because he feels his daughter "deserves exactly the same rights, privileges and obligations of full participation in citizenship in this country as they enjoy, including the right enter into a civil marriage with her chosen love without restrictions of sexual orientation or gender identity."

Dolores Huerta, the President of the Dolores Huerta Foundation for Community Organizing and co-founder of the United Farm Workers, says it is the responsibility of parents with gay children to work for equality for their gay children. She says "ensuring that our children are loved, respected and treated with dignity is what every parent wants. However, this will only happen if mothers and fathers take the first step and not allow their gay child to be treated as a second-class citizen. Gay and lesbian children should have equal rights and equal opportunity to a happy successful life."

Maurie Davidson, social worker and PFLAG mom, who is actively involved with Straight for Equality, a national outreach and education project of PFLAG that empowers straight allies to support and advocate for LGBT people, agrees with Huerta. Maurie is adamant about eliminating marriage discrimination and repeatedly travels to the state capitol to lobby equal marriage rights for gay people. She asks, "Why is it necessary for my child to be denied rights that I have had my entire life as a heterosexual woman? My daughter and daughter-in-law work diligently, pay taxes, own their own home and have two beautiful children, my grandchildren. No family need be a second-class family in the eyes of the law."

Maurie knows that as more straight parents like her come out, and especially as the list of celebrities who are open about their LGBT kids come out —Cher, Barbra Streisand, Tom Hanks, Marie Osmond, former Vice-President Dick Cheney, San Diego Mayor Jerry Sanders among others— and work toward their children's equality it will show that LGBT people come from all walks of life, all classes, and all races.

In 2008, Maurie got to be the mother of the brides after the California State Supreme Court granted same-sex couples the right to marry, and her daughter, Lisa, legally married her wife, Robin. Maurie says, "I only want for my daughter and daughter-in-law and their children what is already a legal right for me." She was deeply disappointed by the passage of Prop 8 and, like many parents with gay children, was shocked by the level of violence directed at them and their gay adult children.

A heterosexual parent of two lesbians reported that his opposition to Prop 8 made him a target. Not only was his home vandalized, according to the parent, "the police ignored it and some neighbors slandered me." Another parent who attended No on Prop 8 rallies reported that she was told she was "going to hell" and reported that her son was "spit on, called names, told he was a demon, a freak of nature, and a pedophile."

It is clear from these accounts that marriage discrimination negatively impacts LGBT people, their children, their family members, and even their straight friends. Marriage discrimination hurts LGBT youth who are growing up in a world that treats them unfairly and denies them the right to dream about a happily-ever-after. Because of marriage discrimination, children of same-sex couples are denied a sense of family, creating distress for them and their parents because they are denied important rights and protections as a family. Giving same-sex couples the right to marry would have positive emotional and psychological effects for these children.

Section Four:
International Marriage Equality

CHAPTER THIRTEEN:
THE GLOBAL HEART: BEYOND
INTERNATIONAL BORDERS

Who hasn't once dreamt of traveling to another country and falling in love with a local? There's a reason that *Eat, Pray, Love* and *Under the Tuscan Sun* were so popular. It's a great fantasy to leave your world behind and find a new adventurous part of yourself that you didn't even know existed.

For those who don't travel, I'm sure at least once in your life you've met an interesting man or woman from another country with a sexy accent and had a fantasy of them whispering sweet nothings to you in French, Italian, Spanish, Swahili, Hindi or whatever. Admit it. That ABBA song is still so popular because they were asking us to sleep with them in French. For most Americans, "Do you want to go to bed with me?" sounds good, but not as sexy as *voulez-vous coucher avec moi ce soir*. For some of us, we are just seeking a romantic encounter or a summer love, but some people's soul-mates do hail from a country other than their own.

Like heterosexuals, gay people travel abroad for work, in the private or public sector, and sometimes meet that someone special and fall in-love. But it's when they wish to remain together or return home with their new mates that the trouble starts for same-sex couples. Permanent residency is a right granted to non-citizen spouses, but in most countries, including the United States, not available to same-sex partners or same-sex spouses. Why are committed and married same-sex couples denied this right? Why can their heterosexual counterparts fall in love and return to their home country and give their mate legal residency, but same-sex couples cannot?

The United States borders Canada and Mexico, and according to Sarah Palin, Russia is just due north of her front porch. Many people cross these international borders everyday, some people fall in love with a guy or gal across the border. Heterosexual Americans have access to laws that give their spouse citizenship, gay Americans do not. This creates heart-break for numerous loving same-sex couples and tragedies for gay Americans. Bi-national couples, couples in which one member is a citizen from a country other than the country the couple is living in, are under the constant threat of separation.

MARTHA'S STORY

Martha met Lin while working abroad in the Netherlands. Lin is Australian. The couple fell in love and were legally married in 2001 when the Netherlands became the first country to recognize same-sex marriages. Nine years later, neither Australia, nor the United States will recognize the couple's marriage and they are living in exile in the Netherlands.

> *"I can bring my dog back to this country, but I can't bring my wife."*
> —Martha McDevitt-Pugh, American living in Exile in the Netherlands, Founder of Love Exiles International.

Out of necessity, Martha and Lin have become actively engaged in the political process to change the immigration and marriage laws in the United States. Martha flies to California as frequently as possible to visit her aging mother. On every trip she visits Sacramento to speak with politicans about the personal suffering that not having equal family immigration rights causes her and her family. She also frequently travels to DC to lobby for the Uniting American Families Act.

Martha never imagined she would have to choose between her family, her country, and the person she loved. Even if the State of California recognized same-sex marriages performed in other countries, because of the 1996 Defense of Marriage Act, Martha and Lin's marriage would still not be recognized by the federal government. As Martha says, "Because of DOMA, I can bring my dog back to the United States, but not my wife." Martha has created an organization entitled, Love Exiles International,[33] made up of same-sex couples who are legally married, but unable to return to their countries because of anti-gay marriage laws. She continues to hope that U.S. senators from her home state, like Diane Feinstein whom she has lobbied for over a decade, will finally sign on to co-sponsor legislation that would give same-sex couples immigration rights.

> *A marriage between a man and a woman is recognized for immigration purposes, but civil unions and gay marriages —even where they are allowed — do not qualify under the Defense of Marriage Act.*
>
> —Adam Francoeur, Policy Coordinator
> for Immigration Equality.

UNITING AMERICAN FAMILIES ACT (UAFA) HR 1024 AND SB 424

Once called the Permanent Partners Immigration Act, the Uniting American Families Act would amend the nation's Immigration and Nationality Act by adding same-sex "permanent partners" to the list of family members that a U.S. citizen or legal

---

33 *Love Exiles International Website www.loveexiles.org*

resident can sponsor for immigration. Under the bill, a "permanent partner" is described as an adult who is in a committed, intimate, financially interdependent relationship with another adult "in which both parties intend a lifelong commitment." The UAFA is supported by the American Bar Association and the NAACP.

The roadblocks to equality for bi-national couples are many. Not only is homophobia at play, and not only are the current laws unfair towards same-sex families, but anti-immigrant sentiment is part of what keeps the UAFA from passing. Many people view a bi-national same-sex couple's situation with skepticism assuming that it is always the foreigner who comes here and wants to stay to exploit America, rather than because they are in-love and loved by their partner and want to stay together as a family and want to contribute to this country. Anti-gay politicians capitalize on their constituents' fear and subterranean racist beliefs to defend their denial of equal family protections for bi-national couples and their families with devastating consequences.

If the UAFA passes, LGBT Americans will finally have the right to sponsor their same-sex partner for immigration and couples like Martha and Lin, who are already legally married, would finally have their marriages recognized in the U.S.

Congressman Mike Honda, a straight Japanese-American from California, sees the connection between the denial of civil rights of Japanese-Americans in the 1940s with the denial of civil rights for LGBT people today. He attributes the internment of Japanese Americans to a "lack of political leadership" against injustice and says that in "almost every civil rights case" this lack of advocacy and leadership is what allows discrimination to persist. He has included immigration rights for permanent same-sex partners in a larger immigration reform bill called the Reuniting American Families Act. However, the bill's sponsor in the senate has removed the section for bi-national same-sex couples in response to pressure from the religious groups. The Catholic church is one of the main opponents.

Shirley's Story

"I have a partner who is a U.S. Citizen, and two beautiful children who are also U.S. Citizens, but not one of them can petition for me to remain in the United States with them."

—Shirley Tan

Shirley Tan grew up in the Philippines. When she was 14 years old her mother and sister were murdered, Shirley too had been shot and left for dead, but survived. She came to the United States on asylum and has lived in California for over three decades. Shirley met the love of her life, Jay, a Filipina American, 23 years ago and the couple had two children together. Shirley, Jay and their twin boys were living their happily-ever-after, when a tragic event occurred.

"Around 6:30am, the doorbell was ringing. Two officers were looking for a Mexican girl they said is using our address. They said that in order for them to close their case they needed to see if the girl is hiding in our house. My partner, Jay, asked to see their identification and badge before she let them in. They asked that we show our ID cards. They got my ID and made a phone call and said that I had an order for deportation going back to May of 2002. I told them that I have a lawyer that is handling my case and I have never been informed of such. I am a housewife and have never broken the law.

They insisted that I go with them to the immigration office. My partner told them that we have to contact my lawyer first and have the lawyer go to the immigration office with us. They handcuffed me. I was taken like a criminal. I was praying so hard for me to wake up, but it was not a dream. My heart was beating so hard, my whole body was shaking and I felt so nauseated with what was happening to me.

When we arrived, I got off with my jacket concealing my handcuff in shame, because it is a public place. It took awhile before they took off my handcuff, then I was asked to put my palms on the wall, feet apart and searched me like a criminal, like I see only in movies. I was given a mug shot and put in a jail cell together with women with different types of criminal offenses.

That afternoon they put a monitoring device on my leg and told me to come back with a plane ticket to the Philippines. I went home that night. I did not eat nor speak to anyone in my family. My kids were asking questions where I had been and I could only say that I had several appointments the whole day.

How many times can a person be persecuted in a lifetime? I cannot go back to the Philippines again feeling scared and afraid for my life."

SHIRLEY'S CHILDREN WROTE LETTERS TO SENATORS TO KEEP THEIR MOM FROM BEING DEPORTED.

"Dear Senator,

My mother, Shirley Tan, has experienced some bad experiences in her life. She was almost killed and she lost her mom and sister at a very young age. Now our mom might have to leave our family. I don't want her to leave us. She doesn't deserve to lose us and we don't deserve to lose her. My other mom (Jay Mercado) is working very hard so my mom doesn't need to go back to the Philippines. The killer who murdered our grandmother and aunt is out there. We're very afraid. We are all she has and I don't want her to lose that too. We need to stay together as a family. We need her here not far away from us. She does everything for us. Our home will not be complete without her. I want my mom here beside us. Please help us senator not to lose our mother. We want her here with us. Help our mom. Please don't let this happen. I hope you understand how much we need her here."

This is only one example of how same-sex couples and their families can be torn apart because they don't have access to the same immigration rights provided heterosexual couples through marriage. Luckily, through extraordinary efforts, U.S. Senator Feinstein sponsored a private bill that allowed Shirley to stay in the U.S.[34] However thousands, of people in bi-national relationships like her, have already left or been deported, forced to leave the country, with or without their loving partners, because same-sex couples are not recognized as family by the U.S. Immigration and Customs Enforcement (ICE) Agency.

There was no legal avenue for San Angelo, Texas Mayor, J.W. Lown, to give his Mexican boyfriend citizenship because the federal government does not recognize same-sex relationships. So, in order for the couple to stay together, Lown who has dual citizenship, resigned from his government post and the couple moved to Mexico.

Eric Affholter, a St. Louis public defender, also tried to find a way to stay together with his partner, Pedro Cerna-Rojas from Peru. Since the couple could not immigrate together to Peru, he asked a heterosexual friend to marry Pedro, so that Pedro could remain in the country. "I just wanted to be able to spend the rest of my life with the person I fell in love with — in this country," Eric said in an interview after federal authorities discovered the details of the fraudulent marriage and deported Pedro. Eric was indicted on criminal charges.

Chris Waddling is from Canada where same-sex marriage has been legal since 2003. He's been with his American boyfriend for seven years and described his frustration with the United States' discriminatory marriage laws. "Last summer, my co-worker from Turkey announced her marriage to her American boyfriend of four years. I too announced my pending marriage to my American boyfriend of seven years. Both of us were look-ing forward to our wedding day, honeymoon, and our future lives with our spouses. The one difference was that my coworker's fiancé was taking steps to sponsor her based on their pending nuptials, but because my husband and I are of the same gender,

---

34 *At the time this book went to print, Senator Feinstein still has not signed on as a co-sponsor of UAFA.*

current U.S. immigration law does not recognize us as anything but strangers."

Waddling goes on to say, "Although my mother was able to sponsor me in 2006, I am not eligible for a visa until 2012, two years after my work visa expires. My only remaining option is to ask my boss to change my job title, shell out tens of thousands of dollars on lawyers, and hope that after years of going through the arduous process of a job-sponsored application, I will achieve the permanent residency status that my straight coworker and others in her situation are allowed through marriage. None of this would have happened if the federal government would allow LGBT Americans to sponsor their same-sex partners and recognize them as legal family, as they do for heterosexual Americans."

Transgender Americans have even fewer rights. Donita Ganzon transitioned from male to female in 1980. Twenty years later she married a man from the Phillipines and they applied for his citizenship. She was honest with the U.S. Citizenship and Immigration Service, or USCIS, and told them of her transition twenty four years earlier. She was told that she was not a "legal woman" and that under the DOMA, her marriage was not legal. Her husband was deported.

COUNTRIES THAT RECOGNIZE SAME-SEX RELATIONSHIPS FOR IMMIGRATION[35]

Some countries that recognize same-sex relationships as legal family relationships and allow the citizens of that country to sponsor their same-sex partners for citizenship include:

Argentina	Australia
Austria	Belgium
Brazil	Canada
Czech Republic	Denmark

---

35 *Please consult an immigration attorney to learn more about specific countries' laws on immigration.*

France   Finland
Germany   Iceland
Ireland   Israel
The Netherlands   New Zealand
Norway   Portugal
Spain   South Africa
Sweden   United Kingdom
Uruguay

REALITIES OF BI-NATIONAL COUPLES:

Because they do not have the legal protections through marriage that heterosexual bi-national couples have, same-sex couples search for creative solutions to stay together. However, because of legal and financial complications, many of these solutions are create other problems.

1. Emigrating

Both partners seek citizenship in one of the sixteen countries that recognizes same-sex relationships or one partner seeks citizenship if the other partner is already a citizen of one of the countries above.

2. Living in Exile

Both spouses remain in the country where they are legally married or partnered because they are unable to return to the United States or other country of origin with their spouse.

3. Living in the United States or Other Country Illegally

In some cases, the non-citizen overstays their visa to remain with their beloved and is now an illegal immigrant risking permanent deportation and a prison sentence. In the U.S., the U.S.

citizen is also risking a prison sentence and loss of career and reputation for aiding an undocumented immigrant.

4. Entering into a fraudulent heterosexual marriage

In desperation, some bi-national couples choose for one or both partners to enter into a fraudulent heterosexual marriage to obtain citizenship to keep the couple together. In the United States, this is a federal offense. The non-U.S. citizen is risking permanent deportation and a prison sentence, and the U.S. citizen is risking a prison sentence and loss of career and reputation.

5. Living Apart

One person lives in one country and the other in another. The couple sees each other as time and money afford which can be extremely costly both financially and emotionally.

6. Living by Visa

Getting a work permit that allows non-citizens to live in the United States or other country as long as they are being sponsored by an employer or while enrolled in a college or university. This is especially tenuous because if for any reason the immigrant loses his/her job, they have a very short window to find another job or they will be deported. In the United States it's two weeks. Also, for those who are in school, they must continue paying tuition and taking a full course-load or they will be deported.

UNITED BY LOVE, DIVIDED BY LAW

Bi-national couples are under considerable stress trying to stay together and this stress can often destroy the relationship as the couple tries to negotiate these challenges. After investing extraordinary amounts of time, money, and energy to stay together, many couples are torn apart. Many chose to leave their birth families and countries of origin behind. For those partners who stay illegally, they will never see their families again because they cannot return once they leave.

All of unjust situations in the United States could be easily remedied by the passage of the Uniting American Families Act (UAFA), which would add same-sex "permanent partners" to the list of family members that a U.S. citizen or legal resident can sponsor for immigration. or by repealing the Defense of Marriage Act. These tragic hardships could be eliminated globally if the remaining countries and provinces who don't recognize same-sex marriage would follow the lead of the sixteen countries that do legally recognize same-sex relationships for immigration purposes.

THE ABSURDITY OF THE LAW

On Valentine's Day 2003, my wife and I asked for a marriage license at San Francisco City Hall. It was our third year in a row of asking for a marriage license. Each year we did this to render visible the discrimination same-sex couples face by being denied the right to marry. We were standing in line in front of two gay men, a bi-national couple. We approached the counter and asked for a marriage license. When the clerk denied us, we turned around and each linked arms with the man behind us and re-approached the counter. This time the clerk immediately handed us a form. "We don't even know these men," I said. "Molly and I have been together for six years and you won't let us marry, but we can each marry a complete stranger off the street?"

"One man, one woman," the clerk replied.

It was crazy that we could have married those men, right there and then, without even knowing them, and marrying the man who was not a United States citizen would have granted him immigration rights and helped him stay in the country. But because the couple is denied equal marriage rights in the United

States, they were forced to the leave the country. They now live together in Canada where they are legally married.

TAKE ACTION NOW

You can help make a difference in the lives of thousands of same-sex couples, including couples like Shirley Tan and Jay Mercado, by encouraging your elected officials to support the Uniting American Families Act. I've included a sample letter below that you can copy and send to your Congressmember or Senator.

SAMPLE UNITING AMERICAN FAMILIES ACT (UAFA) LETTER

The Honorable Senator Feinstein
One Post Street, Suite 2450
San Francisco, CA 94104

RE: SUPPORT Uniting American Families Act S.424

Dear Senator Feinstein:

Please support the federal Uniting American Families Act (UAFA), which would remove legal barriers to immigration by permanent same-sex partners.

U.S. immigration policy is largely based on the principle of family reunification, which allows U.S. citizens and legal permanent residents to sponsor their spouses (and other immediate family members) for immigration purposes. Same-sex partners of U.S. citizens and legal permanent residents, however, are not considered to be family, and thus cannot be sponsored by their partners for family-based immigration. This is true even for couples that are legally married or recognized as married in Massachusetts, Connecticut, Iowa, California and New York. Because of this inequity, thousands of lesbian and gay bi-national couples are kept apart, torn apart, or forced to stay together illegally, with one partner living in constant fear of deportation.

According to the 2000 Census, approximately 35,000 bi-national same-sex couples currently live in the U.S. At least sixteen other countries already have immigration policies allowing the sponsorship of same-sex partners: Australia, Belgium, Brazil, Canada, Denmark, Finland, France, Germany, Iceland, Israel, the Netherlands, New Zealand, Norway, South Africa, Sweden and the United Kingdom.

The UAFA was introduced by U.S. Senator Patrick Leahy (D-VT) and Congressman Jerrold Nadler (D-NY) on February 12, 2009. The proposed legislation would amend the nation's Immigration and Nationality Act by adding same-sex "permanent partners" to the list of family members that a U.S. citizen or legal resident can sponsor for immigration. Under the bill, a "permanent partner" is described as an adult who is in a committed, intimate, financially interdependent relationship with another adult "in which both parties intend a lifelong commitment."

I urge you to become a supporter and to urge the United States Senate to pass, and President Obama to sign, the UAFA and support the removal of legal barriers to immigration by permanent same-sex partners.

Sincerely,

CHAPTER FOURTEEN:
MARRIAGE EQUALITY IS A GLOBAL ISSUE!

Marriage is a world-wide, universally recognized relationship status. Therefore, equality is not just an issue that is limited to the United States or Western Countries. Marriage equality is a global issue. Same-sex loving people exist all over the world and always have. Marriage allows them the same rights and relationship protections their heterosexual counterparts have.

Unlike the United States, where marriage for same-sex couples is only recognized in 10% of the states and not at the national level, several countries have already provided their gay and lesbian citizens with national marriage rights: The Netherlands (April 2001), Belgium (January 2003), Canada (June 2005), Spain (June 2005), South Africa (November 2006), Norway (January 2009) Sweden (April 2009), Portugal (June 2010), Iceland (June 2010), and Argentina (July 2010). Additionally, while Israel does not allow same-sex couples to marry, the country does recognize same-sex marriages performed in other countries and while the country of Mexico does not allow same-sex couples the right to marry, the region of Mexico City does (March 2010). Nepal is also expected to legalize same-sex marriage in 2010.

GLOBAL EQUALITY. ARE WE THERE YET?

There are also several countries that provide same sex couples recognition and protection, though not yet marriage. They include:

Andorra	Austria
Australia	Colombia
Czech Republic	Denmark

Ecuador	Finland
France	Germany
Greenland	Hungary
Ireland	Luxembourg
New Caledonia	New Zealand
Slovenia	Switzerland
Uruguay	United Kingdom
Wallis and Futuna	

Some parts of Mexico and Venezuela recognize same-sex unions and the list continues to grow. But as mentioned previously, most gay people living in these "marriage-lite" countries are not satisfied with their separate and unequal status. In the UK, same-sex couples continue to pursue legal marriage, as do gay Aussies, because they are discontent with civil unions.

Moninne Griffith of Marriage Equality Ireland says, "Marriage equality is so important in Ireland because the status of being married carries so much weight in Irish society, in our laws and under our Constitution. In Ireland, the family based in marriage (with or without children), is protected by the Constitution from attack and must be guarded with special care. This means that other families (with or without children) do not have this special elevated and protected status in Irish law and can and have been actively discriminated against in our laws."

Griffith is for full marriage equality and has come out against the Civil Partnership legislation, which she says "stops short of recognising our families as equal to other families and completely ignores the existence of our children." Griffith feels that the Civil Partnership legislation, "Enshrines a separate legal institution for the recognition of our relationships which will further stigmatise us a different and less than equal. This is why we must continue to fight for equality – for ourselves, for our families, for our children. Equality is not a luxury item."

Niall Crowley, an Irish marriage equality advocate agrees with Griffith. Crowley said at a rally for marriage equality in Ireland that a "Civil Partnership Bill is not just shaped by backlash against equality, it also serves as an active part of the backlash. It is designed to act as a block to the achievement of equality for lesbian, gay, bisexual and transgender people."

Like most of the states in America that tried civil unions and then decided to upgrade to marriage equality for same-sex couples, several governments who also started with "marriage-lite" alternatives, have expressed a commitment to creating gender-neutral marriage laws (Uruguay, Luxembourg, and Slovenia) and several countries are considering allowing same-sex couples to marry in the near future (Nepal and Venezuela).

> *More than 50% of the EU recognizes some form of same-sex partnership*

THAT'S AMORE!

In Italy, several attempts have been made to pass legislation granting marriage to same-sex couples. According to Arcigay, the Associazione Lesbica e Gay Italiana, 33 provinces have some sort of same-sex partnership registry or *unioni civili*,[36] but opposition has defeated attempts at marriage equality and any form of national partnership rights for same-sex couples.

Italian journalist and novelist, Delia Vaccarello, and the woman she would love to marry her partner Anna. Both want to see legal marriage for same-sex couples in Italy in their lifetime. However, because of the powerful influence of the Pope and Vatican City, Anna doubts this will happen. Delia is more hopeful. She believes that eventually there will be some sort of

---

36 *http://www.arcigay.it/tutti-registri-delle-unioni-civili*

national registration for same-sex couples and that it will lead to the recognition of same-sex marriage. Both want marriage now and find it very painful that they are denied this right. Delia does not understand how her country can "make war on love." She believes that other gay Italians want marriage too. "Many people want the stability" that marriage brings, she says. She also emphasizes that Italian LGBT parents and their children need family protections that come with the right to adopt and marry, but she feels that "a law acknowledging same-sex couples would be a great achievement, a first important step."

In November 2008, twenty-three same-sex couples calling themselves the "Civil Affirmation" campaign went to city halls in Florence, Venice, Ferrara and Trento. After being denied marriage licenses, they filed lawsuits. One lawsuit filed by a couple pointed out that laws in Venice's Civil Code are gender-neutral with regard to marriage. The couple was represented by attorney, Rete Lenford, who is working to bring civil rights to Italy's LGBT population. They argued that the Civil Code's mention of protecting human rights and its "prohibition of discrimination on grounds of personal conditions" should guarantee equal marriage rights for same-sex couples.

The need for equal marriage rights became even more important for Italian couple Francesco Zanardi and Manuel Incorvaia, after Zanardi was hospitalized with serious injuries resulting from a gay bashing while on vacation in Greece in September 2009. Franceso realized that had he died, his partner, Manuel, would not inherit their home as a spouse would and would have no survivor rights or benefits.

LIVE AND LET LIVE

In many countries, LGBT people are still working to secure the most basic human rights for LGBT people, including the right to be in a same-sex relationship and to gather peacefully and safely in public. In Poland and Russia, gay pride marches are still banned and people are arrested for gathering in public places for gay rights. In the rare cases when gatherings were allowed, police have stood by while crowds of protestors threw acid and rocks at LGBT people and their supporters. In other countries, like Slovakia and the Czech Republic, gay pride celebrations are allowed, but often cancelled because of the inability of the police to protect LGBT people from violent protestors.

Worse still, is that LGBT people are treated as criminals in many countries. For example, gay people in Fiji, Samoa, Tonga, Jamaica, Guyana, Belize, and dozens of Middle Eastern, South Asian, and African countries can be thrown in prison for several years for engaging in same-sex behavior. In May 2010, a same-sex couple who were having a private wedding ceremony in their home in Malawi when police broke in and arrested them were given a fourteen year prison sentence.

People identified as gay, lesbian, bisexual or transgender in Saudi Arabia, United Arab Emirates, Iran, Nigeria, Yemen, Sudan and Mauritania, where being gay is a crime punishable by death, are executed by the government.

The country of Uganda, influenced by U.S. right-wing fundamentalist Christians, are considering instituting a shocking new policy to kill gay people and punish anyone who knows a gay person and does not turn them over to the government. Sound familiar?

While homosexuality is not a crime in Iraq, fundamental Islamic zealots view homosexuality as a sin against Islam. Incited by radical Shiite religious clerics who say gays are feminizing Iraqi men, the Iraqi militia has gone on a killing spree against gay men. Eye witnesses have reported watching Iraqi Militia forcibly remove men who are allegedly gay from their homes. When next seen, these men have been shot through the head, their bodies dumped in isolation. According to a Human Rights Watch report, some men were found with their "anuses glued shut." Additionally, several gay men have received death sentences for simply belonging to an organization, called "Iraqi LGBT."

SPEAK OUT

Marriage equality is a global human rights issue and we must work to end the injustices against all of our gay, lesbian, bisexual, transgender and intersexed brothers and sisters around the world and in our own backyards. I invite you to become an international love warrior and to speak out against all injustices against LGBT people.

Section Five: Strategy

Chapter Fifteen:
The Psychology of Discrimination

Dehumanization is the process by which members of a group of people assert the "inferiority" of another group through subtle or overt acts or statements. Once you dehumanize a segment of people it is easier to take away their rights, deny their common humanity, and treat them in far harsher ways than you would other groups of people. Again, I refer back to shameful moments in United States history where xenophobia and dehumanizing stereotypes resulted in: interning Japanese-Americans, denying Chinese-Americans the right to education and marriage, enslaving and segregating African-Americans, keeping Jewish Americans from attending certain universities and belonging to country clubs, and stripping Native Americans of their land, culture, language, and children.

The Psychology of Discrimination

Homophobia is defined as a fear or irrational dislike of homosexuals and homosexual behavior. It can be likened to xenophobia a dislike, fear, and hatred of foreigners or strangers and anything foreign or strange. Vocal opponents of marriage equality play on existing fears, stereotypes, and homophobic hysteria to dehumanize LGBT people.

Some opponents of equal marriage use subtle homophobic messages. They talk about having gay friends and say they think that gay people should have some protections, just not equality, (like we are pets who can have table scraps, just not sit at the table). Other opponents make overt statements like "love the sinner, hate the sin," which is related to an erroneous belief that being gay is a choice and that gay people are morally inferior. Some out right lie.

During the Proposition 8 campaign to take away same-sex couples' constitutional right to marry, anti-gay opponents scared parents with images of their children being taught about gay sex in the first grade.

And people fall for it! Why? Because the opponents of marriage equality did a good job using dehumanizing tactics to make gay people the "other." They played on people's existing fears and homophobia. The years when gay people had to stay hidden allowed stereotypes that gays were "perverts and pedophiles" and other untruths to pervade our culture's perceptions of gay people.

In California, polls found that pre-election more people were in support of marriage equality than opposed it, but as the campaign unfolded, the numbers turned. The Yes on 8 Campaign was effective and persuasive. They utilized manipulation strategies to deeply stir irrational fear and emotions in people. For example, Ron Prentice, President, of the California Family Council, an anti-gay religious organization that advocates the benefits of family and marriage for straight families by working to undermine the rights of gay people and their families, worked with Protect Marriage, the official organization for the Yes on 8 campaign, to distribute booklets to churches that were chock-full of malicious lies and false information about gay people and gay marriage. Included in the materials was a document entitled "21 Reasons Why Gender Matters," which suggested that children being raised by gay and lesbian parents were subject to "gender disorientation pathology." —at term that these people invented that has no scientific or psychological basis.

According to this slanderous literature, "Gender disorientation pathology" again a made up condition that they say either results from being gay or having gay parents, "encourages the sexual and psychological exploitation of children."[37] Prentice also stated in campaign materials that "the sad truth is that homosexual abuse of children is higher than heterosexuals. Gender orientation pathology increases the risk that children will suffer sexual exploitation. It is our duty to protect them." Never mind the decades of psychological research which shows that children raised by gay parents are just as healthy and well-adjusted in all aspects as children raised by heterosexual parents or that instances of child sexual abuse are higher among heterosexual males.

However, Prentice was not the only Yes on 8 leader promoting this kind of misinformation. Dr. William "Bill" Tam, of the Traditional Family Coalition of California, also intentionally misled voters. He organized numerous rallies within the Bay Area Asian American community and authored campaign materials that advised people that the gay agenda is to "legalize sex with children." One campaign document stated that if gay marriage were allowed to continue in California "more children would become homosexuals." Maybe more LGBT people would be open and honest about who they are, rather than lying, hiding, and living double-lives where they engage in sham relationships and marriages, at the expense of their straight spouse, as part of their cover up, .

Yes on 8 materials also argued that if same-sex couples have the right to marry, children would be taught about gay sex in elementary school. In response, Jack O'Connell, California State Superintendent of Public Instruction, set the record straight, so to speak, in a Prop 8 television commercial that this was not at all true. But it's this exact kind of misinformation that turns rational adults into hysterical parents.

While they have no rational argument for keeping marriage licenses out of the hands of gay people, our right wing opponents are relentless in their efforts to tap into the irrational fears some heterosexual voters have of gay people. They effectively

37 http://www.familyaction.org/Articles/issues/sexuality/gender-matters.htm

manipulated enough voters with fear of the "unknown" that gay Americans were stripped of their legal equality.

In the absence of personal experience with real gay people, many heterosexuals are vulnerable to stereotypes promoted by religious organizations and anti-gay groups. People need to be exposed to the truth of the diversity of who we are and how we live our lives. Until real images of LGBT people in loving, committed relationships are made visible, heterosexuals will continue to fall victim to stereotypes and myths that gays are child molesters, sex addicts. And this is why, as I will repeat throughout this book, LGBT people and family members and friends of LGBT people need to continue to come out, so people can see that we don't have three eyes or ten arms. That with the exception of our sexual orientation and/or the fact that we were born in a body that does not reflect our gender identity) LGBT are the same as heterosexual people. Although some would argue that we are a little more fabulous and creative.

CURING HOMOPHOBIA: A PSYCHOLOGICAL APPROACH TO EQUALITY.

To identify with someone who you initially perceived as different, you must first become more familiar with them and their culture. Familiarity will allow you to see the past the differences to the commonalities between you.

When someone has a fear of something—a phobia—psychologists treat the phobia by providing the client with facts and education in order to demonstrate that this fear is irrational. Gradually the person is exposed to the thing they are fearful of and they see that the feared outcome did not happen. There was no real threat all along.

Because opponents play on fears of gay people, we must neutralize this homophobic hysteria like we would a phobia.

There are 3 stages to cure any phobia
1. Accurate Education
2. Exposure
3. Response Prevention

I will discuss each stage in detail and how we can apply it to winning/keeping marriage equality for same-sex couples.

1. Accurate Education

- We must clearly state the positive value of diversity and equality as American values and how equal rights leads to equal respect for all, reduces hate crimes, fosters an environment of mutual respect for differences, and reduces dehumanization and bias speech aimed at other groups.
- We must show psychological studies that prove marriage is correlated with increased health and wellness for both heterosexual and same-sex couples and that marriage discrimination is correlated with increased distress in LGBT people and a more divisive, dangerous and intolerant environment for all.
- We must educate people about the 1,138 federal rights and hundreds of state rights that allow families to care for each other in the hospital, make medical decisions, file joint state taxes, have shared parentage of their children, inherit without a will, etc.
- We must have culturally competent messages and messengers who reflect the diversity of our varied communities.
- We must show the harms that denying equality to similarly situated same-sex couples and their children can cause.
- We must have same-sex couples describe how "marriage-lite" alternatives are viewed and treated as an inferior status for them and their children and how that makes them feel.

- We must be proactive about educating people about the separation of church and state, so they are clear that their Catholic church will not have to marry same-sex couples, and that their local Unitarian Universalist and United Church of Christ churches already do. This isn't about religion. This is about the government treating all people equally.

- We must have parents describe the pain of witnessing their gay children being treated with contempt by society and how their gay children have the same hopes and dreams of getting married and having a family as other children do, only with a same-sex spouse.

- We must have gay people describe how legislating unfair separate and unequal treatment towards one group in society sends a message that it is okay to discriminate and hate gays.

- We must correct inaccurate perceptions about what children are taught about sex and adult relationships in elementary school and show how legal anti-gay discrimination allows anti-gay bullying of LGBT kids and kids with LGBT parents.

- We must remind people that anti-gay forces are intentionally misleading people to create massive fear. When fear or a need for power take hold of people's brains they will act in shocking and horrifying ways.[38]

- We must remind people to recognize the pull of hysterical homophobia, just like acknowledging vestiges of racism and sexism, because the tactics anti-gay forces use are powerful and may pull them backwards.

---

38 *For examples of how fear and power cause normal people to act in inhumane ways check out Phillip Zimbardo's Stanford Prison Study and his book The Lucifer Effect. Also Stanley Milgram's obedience studies.*

ACCURATE EDUCATION CAN OVERCOME FEAR BY CREATING COGNITIVE DISSONANCE

Cognitive dissonance is an uncomfortable feeling caused by holding two contradictory ideas at the same time. The theory proposes that people will eliminate the uncomfortable feelings caused by holding two opposing viewpoints by either adjusting their attitudes, beliefs, and behaviors, or by justifying or rationalizing why they believe or act the way they do. Accurate education can create cognitive dissonance between their irrational feelings of homophobia that lead them to believe that gay marriage will hurt them and the reality that it won't.

> *How many gay marriage opponents eat shrimp and wear leather shoes which are also abominations unto God?*

Cognitive dissonance can be created for the person who sees themselves as fair-minded but voted for marriage discrimination by sharing the real, painful impact marriage discrimination has on real people and their families. Similarly, asking people how they can hold strong Biblical beliefs about homosexuality being an "abomination," but eat shrimp or wear shoes made of leather, when shrimp eating and wearing leather shoes are also Biblical abominations in Leviticus. Creating cognitive dissonance by activating these internal contradictions, or calling forth a higher self, will be more effective than simply making requests for them to "be fair." Calling forth a higher self will create the internal pull for them to want to change their attitudes or beliefs to get back in alignment with themselves, and to reduce their dissonance. I will speak more about this in a moment.

2. Exposure is the second part of addressing any phobia. This means exposing the person to what they fear repeatedly.

Exposure is showing people things over and over again until the shock or impact is minimized, neutralized, or gone. In a more sinister way, this is how we have all become more tolerant to violence on TV. In a more positive way, this is how Americans, 80% of who were against interracial marriage in 1968, became more comfortable with married couples from different racial backgrounds. Think of *I love Lucy*, the first television show with an interracial couple. How many people today would even think of *I love Lucy* as a show with groundbreaking social and political implications? How many viewers today would care that Ricky was Cuban and Lucy was white? Same approach with interracial couple Tom and Helen Willis on *The Jeffersons*.

People must be exposed to repeated positive images of same-sex couples and their families to realize our shared humanity. Unfortunately, depicting gay characters on TV and in the movies was not allowed by Hollywood executives for decades. Today, there are no longer these kinds of enforced prohibitions, but as recently as 1998 the Ellen Show was cancelled shortly after Ellen Degeneres and her character on the TV show "came out" and began having a relationship with a woman.

Gay people need to present as married couples. In daily life, gay people must also claim the words "spouse," "husband" and "wife," if they expect heterosexuals to support them as married couples. If we say "partner," they'll say "partner," and that's all they'll see "domestic partners."

SHOW AND TELL

I emphasize the need to show the impact of marriage discrimination in our educational campaign for marriage equality, rather then just putting our messages out there. If you are reading a book or watching a movie, you will feel more connected to a passage or a scene in which you are shown something about a person's character, rather than told. The same is true for campaign commercials and literature. Imagine these examples below, one commercial shows and the other one tells. Which one has a bigger impact on you?

Commercial #1: There is a loud crashing noise. A plane has just hit the World Trade Center. We see Rev. Michael Judge rush into the burning World Trade Center, smoke is everywhere, objects are falling around him. We can see he won't make it out alive. He kneels by the dying fire fighter and reads him his last rites. Sweat beads on his forehead as he moves on to hold the hand of dying woman, and then the screen goes dark and the message reads: "Rev. Michael Judge, was a heroic gay man who served the church and his country. He lost his life by going into the World Trade Center on 9/11 to administer last rites to the dying."

Commercial #2: Still photo of Michael Judge with voice over. "Rev. Michael Judge, was a heroic gay man who served the church and his country. He lost his life by going into the World Trade Center on 9/11 to administer last rites to the dying."

GAYS ON DISPLAY

Most people only see real gay people when the news media rolls images of a Gay Pride parade or they see stereotypes of gay people on TV shows that depict gay men as perpetually single and silly, like Jack on *Will and Grace,* and lesbians and transgender people as serial killers like *Monster* and *Silence of the Lambs.*

In the movie *Bruno,* Sasha Cohen plays a gay character who embodies almost all gay stereotypes and who interacts with the real world to elicit shock. In one scene, Bruno has entered a wrestling match. He and another actor are locked in a wrestling cage, and instead of wrestling one another they kiss. The redneck audience is so disgusted by this kiss that they actually try to physically hurt the two men by throwing beer bottles and metal chairs at them.

If people are moved to violence by seeing two men kiss then we must show more images of tenderness between two men until it no longer solicits homicidal rage. If they are horrified by seeing two gay parents with their children, then we must show them that. They must see images of us in-love, they must see images of us as families. We need to get them used to seeing us, so the shock value wears off and they can start to see us as just other human beings doing the same things they do, go shopping, pay bills, rake leaves, eat dinner, fight over what TV show to watch. We must do everything in our power to pro-actively humanize and normalize ourselves, our love, and our families, to our opponents. Eventually, people will be able to look through the difference and see our common humanity. So what there are two gay guys holding hands, how's your steak?

3. Response Prevention is the third piece of curing a phobia.

In addition to receiving accurate education related to the feared object and being exposed to the feared object, people need to be supported to prevent their sliding back into homophobic hysteria. In cases of physical phobia, response prevention means not letting people escape from that which they are afraid of. For example, if you have a fear of birds, making you remain in a room with a bird and not letting you leave will eventually allow you to work your way through the extremes of terror and panic. Your breathing would slow down, your heart beat would return to normal, and as you saw that the bird was not interested in pecking your eyes out, your fear of birds would gradually subside. You would see that Hitchcock's *The Birds* was all made up and your fears were unfounded.[39]

In order to cure a marriage equality phobia, we must flood people with images of loving same-sex couple and their fami-

---

39 *Okay so this may be a bit simplistic. You could choose to hire a psychologist to help treat your phobia, but the general mechanics apply. Education, exposure, response prevention, voila!*

lies and we cannot let them off the hook. The message must be framed in terms of anything less than marriage equality is discrimination. You are either for equality or you support injustice and discrimination. You can't have it both ways. This can be addressed through how we frame the message as an "all or nothing" issue, which keeps people from comfortably escaping back to old beliefs.

In order to effectively implement this part of desensitizing people who are phobic of gay marriage there can be no room for apologetic, fence-sitters. We must erase the buffer zone that allows people to choose civil unions and not full equality. You are either for full equality or you accept and allow injustice and inequality! It's simple. We must be bold in framing the message. Most campaigns for marriage equality have not been bold, as I will discuss in the Chapter *Why Prop 8 Passed.*

We must explicitly state that civil unions, whether they come with what looks like all the rights or not, allows people to continue to discriminate and treat gay people as second-class citizens and robs them of full participation in the fabric of society (marriage and family). Additionally, we must ensure that people have the opportunity to engage in new ways with LGBT people, by meeting real LGBT people at supermarkets, in places of worship, at educational forums, etc, so that they can see real people, not just the wild and crazy gay pride parade images that they hold in their minds. Gay pride parades are not bad—it's just that they need to be in context, no one views straight people only in the context of how they act at Mardi Gras celebrations.

Imagine if we judged all heterosexuals by how they dressed and behaved at Mardi Gras and if we focused on the most outrageous person and held them up as example of your average heterosexual.

Let's look at a few beliefs where there is strong pressure for people to choose a new position and not go back to their old one. For example, it would be very hard to convince most people in society to go back to believing that the world is flat, even though at one time professing that the world was round could get you killed. To return to a belief that the world is flat would make you seem ridiculous. Or a better example might be that many readers at one time likely believed in Santa Claus. But I bet I couldn't get you to believe in Santa Claus again, because you would feel more uncomfortable being in your former belief (Santa Claus is real) than in your new belief (Santa Claus is not real).

SO, WHAT DOES THIS MEAN FOR MARRIAGE EQUALITY?

1. If we are going to end discrimination against LGBT people we must take an unflinching stance that LGBT people are equal, whole, complete human beings.
2. We must see that the love two men share, or the love that two women share, is as wholesome, beautiful, spiritual, innocent, tender, and valuable as the love a man and a woman share.
3. People must see repeated images of same-sex couples and their families on TV, in the movies, and in real life.
4. People must hear real life stories of LGBT people.

It is then, that they will find that it takes more effort to hate, than love.

GROWING PAINS

You can't cure a phobia by letting the person stay in their comfort zone. People will feel uncomfortable growing and stretching, but they won't change if we let them stay in their comfort zone and by holding on to their prejudice. We must make them feel the discomfort of believing that two water fountains—one for gays and one for straights—is fair. It's not fair! Civil unions ≠ marriage. Separate is not equal. So, we need to stop saying it is okay. It's not okay to discriminate and treat people unfairly. People must feel uncomfortable with taking a stance that denies people full equality. They must see that this is discrimination and wrong and that they can only be comfortable again by shifting to and embracing a pro-marriage equality position because it's the right thing to do!

MARRIAGE EQUALITY EXPRESS

The movie *The Express,* based on the real-life story of football legend, Ernie Brown, shows a great example of the cognitive dissonance that a white Syracuse University football coach experiences as his star Black player, Davis, challenges his innocent bystander approach to segregation in the late 1950s. The white coach accepts black football players on his team but agrees with white society only allowing blacks a limited role on the field (and essentially in life). He sends the message to Davis that he must know his place, for his, and the team's sake.

There is a pivotal moment when the team is playing at West Virginia University and the coach pulls Davis from the football field to let a white player score the touch down. His justification to Davis is that the whites of West Virginia cannot accept a black person succeeding or exceeding white players, essentially, he doesn't want to make the whites uncomfortable, or worse violent. There is a real possibility that they may riot if "tradition" is not upheld.

Davis confronts the coach on his own ingrained white supremacist beliefs and his acquiescing to the second-class treatment of African-Americans. Davis pushes the coach to look at how his "let's not rock the boat" stance willingly sacrifices black people's rights to keep white people comfortable in the presence of an exceptional black athlete. In other words, he shows the coach how he has placed a higher value on white people's feelings than black people's human rights. He tells the coach how profoundly wrong and painful this is which finally strikes a chord in the coach and he is able to see his own bigotry and cowardice. He is clear that instead of standing up for equal treatment and respect for blacks, he has cowered and conformed to the status quo, and thereby perpetuated discrimination.

Davis's consistent unwillingness to settle for less in his life, his refusal to leave the game the next time he has a chance to make a touch down, and his ongoing challenge to the status quo, creates extreme cognitive dissonance in his coach and his white teammates who had previously taken their white supremacy for granted and didn't see it as hurting anyone. Inspired by Davis's convictions in his own inherent equality as a human being; his white coach, white teammates, and the white officials in the football league, who had only tokenized black athletes before; begin to embrace a new standard by which they view blacks and their right to equality. They have shifted their consciousness and become his allies.

LEARNING FROM EXAMPLE

Another principle of psychology that can be effective is observational learning or modeling. We should not underestimate the power of having straight people talk about their own homophobia and how they got over it and became supporters of equality. Many of the straight preachers I have done marriage equality work with over the years first faced their own fears and prejudices and are now some of the greatest allies. It shows that even people who appear wedded to their intolerance or blinded by misinformation can become more accepting and even powerful advocates for LGBT people, which is why I remind my fellow advocates of equality that someone's first reaction or response is not necessarily their last. People are always evolving.

A CHANGE OF HEART FOR MARRIAGE EQUALITY

Ed Fallon, Iowa State Representative (D-Des Moines), who spoke before the Iowa house on civil marriage equality, had a similar change of heart for gay people. He said in his speech to the house on February 20, 1996, "I've never hated homosexuals, but I used to fear them. When I was a kid growing up, the worst name you could call someone was a gay loser." Fallon recalls growing up with "the stereotype of the highly aggressive, promiscuous gay man seeking countless, anonymous relationships. This is the stereotype I grew up with that contributes volumes of ignorance and fear. I've come to learn that this stereotype, like most stereotypes, is based on hearsay, not facts. The rogues who may fit the description are the exception, just as there are male heterosexual rogues who are aggressive, promiscuous, and constantly hitting on and harassing women. In my evolving experiences with homosexuals, familiarity has displaced ignorance and dispelled fear."

Ed continues to be a courageous leader for marriage equality. He and his wife, Lynn are at the forefront of changing the hearts and minds of their fellow Iowans with their organization, I'm For Iowa.

San Diego's Republican Mayor, Jerry Sanders was staunchly against gay marriage when he ran for office, (though he supported civil unions and domestic partnerships), and he intended to veto a resolution passed by the San Diego City Council in support of marriage equality. But then he had what he calls "a change of heart."[40] Mayor Sanders is an incredible role model of courage, growth, and heart and now says that he sees he was blind to his own prejudice that allowed him to believe the lesser status of civil unions were equal to marriage. Here's his description of his personal evolution.

---

40 *Here is a link to the youtube video where he discusses his personal evolution to becoming a supporter of marriage equality. Make sure you grab a Kleenex.* http://www.youtube.com/watch?v=0rfea8iEGNw&NR=1

"My plan was to veto the resolution. My opinion on this issue (gay marriage) has evolved. The arrival of the resolution, to sign or to veto, in my office late last night, forced me to reflect and search my soul for the right thing to do. I've decided to lead with my heart, which is probably obvious at the moment. [He says choked up with emotion.] To do what I think is right and to take a stand on equality and social justice. The right thing for me to do is to sign this resolution.

For three decades, I've worked to bring justice, enlightenment, and equality to all parts of our community. As I reflected on the choices I had before me last night, I could not bring myself to tell an entire group of people in our community they were less important, less worthy, or less deserving of the rights and responsibilities of marriage than anyone else simply because of their sexual orientation. A decision to veto this resolution would have been inconsistent with the values I've embraced over the past thirty years.

I do believe that times have changed and with changing time and new life experiences come different opinions. Two years ago I believed civil unions were a fair alternative. Those beliefs in my case have changed. The concept of a separate, but equal, institution is not something I can support. I have close family members, friends and members of my personal staff who are gay. I want for them the same thing that we all want for our loved ones—to find a mate whom they love deeply and who loves them back. Someone whom they can grow old together and share life's experiences, and I want their relationships to be protected equally under the law. In the end, I couldn't look them in the face and tell them that their relationship, their lives, were any less meaningful then the life I share with my wife."

To remove homophobia, as an obstacle that stands in the way of equality for LGBT people, the public must have accurate information about LGBT people. They must see real images of loving same-sex couples and their families and the hardships they experience by being denied marriage equality. And straight allies must confront their own discomfort and heterosexual privilege and take an unapologetic position on equality for all. Supporting anything less than marriage is discriminatory and wrong.

Chapter Sixteen:
Equality Up for a Popularity Contest

Let's Vote on It!

On my first marriage equality book tour through the American South in 2004, I visited the Ralph Mark Gilbert Civil Rights Museum, in Savannah Georgia where I saw historical photos of angry white segregationists in the 1960s holding picket signs that read:

"Is this equal rights?"

"We demand our equal rights."

"Out with the NAACP!"

"Did you vote for this?" (referring to integration)

"Where is your child today?" (to frighten white parents that their children were now surrounded by, OMG, black children. Ahh!!!)

These white segregationists held a march because they believed African-Americans having equal rights would take away their rights. These white folks were talking about their own rights being jeopardized by black people being granted equality. They didn't want to share equality with blacks and felt that they had a right to vote to take away black people's civil rights.

Sounds crazy, right? It should sound eerily familiar. I think it goes something like..."*Gay people having marriage rights will take away rights from straight people,*" and "*Gay marriage violates my religious freedom.*" In America, one group's right to be superior over another group should never be justification for denying equality under the law. As we have learned in other contexts, while some may be uncomfortable with losing their supremacy over others, that is not a good enough reason to keep things status quo and continue to disenfranchise and deny people fundamental civil rights.

Despite the obvious flawed logic in "voter's rights" arguments, anti-gay groups continue to distort government efforts to create equality for gay Americans as infringements on the rights of people to vote, much as white segregationists once did. For example, Brian Brown, Executive Director, of the National Organization for Marriage (NOM), which was founded in 2007 to oppose same-sex marriage in state legislatures and to "protect marriage and the faith communities that sustain it," sent out an e-mail to NOM's e-mail list stating that "protecting your right to vote for marriage without fear or favor has become a key part of NOM's mission." This e-mail was sent out during the federal trial challenging Proposition 8 in order to create the impression that our justice system, which operates on a system of checks and balances, should not have the ability to weigh evidence and make measured decisions. This group believes marriage rights decisions should only be made by popular vote. Imagine what this country would be like today if we had put slavery, women's and black people's rights to vote, and interracial marriage up for a popular vote?

CALIFORNIA SCREAMIN'- OUTR8GEOUS PROP 8

On November 4, 2008 a slim majority of California voters stripped constitutional rights from a recognized and discriminated class in a ballot initiative campaign that ended with 52% in favor of eliminating marriage rights for same-sex couples and 48% against. Literally, overnight, the right for all people to marry was taken away and an insertion of discrimination soiled the California State Constitution. On November 4th same-sex couples were getting legally married and the day after the election they were turned away at the marriage license counter.

Proposition 8 is literally written into the California State Constitution as an exception to the equal protection clause. Article 1, Section 7 of the California Constitution guarantees that: "A person may not be deprived of life, liberty, or property without due process of law or denied equal protection of the laws." And now since Prop 8 passed the words *"Only marriage between a man and a woman is valid or recognized in California,"* have been inserted into the equal protection clause of the California Constitution. This sentence limiting a person's rights is *the sole exception* to California's equal protection clause. It's shocking to consider.

Marriage equality advocates hoped that the California Supreme Court would declare the initiative unconstitutional and repeal Proposition 8. Eighteen thousand same-sex couples waited anxiously for six months, after hosting joyous wedding parties and exchanging vows in front of friends and families who had traveled from afar in a flurry to celebrate with us, wondering if our marriages were even still valid. We had had no time for honeymoons as we campaigned for our right to stay married.

And in another setback, on May 26, 2009, the California State Supreme Court upheld Proposition 8 stating that the California initiative process may be broken and unfair, but the court was helpless to change the system that allows a bare majority of voters to change the California Constitution to discriminate against anyone. Mind you it takes two-thirds of the legislature to pass the California budget, but only 50% plus one vote from California voters to take away Constitutional civil rights from any unpopular minority group. The court did uphold the marriages of the 18,000 same-sex couples married between June 16 and November 4, 2008. So, Molly and I are still legally married (and it only took 13 years).[41]

---

41 *Now that that's clear, feel free to send wedding gifts or better go to my website* www.davinakotulski.com *and make a contribution so that we can continue doing marriage equality work.*

In California, it is now fair game to vote on people's constitutional rights and the California court system can't, or won't, do a damn thing to stop a majority from having a popularity contest with the rights of a minority group. The California State Supreme Court rubber-stamped the right of a majority to take away the constitutional rights of a group, that only a year earlier, they had guaranteed, setting a dangerous precedent that any minority group rights are subject to the whim of a popular vote.

Letting majorities decide the civil rights of minorities has led to some of our nation's most shameful acts. Take, for example, the internment of Japanese-Americans during WWII, denying Blacks basic civil rights, and denying Chinese Americans the right to own land, marry whites, and receive public education. One only needs to open a history book to see that human beings are capable of great injustices against their fellow man, coming from a selfish place of "just us," rather than justice. But no less damaging, is the sin of apathy—staying silent and unmoved in the face of another's suffering

But history will remember the names of Sojourner Truth suffragist and abolitionist, and her contemporary Harriet Tubman suffragist and abolitionist with the Underground Railroad; Susan B. Anthony, Elizabeth Cady Stanton, and Lucretia Mott, suffragists who devoted their lives to securing women's equality and voting rights; Raul Wallenberg, a non-Jew who put himself at great personal risk to hide Jews from the Nazis, and was ultimately murdered for his humanitarianism; and Gavin Newsom, San Francisco Mayor, who in 2004 fearlessly and courageously stood up for LGBT people by changing the law in San Francisco to allow same-sex couples to marry.

"For politicians to put aside someone else's rights so they can get ahead politically...I'm never going to be that person." Newsom said at a Commonwealth Club meeting in March 2009.

"There's nothing more insidious than the politician who says 'I'm with ya, I agree with ya' and then they go out in public and say something totally different...or they wait for a public opinion poll and say, 'I've evolved on this position.'"

I agree. Politicians need to stop talking out of both sides of their mouths. There is no middle ground on this issue. To say "I believe in equality for LGBT people, but believe civil marriage should be limited to a man and a woman" is a contradiction. It's also disingenuous. John Edwards, shame on you for using the Bible as the reason you don't support civil marriage for same-sex couples. What does your Bible say about what should be done to an adulterer who fathers children out of wedlock?

> *"Cowardice asks the question - is it safe?*
> *Vanity asks the question - is it popular?*
> *Expediency asks the question - is it political?*
> *But conscience asks the question - is it right?*
> *There comes a time when one must take a position that is neither safe, popular, or political; but because it is right."*
>
> —Dr. Martin Luther King, Jr.

WHY NOT SHARE?

For years gay people have styled your hair, decorated your fabulous wedding cakes, created breathtaking floral arrangements, planned your weddings, and even officiated at your weddings, and some of you still don't want to share the joys of marriage. What's up with that?

The movie *Wedding Wars* aptly shows this double standard. In the movie, John Stamos, plays a gay man named "Shel." Shel's brother gets engaged the daughter of his boss, a political candidate running for Governor. Instead of asking Shel to be his best man, the brother asks Shel to be the couple's wedding planner. While Shel is working to create a magical wedding for his brother and future sister-in-law, his brother is writing anti-same-sex marriage speeches for his boss. Upon learning this ugly truth, Shel goes on strike and refuses to serve as his brother's wedding planner.

You can't be a true friend or family member to a gay person and refuse to support marriage equality. It is a betrayal to your relationship with them and a denial of your shared humanity and equality.

Why not let us share in wedded bliss, love, connection, family, stability? Or, as performer, Dolly Parton says, let gays "suffer just like us straight couples do." Sharing may mean letting us experience the hardship and disillusionment that comes from a failed marriage and divorce. You can hold out your shoulder and box of Kleenex, just like we do for you, and when we're ready, look at our internet profile before we post it on Gay.com.

TAKE ACTION NOW

If you are straight and you want to make a difference, you can become an ally for the LGBT rights movements by taking The Straight for Equality Pledge at www.straightforequality. org. The pledge says: "As a Straight Ally I am committing myself to supporting and advocating for gay, lesbian, bisexual and transgender (GLBT) people. I will come out as a straight ally. I will acknowledge and work on any uncertainties I may have in coming out as a straight ally, and, as I grow in confidence, I'll increasingly let my family, friends, and colleagues know that I support equality for GLBT people. I will speak up. Whenever I have an opportunity, I'll say something supportive of GLBT people, whether I'm responding to a homophobic joke or remark, commenting positively about a current event, or making the case for equality in a discussion." Take the Straight for Equality Pledge and share it with others. Your active support is needed to make the world a more inclusive place for GLBT people and their families.

Chapter Seventeen: Why Prop 8 Passed

Einstein put it best when he said, "Insanity is doing the same thing over and over again and expecting different results." We have fought and lost over 30 ballot measures on marriage equality. Despite this record, marriage equality campaigns continue to employ similar messaging and campaign strategies that seek to persuade voters that the measures are "unnecessary and unfair." This messaging alone is unemotional and ineffective. We need campaigns that are clearly pro-marriage equality and pro-gay people.

Pollsters and campaign professionals hired by our community tell us that public education campaigns and beating ballot measures are two totally different things. They argue that the only way to win is to aim at the swing voters who might be persuaded to vote for equality if we can convince them that the issue at hand is not gay rights, but fairness. Unfortunately that does not seem to work because in the process it appears that they are trying to trick people by not including images of gay people and the "gay" and "marriage." This is an issue of fairness for gay people and if you keep them out of the equation it looks like a trick or a cover up, or worse, it sends the unintended message that gay people getting married should be hidden because it's shameful. Contrast that approach with the direct approach of showing gay people and telling stories about how marriage denial is unfair because of specific reasons and specific people who are harmed by this discrimination, rather than just posing it as a theoretical issue.

Marriage equality activist and author, Evan Wolfson talks about the concept of "losing forward' which means, that you run a campaign in such a way that even if you lose, you gain ground by educating voters about the specific harms of marriage discrimination and by sharing the stories of same-sex couples and their families. A campaign that has straight spokespeople telling other straight people that there is nothing to worry about is ineffective. It is also not "losing forward" because people are no more educated or informed about the issues of marriage discrimination than before the campaign began. This is truly a disservice to our community and has to stop.

We must try something new. I believe passionately that future campaigns must show both how gay people are harmed by inequality and deserving of equal rights at the forefront. Not showing gay people when our civil rights are at stake is homophobic and downright nuts. Can you imagine trying to sell detergent in a commercial that never shows any detergent and just hints at what the product being sold is without even naming it? Campaigns can not be homophobic and expect to win equality for LGBT people.

We need ads like the one below that put a human face on marriage discrimination and leave viewers with some sense of the lasting harm of marriage discrimination as they go to the voting booth.

SAMPLE PRO-ACTIVE MARRIAGE EQUALITY COMMERCIAL

Visualize young boy in bed, being tucked in by mother.

"Mommy I'm scared."

"You don't have to be scared, Ezra, there aren't any monsters here."

"No, Mommy I'm not scared of monsters, it's just that…"

"Why are you scared, Ezra?"

"Billy, at school, told me that if Proposition 8 passes, the state may come and take me from you and Mama because people hate families like ours."

"Oh baby," Mother hugs child, tear runs down her face, "Mama and I are doing everything we can to fight Prop 8. There are still a lot of people out there who don't understand and are afraid because they don't know any better. That's why me and Mama are out talking to people about our family and urging them to vote no on Prop 8."

"Can we show them pictures of my birthday?"

{Other mom walks in}

"And Mama can you make them cookies?"

Second mom kisses her son on top of the head. "Sure Ezra, we can do that. Now you need to get some sleep. Goodnight son."

Announcer: "Prop 8 hurts children and families. Prop 8 strips equality from our Constitution and jeopardizes families. Vote no on Prop 8."

There was nothing like this in the 2008 campaign ads. It's not rhetoric, it's not intellectualized—rather, it's human, it has emotion, it educates, and it's the truth.

FRAMING THE MESSAGE

I want to begin with telling you about how the LGBT leadership in California failed to fall forward, not once, but twice because it failed to use pro-active messaging in the campaigns. It was a *very* painful learning experience that cost us our marriage rights, hurt our children, and has led to an increase in animosity towards LGBT people, as well as emboldened our opposition. We must learn this lesson, so I invite you to pay close attention to what I'm about to share and to re-read this until the learning is in your bones.

In 1999, Senator Pete Knight of Palmdale, California gathered enough signatures to get Proposition 22, an anti-gay marriage initiative on the ballot. Prop 22 was a regular law, it was not a constitutional amendment. A law can be changed by a court ruling, a legislative bill signed by the governor, or by another vote of the people. A state-wide constitutional amendment, however, can only be reversed by the vote of the people, which is what motivated the religious right to go for a slam dunk in 2008.

When the Prop 22 campaign started in 1999, the LGBT community in California was in no way prepared to counter the attack. There was no state-wide LGBT infrastructure and the majority of LGBT people were not actually interested in getting married. In fact, some were hostile to the idea. At the time, they either saw marriage as a patriarchal institution they didn't want to be a part of, or were not ready to commit, or just never thought gay marriage would come about. They were, however, against the idea of someone taking away theoretical future rights, but for most gay people in 1999, there was a limited awareness of the impact of the denial of marriage rights on their relationships.

The "No on 22" Campaign, formed to defeat the "Knight Initiative," did not show gay people in its advertising. Instead they featured straight white men saying things like "You don't have to be for gay marriage to be against this initiative." Sending the message—actually *paying for the message*— that it is "okay to be against gay marriage." Think about that for a minute. You don't have to be for equality, to be against the Knight Initiative. Well, if you weren't for equality and equal marriage rights then what were you for?

"You don't have to be for Barack Obama to vote for him."

Sounds crazy doesn't it? If we had voted on interracial marriage in 1966 do you think it would have been a compelling message to say, "You don't have to be for interracial marriage to be against the ban on interracial marriage?" Or "The ban on interracial marriage is mean-spirited and unfair." Not very effective!

If you want to win, or at least fall forward, wouldn't you talk pro-actively about the benefits to society of allowing couples who love each other to marry, (e.g. ending bigotry, supporting diversity, teaching tolerance, and helping families protect one another with marriage rights like hospital visitation, parentage, health insurance, medical decision making, the right to inherit their shared property without a will, filing joint taxes, etc.).

Well, we didn't in 2000 with Prop 22 and the same luke-warm messaging showed up in the No on 8 campaign in 2008. Below is a real No on Prop 8 commercial entitled **"Conversation Ad."** [42]

Woman 1: Here's our niece, Maria and her partner, Julie, at their wedding."

Woman 2: Crinkles up nose. "Listen, honestly, I just don't know how I feel about this same-sex marriage thing."

Woman 1: "No, it's okay, and I really think it's fine if you don't know how you feel, but are you willing to eliminate rights and have our laws treat people differently?"

Woman 2: "No."

Announcer: "Don't Eliminate Marriage For Anyone, Vote no on Prop 8."

---

42 Check out the Conversation Ad on youtube. http://www.youtube.com/watch?v=vB0lZ8XbmJM

Now let's dissect this for a minute.

"PARTNER"

The couple they were talking about got legally married, yet they used the word *partner*, not *spouse*. This sends the message that— two members of the same-sex in a relationship are "partners", not "spouses." This is not a real marriage, so domestic partnership is enough.

"SAME-SEX MARRIAGE THING"

We are paying to have a commercial in which our marriages are called a thing? Need I say more about how ineffective, counter-productive, and harmful to the cause this messaging was? Couldn't she have at least said: "I just don't know how I feel about same-sex couples having the constitutional right to marry?" It lifts the bar. It states our frame. Whose side were those commercial makers working for?

"IT'S OKAY"

No, it's not okay to be homophobic and it's not okay that we wasted $43.3 million dollars on ads like this!

"ARE YOU WILLING TO ELIMINATE RIGHTS AND HAVE OUR LAWS TREAT PEOPLE DIFFERENTLY?"

Okay, this one makes me crazy. It's so neutral. It lacks any real impact about how this is going to harm real people. It lacks emotion and conviction too! She went to the wedding and she loves her niece, how about modeling how a supportive aunt would really respond? My aunt would get up from the table and tell her to get over her narrow-minded self.

This isn't about treating us "differently," it's about discriminating against gay people and taking away their constitutional rights. This was not a time to be understated. Civil rights here one day, civil rights gone the next!

Our opponents were flashing red WARNING lights like someone was taking away their rights and stealing their children from their beds! Yet our own ads were making polite conversation. Yes on 8 boldly framed the message that they were being victimized and that they were losing rights. They found a way to make straight people believe that gay people continuing to have marriage rights would take away their religious rights and force schools to teach about gay families. None of this was happening. Gays were marrying and churches that didn't want to perform same-sex marriages weren't. Explicit, unsparing language was in order.

DON'T ELIMINATE MARRIAGE FOR ANYONE

Hey, no one was coming to take away straight people's marriages and I mentioned earlier, even convicted wife-killer, Scott Peterson, can say "I do" from death row. It was gay people's marriages that were under attack. Our campaigns need stronger language if we are going to defeat these initiatives. It's better to say:

"Stripping away civil rights is never the right thing to do. Equality means equality for everyone."

"Disapproval does not justify taking away someone's constitutional rights."

"It's wrong to use religious beliefs as a justification to take away people's civil rights."

"It's wrong to hurt gay people and their families. Same-sex couples need marriage protections too. Let's keep marriage equality in California. Vote NO on Prop 8!"

"Our state court affirms that gay people have a constitutional right to equal protection under the law, including the right to marry. Taking away that right creates a second-class status in

California. All Californians should be first class citizens. Vote No on Prop 8."

"Gay Americans should have the same rights and protections for their families as straight Americans do."

"ARE YOU WILLING TO ELIMINATE RIGHTS AND HAVE OUR LAWS TREAT PEOPLE DIFFERENTLY?"....."NO."
She said "No." And if you listen to the commercial, it's the wimpiest "no" I've ever heard. This is supposed to be a persuasive commercial. I think the answer should have been a resounding "Hell No!"

Or, she could have said:

"No, of course not," shaking her head, "What was I thinking, I'm sorry."

"No, that would be wrong!"

"No, that would be un-American!"

"You're right, it's wrong to discriminate and take away people's rights. We really shouldn't even be voting on people's constitutional rights like it's some kind of popularity contest. I'm voting NO on Prop 8. Everyone deserves equality."

Are you banging your head against the wall yet?

THE FAILURE OF THE NO ON PROP 8 CAMPAIGN IN CALIFORNIA

Shortly, after the loss of Prop 8, former No on 8 campaign director, Steve Smith, met with LGBT Democrats in Sacramento and told them, that he believed that the No on 8 Campaign failed for the following reasons:

1. No on 8 didn't have as much money as Yes on 8.

(This was inaccurate! No on 8 raised $43.3 million and Yes on 8 raised $40 million).

2. No on 8 failed to define the issue clearly, instead choosing to wait to have a strategy until Yes on 8 had defined the issue as one of gay marriage being taught to kids in schools.

3. Yes on 8 bought more TV ads.

Smith shirked responsibility for the failed campaign by stating that he underestimated the Yes on 8 campaign's ability to raise funds and create a strong strategy to repeal equal rights for same-sex couples. He also blamed the loss on an inaccurate field poll that suggested No on 8 was winning, when apparently campaign leaders knew that the field poll(s) were inaccurate all along. However, they chose not to release that information until October, only weeks before the election.

It was also reported that Smith excused the No on 8 Campaign for its tragic failure to create effective messaging because, he said polling suggested that using the word "discrimination" offended minority groups, especially African-Americans.[43] The campaign chose to use the phrase "treat people differently" because it "polled nine to ten points higher that using the world discrimination." Smith, along with other paid campaign consultants and the No on 8 Executive Committee,[44] approved the primary campaign messages "Don't eliminate marriage for anyone." "Prop 8 is unfair and wrong" and "Keep government out of all our lives, vote no on Prop 8."

Additionally, despite wide-spread concern about the campaign's failure to define the issue and actually show same-sex couples and their families, Smith defended the ads run by the campaign. Media handlers from the No on 8 Campaign told same-sex couples doing media interviews not to bring their children because research showed that seeing same-sex couples marry or with children made people want to vote against marriage

43 November 13, 2008
44 The initial No on Prop 8 committee was made up of Dolores Jacobs of the San Diego LGBT Center, Lorrie Jean of the Los Angeles LGBT Center, Geoff Kors of Equality California, Andy Wong of Asian Pacific Islander Equality, and Kate Kendell of the National Center for Lesbian Rights.

equality. This may also explain why the No on 8 Campaign didn't show gay people in their commercials.

It seemed like gay campaign leaders and straight political consultants decided that gay people were so scary to non-gay voters that they refused to show our faces or acknowledge that 18,000 same-sex couples were happily getting married at this exact time surrounded by their friends and families and asking for donations to the No on 8 campaign in lieu of wedding gifts. Nor did we see real-life dramatizations of the harms of marriage discrimination experienced by our families.

How can we expect to win and hold on to the institution of civil marriage when are own executive campaign committee doesn't think we are palatable enough to be in our own commercials? How can we get non-gay voters to see our shared humanity when we spend $43 million dollars on advertising that excludes gay people?

No on 8 saw this differently, at the February 2009 Creating Change Conference, an annual LGBT advocacy gathering, former No on 8 Executive Committee member Kate Kendell said that, "seeing us getting married freaked people out."[45]

At this same Conference, another Executive Committee member, Geoff Kors told participants that the No on 8 Campaign chose not to message about "differences in rights. That's not what marriage is about ... it's about love, it's about dignity, it's about acceptance, it's about respect. That was sort of where we were going, that was our original thing." Kors also emphasized that the initial No on 8 messaging was not about eliminating rights, "it was about eliminating that joy."

When I watch the official No on 8 campaign commercials, none of them evoke joy. Virtually all their ads had ominous music with cold voice-overs.

The No on 8 campaign leaders went on to say that commercials also steered clear of using the word "marriage," so that they

---

45 *See BAR article No on Prop 8 "regrets tour" hits Denver Confab 2/5/09 by Zak Symanski*

wouldn't offend religious groups or alienate people who choose cohabitation. The campaign was trying so hard not to offend anyone that they failed to come up with an effective reason why marriage matters and in the process lost LGBT Americans' right to marry in California.

No on 8 executive committee member, Lorri Jean who also spoke at the Creating Change panel reflected on the Yes on 8 ad about a girl reading a book about Two Princes Getting Married and jokingly proposed a response commercial, that went "You're right honey, you can marry a princess, and isn't that wonderful? You can also marry someone of [a different] race. And you know what, you don't have to get married; in fact I think you should consider whether you want to participate in that patriarchal institution." Patriarchal institution? Perhaps No on 8 failed because some of the No on 8 executive committee membership held ambivalent views about marriage.

PROP 8 CAMPAIGN TURNED ITS BACK ON SPIRITUAL LEADERS

The California Council of Churches and California Church IMPACT located in Sacramento, California, have over 1.5 million members from Protestant and Orthodox Christian communities in 51 different denominations and judicatories, as well as allies from other faith traditions. In spite of working for marriage equality for same-sex couples for many years, CCC and CCI complained that their services were not tapped. They were told by No on 8 campaign organizers that religious leaders would confuse voters on the distinctions between religious and civil marriage and that using clergy as messengers would turn off would-be marriage equality voters whom research suggests are less religious than people who are against gay marriage.

The lack of confidence in using faith leaders as spokespeople was not actually shared by the community. In response to a Marriage Equality USA survey of over 3,100 people, respondents reported that clergy leaders would have been the most effective messengers to help defeat Proposition 8. It's time to stop thinking of the church as our automatic opponent. There are more religious allies that most of us realize.

How They Framed Us!

While No on 8 failed to show gay people or emphatically supportive straight people, the Yes on 8 campaign were happy to show their versions of "gay people." One dramatization of a same-sex couple that appeared in Yes on 8 TV commercial featured two gay Dads with a confused daughter.[46]

Two men are sitting on separate couches talking while their little girl is on the floor playing with a doll. Sad music plays in the background. She turns to one of the men.

Girl: "Daddy, where do babies come from?"

The two men look at each other their mouths wide open.

First man: "Mommies have babies dear, that's where they come from."

Girl: "Do boys ever have babies?"

First man laughs: "No dear, only mommies."

Girl: "Megan says that you have to have a mommy and a daddy to have a baby."

Second man: "Maybe we should spend a little less time over at Megan's house."

---

46 *Where Do Babies Come From Yes on 8 Commercial* http://www.youtube.com/watch?v=75J3TN9Zzck&NR=1

First man upset with other man says: "What Megan means is that it takes a man and a woman to make a baby? That's all."

Girl: "She says that mommies and daddies have to get married first."

The two men become uncomfortable.

First man: "No, sweetheart you don't have to be married to have a baby."

Girl: "Then what is marriage for?" The child looks confused.

The men look confused, embarrassed, unable to answer their daughter's question.

Announcer: "Let's not confuse our kids. Let's protect marriage, by protecting the real meaning of marriage—only between a man and a woman. Vote Yes on Prop 8."

The Yes on 8 people dramatized a gay family as clueless and unable to advocate for ourselves. And perhaps we were, because we spent $43.3 million dollars and didn't do anything to educate people about why we need marriage equality.

Our opponents also used the words "gay" and "marriage" together in a sentence. They weren't afraid of the word gay. But the No on 8 Campaign seemed to be. No on Prop 8 ads never used the word gay.

Here's what Yes on 8 said in their "Children Will Be Taught About Gay Marriage In the Schools Ad"[47] "When Massachusetts legalized gay marriage, schools began teaching second graders that boys could marry boys. Teaching children about gay marriage will happen here unless we pass Proposition 8." Clearly

---

47 *Children Will Be Taught Gay Marriage Yes on 8 Ad http://www.youtube.com/ watch?v=0PgjcgqFYP4&NR=1*

this was a load of manure, but it worked to scare enough people to vote against marriage equality.

12 REASONS WHY THE "NO ON PROP 8" CAMPAIGN FAILED:

1. It failed to frame the message effectively.
2. It did not show same-sex couples and their families and did not tell about our families and how marriage discrimination hurts us and our children.
3. It did not use progressive clergy or people of faith as messengers.
4. It did not empower leadership in our communities of color and it did not use our resources to reach out to communities of color or non-English speaking voters.
5. It failed to be pro-active in our framing of the message and failed to provide basic education about marriage, government, the separation of church and state, and why we need marriage recognition at the state and federal level.
6. It played from a top-down model where power was kept in the hands of the few and failed to empower the grassroots with resources, confidence and a platform to get out and help change hearts and minds.
7. It relied too heavily on TV commercials (terrible TV commercials) and phone banking (which polls show is the least persuasive method of contacting and moving voters).
8. It failed to have a community outreach component, including door-to-door canvassing, public forums and debates.
9. It used radio and newspaper ads sparingly.
10. It didn't utilize endorsements from celebrities and other civil rights leaders.
11. It allowed this to remain a gay issue and not an equal rights issue.
12. It didn't take our opponents seriously enough and didn't alert the community until it was too late.

In summary, Prop 8 passed by because the No on 8 Campaign failed to rise to the occasion with a pro-active, positive portrayal of same-sex couples; failed to call out Prop 8 for what it was — "discrimination;" and ran a top down campaign that restricted decision making to the hands of too few people and failed to use a grassroots, community collaborative approach that worked for the Obama campaign and for the ultimately successful Yes on 8 Campaign.

Chapter Eighteen:
Do's and Don't for Marriage
Equality Campaigns

"Prop 8 didn't win because of the Mormons. It won because we created superior advertising that defined the issues on our terms; because we built a diverse coalition; and, most importantly, because we activated that coalition at the grassroots level in a way that had never before been done."

—Frank Schubert, Yes on 8 Campaign Director

An Open Message to Marriage Equality Campaign Directors

You are in a very important position. People's lives are in your hands. We cannot afford to keep making the same mistakes year after year, campaign after campaign. So, learn from the mistakes of previous campaigns (and there's at least 35 now to learn from) and from the success of the Yes on 8 Campaign. They did everything that the No on 8 Campaign should have done, (except lie and cheat since there's never a good reason for us to ever do that).

Secondly, if you do not believe that 110% marriage is a valuable rite of passage and relationship choice for all people, give up your seat to someone who does. We can't afford to have leaders who don't believe in marriage leading the charge. We need passionate people who are completely devoted to marriage and marriage equality. People with cold feet need not apply.

Thirdly, you must address any residual homophobia you might be holding on to. Campaigns for full equality for LGBT people need to sing the praises of LGBT people. We need to be glorified for the kind, loving, intelligent, beautiful souls that we are. If you are straight and leading a campaign for gay equality

191

and you don't see LGBT people as your full equal, step out of the way! We don't need charity or sympathy, we need respect and equality.

Next, campaign committee members need to get out of the gay ghettos and into the mainstream. Many of you are surrounded only by LGBT people and you don't spend enough time talking with non-gay people, especially more conservative straight people, and hearing their thoughts and impressions to know what inspires them and changes their hearts and minds. You cannot lead our community to equality if you are not an actual ambassador. So, get out there and mingle.

Finally, I urge you to take this list of Do's and Don'ts very seriously.

DO'S AND DON'TS FOR MARRIAGE EQUALITY CAMPAIGNS AND CAMPAIGN COMMITTEE LEADERS

1. GET INTO YOUR HEART.

You can't change hearts if you stay in your head. Stop trying to change minds and instead speak to people's hearts. This is a movement about love. A survey of 1,066 voters, done by San Francisco pollster David Binder for the Equality California Institute, found that 73 percent of those who voted to ban same-sex marriage said there is no argument that would have changed their mind. That is why we must appeal to their emotions and change hearts, not argue with their minds!

2. TELL COMPELLING, TEAR-JERKING STORIES

My heart is heavy from the loss and suffering marriage discrimination has caused the people I love and the strangers I've met over the past ten years who have shared their stories with me. I've seen anti-gay discrimination destroy lives and families. I can tell you about suicides, split ups, children being taken from their parents, people being deported, exiled, dying alone in hospitals, men and women who were unable to claim their spouse's body and make burial decisions for them, people being separated from their loved one after they were severely injured because a homophobic family member stepped in to claim their next-of-kin-power-of-attorney status to keep the couple apart. Why don't we see any commercials about these hardships caused by marriage discrimination? Tell our stories!

3. FIGHT EMOTION WITH EMOTION

The court of public opinion is much different than the actual courts. The public is more influenced by how they feel about something. So, pair facts and emotion. The pro-active commercial I discussed in a previous chapter that would at least allow us to fall forward even if we lost the campaign. Here are two more real-life examples I offer as suggestions.

1. "There are hundreds of rights denied same-sex couples, but the one that William Flannigan needed most was the right to be with Robert in the hospital. Despite twenty years together, the hospital emergency room staff would not recognize their relationship. They allowed straight spouses access to the emergency room, but denied William."

2. "Marvin and Bill were registered domestic partners together for 51 years, but the guy at the funeral home refused to recognize Marvin's legal rights to make medical decisions for Bill. The aging senior was forced to move his beloved's body to another mortuary." Could show a lifetime of photos together and end with the funeral director scenario, for example.

Another ad, with a more positive spin that Molly imagined, had John Cougar's "Everyone Needs a Hand To Hold On To" song playing in the background and showed parents walking their son or daughter down the aisle to their waiting same-sex fiancé, or with a passing mixture of loving straight and gay couples from all races, backgrounds, religions, and professions singing along with the song, much like the old coca-cola commercial where the bottle is passed from person to person.

4. Show Gay People and their Children

To win, you must show gay people on the TV ads. If people don't see our shared humanity and value our relationships how can we ever get them to vote on our behalf.

5. Use Actors and Script-Writers

While it's important to have some personal testimony commercials featuring gay people, their children, and supportive parents, we must also utilize actors and script writers whose business it is to create drama and tell uplifting and/or tear-jerking compelling stories.

6. Dramatize!

Our opponents do this to the point of lying. We can do it and still stay truthful by depicting real life situations that actually have occurred again and again.

We must dig deeper and share the real pain and costs of discrimination. We need to create commercials that show a suicidal gay kid who wants to kill himself because he is being harassed at school and doesn't feel like he will ever be able to have a normal life, like to marry the man he loves and have a family. *Brokeback Mountain* was so effective because it showed the harm to straight and gay people when people are not supported for who they are and are forced to hide.

The No on 8 spokespeople, were dry, uncomfortable, and impersonal. The ads lacked real drama, emotion, and passion. They were preachy. They did not dramatize effectively or tell real stories because again the No on 8 Campaign refused to clearly define the issue as one of discrimination and failed to plunge into a passionate campaign defending equality.

While the Yes on 8 Campaign clearly defined the issue as something worth defending. They captured real drama, emotion, and passion in their "I Can't Teach Gay Marriage: Teacher Takes A Stand" Commercial.[48] This commercial plays on homophobia and irrational emotion and it completely creates a different focus. Viewers are not thinking about same-sex couples wanting to get married. They are suddenly thinking about their second-grade children learning about sex-which is a topic that makes parents, gay or straight, uncomfortable. They do a classic bait and switch. The commercial also sets up tension and falsely creates a loss of personal freedom for the teacher. No one wants to be "forced" to do something against their will.

It's maddening that the Yes on 8 people lied and did so with shocking finesse, but they did and they won. Our opponents play on *fear*, we must tug at *heart strings* not make compelling intellectual arguments. We need professional consultants and campaign managers who use heart power, not just brain power, in crafting a campaign. We also clearly need leaders who will pro-actively define our position, which leads me to point #7.

7. Be Pro-Active, in defining the Marriage Equality Position rather than Simply being Defensive in Advertising about it's "not" about.

Don't wait to see what our opponents will do. Come out swinging, boldly frame the message first! For example, create a pro-active commercial told from the point of view of a straight male supervisor that capture people's hearts.

Sample Commercial- "When Jane's partner, Sally, was diagnosed with cancer, I wanted to give her time off, but since they weren't legally married I was told that I would get fired if I did that. All of her co-workers supported her too. They even said that they would donate a day of their leave to Jane. I had to explain

48 I Can't Teach Gay Marriage: Teacher Takes A Stand Commercial
http://www.youtube.com/watch?v=U8j2y9WtTPw&NR=1

to them that because of state and federal laws, they couldn't help Jane either. Sally didn't have anyone to take care of her and Jane had to quit her job. If they had been legally married, this would not have happened. Denying couples like Sally and Jane equal rights is unfair and that's why I am voting No on 1 which would take away the right of same-sex couples to marry."

8. DON'T RELY TOO MUCH ON FOCUS GROUPS AND POLITICAL CONSULTANTS.

Focus groups' discomfort with gay people as parents was allegedly the reason the No on 8 campaign told couples set to be interviewed for media interview not to discuss or show their children. My wife, Molly McKay, Media Director of Marriage Equality USA, believes this was a huge mistake. She told the *Bay Area Reporter* following the passage of Proposition 8, that "We need to use our moral compass and check every bit of advice we get from political consultants against it. A big part of the marriage issue is protecting our children and it's important for us to include them. Same-sex couples and their kids are really important ambassadors. One fourth of all male couples and one third of female couples are raising kids. It's a mistake not to talk about the real life impact [marriage discrimination has] on our families and our kids."

9. WATCH YOUR LANGUAGE-STICKS AND STONES MAY BREAK ARE BONES, BUT WORDS WILL REALLY, REALLY HURT US!

Don't say, "You don't have to be for gay marriage to be against this mean-spirited proposition." (Prop 22 campaign commercial language March 2000).

Don't' say, "No matter how you feel about marriage, it's wrong to treat people differently." (Prop 8 campaign commercial language November 2008).

During the last week of the No on 8 Campaign, Senator Diane Feinstein[49] appeared in a No on Prop 8 commercial that

49 *Diane Feinstein No on 8 Commercial* http://www.youtube.com/watch?v=lVu4tLg5gdg

ended with Senator Feinstein saying, "No matter how you feel about marriage, vote No on Discrimination." I have to say it was a step up from don't "treat people differently," which is a luke-warm invitation to Vote no on marriage discrimination. But look at her words more carefully. This sentence "even if you are against gay marriage" immediately draws moderate voters back to checking in with their anti-gay marriage feelings, which is self-defeating.

Remember how afraid some white people in the segregated south were of black people? They were irrationally fearful of what would happen if their children attended school with black children. Would it have been strategically wise to say "no matter how you feel about integration" and intentionally draw white people back to thinking about the irrational fears and stereotypes of black people that perpetuated segregation in a campaign ad and then ask them to vote to support a school desegregation bill? Wouldn't it be self-defeating for a campaign on school desegregation aimed at fence sitting fearful white voters to have said "No matter how you feel about your children going to school with black children, vote for school desegregation."?

Also, why evoke someone's feelings by saying "no matter how you feel…" only to then turn around and tell them to ignore their feelings? We have a whole psychology industry telling people to trust their gut and respect their feelings. Wouldn't it have made more sense to help them connect with their higher self, rather than their fearful one? A message with a higher call to action would have been, "Equal protection under the law. No exceptions. Vote No on Discrimination. Vote No on Prop 8." Or "Vote No on Discrimination, vote no on Prop 8."

Unlike the No on 8 campaign, the No on 1 Campaign in Maine showed real gay people and their families. However, the Maine Campaign showed ads that had more of a "live and let live" message, rather than a pro-active marriage equality message, including failing to use the words "marriage equality" in two of the initial highly promoted ads.

No on 1 Maine "Sam Putnam" commercial.

This commercial was seen as a huge breakthrough because it showed a same-sex couple with their son, Sam. However, there were flaws with this commercial's language and messaging.

Video of teenage boy standing on porch with one woman on his left and one woman on his right. Voice over begins, "I'm Sam Putnam, I have two moms, we are like every other average family."

Commercial moves to Sam testifying before a legislative committee flanked on either side by two women.

Sam-"I consider my mom's partner, my step-mom, but society doesn't, my school doesn't, my doctor doesn't, sometimes my friends' parents don't either. My family doesn't mean to other people what it means to me."

Jennifer Putnam-"We are just like a lot of other families in Maine. We have our ups and downs, and we stick together and we love each other."

Sam-"We can't be seen as lesser and if you vote no, then it will help change that, please do the right thing."

Since this is supposed to be an ad persuading people to support marriage equality, I'm going to restate this commercial as if it were a product we're selling so you can see its weaknesses.

Video of teenage boy standing on porch with one woman on his left and one woman on his right. Voice over begins, "I'm Sam Putnam, I have a Hoover vacuum Cleaner, it's just like every other average vacuum cleaner."

Commercial moves to Sam testifying before a legislative committee flanked by his vacuum cleaner. Sam-"I consider my vacuum cleaner to be good, but society doesn't, my school doesn't, my doctor doesn't, sometimes my friends' parents don't either. My vacuum cleaner doesn't mean to other people what it means to me."

Jennifer Putnam-"The Hoover vacuum cleaner is just like a lot of other vacuum cleaners in Maine. It has its ups and downs, but we stick together and we love each other."

Sam-"Hoover vacuums can't be seen as lesser and if you buy our product then it will help change that, please do the right thing."

Okay, I realize that doesn't directly translate, but how compelled are you to buy a Hoover vacuum, based on this commercial? Let's rewind and play it back slowly.

"CONSIDER"

Sam-"*I consider my mom's partner, my step-mom, but society doesn't, my school doesn't, my doctor doesn't, sometimes my friends' parents don't either. My family doesn't mean to other people what it means to me.*"

First, Sam uses the word "consider" with regard to his step-mom. According to the Merriam-Webster Dictionary, consider means to "think or ponder, heed or regard." It is a dispassionate, intellectualized term. It is not heart-felt and it is not assertive. He also doesn't even use his "step-mom's" name, he calls her "my mother's partner," which is also dispassionate. How about? "Michelle is my other mom."

He then goes on to talk about all the people who disagree with his belief that Michelle is his step-mom. He mentions a laundry list of people in his life that totally reject the notion that's he's selling: society, his school, doctor, and even his friends' parents.

I'm not picking on Sam, he's a kid. I'm picking on the professionals that were ostensibly steering this commercial. The commercial needed to assert how marriage would improve this family's life and it didn't.

Isn't this stronger?

"Michelle is my other mom, and we were so happy in May of this year when the Maine legislature finally recognized my family by providing my parents with the opportunity to marry. Now, outside special interest groups are trying to take away that right to keep my parents from marrying and having the legal recognition and protections that we need as a family."

"WE HAVE OUR UPS AND DOWNS"

Jennifer Putnam-"We are just like a lot of other families in Maine. We have our ups and downs, and we stick together and we love each other."

For God's sake now is not the time to tell people your product is flawed. That's what the other side is doing. This is your 30 seconds to shine. Tell us about the good stuff. And not to be harsh, but you'd better "stick together" and "love each other," because that's what families do, especially families with healthy parents. By saying this, the commercial almost makes us think twice about the truth of this.

Also, "we are just like a lot of other families in Maine," sounds sketchy. Which "other families?" You've not anchored us to anything positive. Are you like the ones with domestic violence and alcoholism, the ones who volunteer at the soup kitchen or the animal shelter, the ones who to religious services on weekends, or the one's who take their kids to soccer practice? Please connect us to something.

The time would have been better spent stating.

"We are a loving family and our family needs equal protections, rights and respect that marriage affords other families. Amendment 1 denies us those protections. Vote No on 1."

"WE CAN'T BE SEEN AS LESSER"

Sam-"We can't be seen as lesser and if you vote no then it will help change that, please do the right thing."

This last statement is so convoluted I almost don't know where to begin. First, Sam the sad thing is that you are your family can be seen as lesser. That's why your family doesn't have equal protection because LGBT people are seen as lesser and thus people feel justified giving them and their families a lesser relationship status and fewer rights under the law. Second, the commercial ends with Sam asking people to do something, but it's not clear what he's asking for. Again I'm not trying to pick on Sam. The script does not say clearly, "Vote No on Amendment 1." In fact, nowhere in the commercial does anyone say, "Vote No on Amendment 1." That's senseless. Worse, somebody approved and paid for this piece of work! Never does this commercial say "support marriage equality." Never do they even say the word "marriage," and that's what it's all about! The commercial should have clearly stated, *"Do the right thing, vote no on Amendment 1."* Or *"Please support our family's right to equal protection, vote no on Amendment 1."*

Finally, where the hell was Michelle in this commercial? Can you imagine a heterosexual couple with a child and not having each parent speak in a family commercial? Commercial makers what do you think not having all of the family members speak communicates to people who already don't believe in the integrity of this family? I'll tell you. It communicates that Michelle is not a "real" part of this family she is simply Sam's mom's partner, not Sam's second parent. It also communicates that it's likely that Sam's mom will have another partner, so why bother taking her seriously.

If I sound mad I am. This is a self-defeating commercial on so many levels. Who is reviewing these commercials for the psychological impact and the subtle homophobic messages that are being conveyed? It makes me upset to hink of the money being spent and the resources expended on these lack-luster commercials.

10. Show, don't Tell

The No on Prop 8 Campaign said "Prop. 8 is unfair, unnecessary and wrong." However, 44 percent of California voters polled disagreed. Campaigns must show, rather than tell, people that same-sex marriage bans are wrong.

11. Use Supportive Clergy in Campaign ads

When polled in the aftermath of Prop 8, people repeatedly cited their religious convictions for why they are against marriage equality. According to David Binder's research, "The influence of the church was a major factor. The religious aspect tended to win over concerns about discrimination." In order to win, marriage equality campaigns must employ clergy as messengers. Voters need to see how and why other people of faith, especially religious leaders, have reconciled their religious beliefs with their convictions for equality for LGBT people. They need to hear from clergy that anti-gay measures increase hate and that God is about loving thy neighbor as thyself. Use supportive progressive clergy. Despite, the stereotypes, many liberals are also spiritual and religious, or would at least like to know that there are believers who have another perspective on gay issues.

12. Educate about the Separation of Church and State

Because religious doctrine tends to be the number one justification for denying same-sex couples civil rights, campaigns must have clergy, religious politicians, and secular politicians talking about the separation of church and state and reminding people of the distinction between religious beliefs and discriminatory state laws. To flesh out this issue, a campaign can ask conflicted voters "How concerned are you that divorce violates some people's religious beliefs? Does this mean we should ban divorce for all?"

Like the environmental group "We Can Solve It" whose commercials bring together opposing political parties to talk about the environment, marriage equality campaign commercials could show a clergy member, a religious politician, and a secular politician sitting on a couch sharing why they believe in marriage equality and why religion should never be used as a reason to justify discrimination in government policy. Why not do a PSA or a proactive marriage equality commercial with liberal Democrat, David Boies and conservative Republican, Ted Olson, two attorneys who are working together on a federal challenge to repeal Prop 8?

13. EDUCATE PEOPLE ABOUT HOW THE SEPARATION OF CHURCH AND STATE MEANS THAT GIVING SAME-SEX COUPLES ACCESS TO CIVIL MARRIAGE WILL NOT FORCE ANY RELIGIOUS INSTITUTION TO PERFORM SAME-SEX MARRIAGES OR TO LOSE THEIR 501c3 NON-PROFIT STATUS.

During the five months same-sex couples were able to legally marry in California, none of them were married in the Catholic, Mormon or Evangelical Churches. None of these churches were ever forced to marry same-sex couples and the only churches that could lose their 501c3 non-profit status are those who violate tax law by going over the amount of money non-profits are allowed for political organizing.

14. EDUCATE PEOPLE THAT THE SEPARATION OF CHURCH AND STATE ALLOWS RELIGIOUS GROUPS THAT DO SUPPORT MARRIAGE EQUALITY FOR SAME-SEX COUPLES TO CONTINUE TO PERFORM THESE BLESSINGS/MARRIAGES FOR SAME-SEX

**COUPLES WHETHER OR NOT THE STATE GRANTS SAME-SEX COU-
PLES THE CONSTITUTIONAL RIGHT TO MARRY.**

In all 50 states, same-sex couples are married in churches and
synagogues by faith groups that believe in equality for same-sex
couples. However, these religious marriages don't come with any
government rights except in states that already grant same-sex
couples the right to marry.

15. CREATE A POSITIVE MANTRA ABOUT MARRIAGE EQUALITY AND FAIRNESS FOR GAY PEOPLE AND THEIR FAMILIES.

Say:
- "It's time to support full equality for gay people and their
  families!"
- 'Our gay friends, family members, co-workers deserve
  equal marriage rights." —"Equality and responsibility
  are family values."
- "I want my gay parents to be able to be legally married."
- "Marriage equality for same-sex couples, nothing less,
  nothing more."
- "Stand on the side of love, not on the side of intolerance
  and bigotry."
- "Gay families deserve equal rights and protections."

16. USE MESSENGERS THAT REFLECT THE DIVERSITY OF THE LGBT COMMUNITY.

Messengers must reflect the ethnic, racial, religious, and socioeconomic diversity of LGBT people and their families. The
Yes on 8 folks did this by including actors representing young
people, people of color, and people of various religious backgrounds, in their "Protect Our Future" Commercial.[50] While No
on 8 commercials appeared to have some diversity, it seemed to
rely more on voice-overs and still photos, and a few token people

---

50 *Protect Our Future* http://www.youtube.com/watch?v=A-jc4ujp9Ok&NR=1

of color, at least until the last few weeks before the vote. Was that the official Prop 8 campaign's idea of diversity?

17. MESSENGERS MUST INCLUDE LGBT YOUTH, LGBT ADULTS, PARENTS OF LGBT PEOPLE, AND KIDS OF LGBT FAMILIES AND HOW MARRIAGE DISCRIMINATION HURTS THEM.

- Show gay seniors talking about senior's issues related to marriage denial, like Social Security, pension benefits, inheritance tax, etc.
- Show parents of LGBT people and why they want all their children to be able to marry.
- Show kids of same-sex couples talking about wanting their family to be treated with equal dignity.
- Show gay youth talking about wanting to grow up and share in the American Dream.
- List the hundreds of rights denied same-sex couples and then pick one and talk about the effect on a specific couple.

18. USE STRAIGHT ALLIES AND PUBLIC CELEBRITIES AS MESSENGERS.

Find and use our straight allies, service providers, police officers. Use American civil rights heroes who've come out in favor of marriage equality, including Congressman John Lewis, Christine Chavez, and Dolores Huerta. Use allies with star power like Brad Pitt, Tom Hanks, Whoopi Goldberg, Ellen Degeneres, Eric McCormack, Drew Barrymore, John Stuart, Stephen Colbert, Stephen Spielberg, Melissa Etheridge, among others for public service announcements or commercials in support of marriage equality. Ellen made her own commercial that No on 8 didn't use. I'm not sure why.

19. MAKE MESSAGES THAT ARE CULTURALLY-COMPETENT AND IN LANGUAGES OTHER THAN ENGLISH.

Over a third of Californians are Latino, yet the No on 8 Campaign printed barely any materials in Spanish. Culturally competent campaign ads and educational materials must be widely available in all relevant languages spoken by voters.

20. EDUCATE PEOPLE ABOUT MARRIAGE RIGHTS.

Your average American does not know that LGBT people are denied 1,138 federal rights. As I mentioned previously, most Americans don't even know what rights and responsibilities come with that marriage license they say "I do" to. They don't understand that marriage rights span all areas of life from birth and parentage rights, to death burial decisions, inheritance, Social Security, employment benefits, the ability to leave work to care for an unrecognized spouse or in-law, something that heterosexual married employees are granted through marriage. They don't know how inadequate domestic partnerships and civil unions are. They don't understand that it's not just a piece of paper at issue, marriage is the fundamental way for families, gay or straight, to protect themselves, their earnings, their possessions, etc.

21. CALL IT WHAT IT IS!

The No on 8 Campaign made a conscious choice not to use the word "discrimination" even though anti-gay groups put a ballot initiative on the ballot to take away gay people's constitutional civil rights. They decided to go with "unfair and wrong." However, they started using the word discrimination a week before Prop 8 passed, and since Prop 8 passed, people have been using the word discrimination liberally. Keep it up. This is a civil rights movement to end discrimination. Just be sensitive and listen to people and don't act like we are the only group to ever suffer. Build alliances for justice for all, if you want good allies, be one.

Also, use the words "marriage" and "marriage equality." This is not the time to talk about "live and let live," people can let us live without letting us live in equality. In California the campaign failed to use the affirmation of the court system for marriage equality. The commercials could have said something like this: "The California Supreme Court declared that denying same-sex couples the right to marry is unconstitutional. Now, special interest groups want to dismantle the court's ruling. It's wrong to try and take away a person's constitutional right to marry. Vote no on discrimination by voting no on Prop 8." They didn't because they catered to the opponent's frame of "activist judges." You can't run a successful campaign that is reacting to the other sides frame and messages.

A similar strategy could have been employed in Maine. "The Maine Legislature and Governor, John Baldacci, signed a bill into law to extend marriage rights to same-sex couples, granting them full equality under Maine law. Now, outside special interest groups have poured money into Maine to take away equality. Having an opinion on something is one thing, but taking away a person's constitutional rights is wrong. Vote no on discrimination by voting no on Question 1."

22. DON'T REPEAT THEIR FRAME

In a No on 8 commercial Senator Diane Feinstein repeats the Yes on 8 frame by saying "Prop 8 is not about schools or children." She would have used her time better by saying what Prop 8 was—an anti-gay ballot initiative to strip same-sex couples of their constitutional right to marry. But instead, she repeated the opponent's own frame.

Do me a favor, try not to think of an elephant? What are you thinking of now, not an elephant I hope? Professor George Lakoff's *New York Times* Best Selling Book *Don't Think of An Elephant* repeatedly states that you should never repeat your opponent's frame. It's like political debating 101. Lakoff says that repeating this gives the opponents argument validity. In this case, it sends the message to people that Prop 8 *is about schools and children!*

Here's another ad that responds to the opposition's frame and again has the horrible phrase "regardless of how you feel about marriage," which is a flashback to Prop 22's "you don't have to be for gay marriage to vote no on 22."

JACK O'CONNELL, CALIFORNIA SUPERINTENDENT OF SCHOOLS COMMERCIAL

The ad begins with a visual of a Yes on 8 ad of a little girl telling her mom that she learned at school that a prince could marry a prince and she could marry a princess. The words "absolutely not true" appear across the screen.

Voice Over: "Have you seen the TV ads for Prop 8? They're absolutely not true says California superintendent of public schools."

Then it shows Jack O'Connell standing in front of his desk.

Jack O'Connell: "Prop 8 has nothing to do with schools or kids. Our schools aren't required to teach anything about marriage. And using kids to lie about that is shameful."

Voice Over: "That's why California teachers and every major newspaper say No on prop 8. Because regardless of how you feel about marriage, it's wrong to eliminate fundamental rights. No on 8. Unfair and Wrong."

Do you see that when you say Prop 8 has nothing to do with kids, listeners hear "Prop 8 has to do with kids!" When No on 8 says "Our schools aren't required to teach anything about marriage." It could suggest that while schools aren't required to, there's nothing stopping from teaching kids about gay marriage in schools which is what those Yes on 8 people said would happen if I don't vote Yes on 8. And now they are telling me to ignore my feelings on marriage and that I'm wrong. That doesn't feel good. I don't trust these people. Note also, that the commercial doesn't decisively tell the listener to "vote no on 8." Actually, if you just listen to the words it says "No on 8, unfair and wrong," sending a message that No on 8 is unfair and wrong. It's subtle, but it's there. Also they replay the most effective Yes on 8 commercial! Wow, free airtime for the Yes on 8 campaign's commercial that's a really smart move.

As mentioned earlier, almost the entire No on Prop 8 Campaign was a defensive campaign that responded or reacted to Yes on 8's framing of the message. We will continue to lose campaigns until we boldly frame the issue on our own terms.

23. TRY HARDER

The best television commercial, entitled "Discrimination,"[51] came out a week before the election. This commercial talked about discrimination against racial minorities in California's history, but it did not strongly connect past racial discrimination to stripping same-sex couples of their constitutional right to marry. Samuel Jackson simply says, "The sponsors of Prop 8 want to eliminate fundamental rights. We have an obligation to pass along to our children a more tolerant, decent society. Vote no on Prop 8."

This ad does not mention that gay people are about to lose their constitutional right to protect their families. It does not mention how Prop 8 will harm our families. If you are not going to be pro-active, at least message things in a more assertive manner and mention gay people. For example, "Today, same-sex couples and their families are under attack. Don't repeat the mistakes of the past. It was wrong to take away people's constitutional rights and discriminate, and it is wrong today. Don't let discrimination win, vote No on 8."

---

51 *Discrimination No on 8 Commercial* http://www.youtube.com/watch?v=Oj-0xMrsyxE

24. USE OUR GAY TALENT!

Our community's legendary flair and creative talents were under-utilized. For just a taste of what could have been, see Marc Shaiman's *Prop 8—The Musical*[52] starring Jack Black, Maya Rudolph, and Margaret Cho.

There were also some creative and funny ads on the internet that never made it to TV. The commercials that mimic the actual Macintosh computer versus PC computers commercials were funny and effective.[53] In these commercials the guy representing No on Prop 8 is like a Mac, progressive and open-minded, and Yes on 8 is supposed to be like a PC, the character is depicted as sexist and conservative.

Here's a sample of one commercial:

No on 8 guy: "I'm No on 8. I maintain the current constitution and give everyone equality in the eyes of the law."

Yes on 8: "And I eliminate rights, but just for certain people, so that's cool."

No on 8: "Right, I'm into fairness and dignity."

Yes on 8: "Yeah, me too."

No on 8: "But you just said…"

Yes on 8: "Just not for everyone. I want to preserve tradition."

No on 8: "By putting discrimination into the constitution?"

Yes on 8: "Yep!"

No on 8: "That doesn't sound like the California I know."

Yes on 8: "Okay, name one thing more important to Californians than stopping same-sex marriage?"

No on 8: "The economy, healthcare, the war, the environment…"

Yes on 8: "Boring. I'd like to see where all this fairness and dignity is going to get you."

---

*52 Google **"Prop 8 The Musical"** or follow this link.* http://www.funnyordie.com/videos/c0cf508ff8/prop-8-the-musical-starring-jack-black-john-c-reilly-and-many-more-from-fod-team-jack-black-craig-robinson-john-c-reilly-and-rashida-jones

53 I'm No on Prop 8 Commercial
http://www.youtube.com/watch?v=b9T7ux8M4Go&NR=1

No on 8: "Yeah me too. We are all Californians. We're all equal. Let's keep it that way. Make sure you, your friends and your family all vote no on Prop 8."

In another one of these ads, the Yes on 8 guy looks at a woman pretending to be the California Constitution and says "I'd sure like to amend her."

Sadly, since these ads were not created by the ad campaign companies they were ignored to our detriment. Try to think outside of the corporate box and utilize talent.

25. DON'T WAIT FOR A CAMPAIGN, START EDUCATING TODAY

We can't wait until our back is against the wall again to start educational media campaigns. We must be focused now on educating everyone. It's been almost two years since Prop 8 passed and this still not happening in California. We need to create proactive infomercials and PSAs that educate people about marriage discrimination. For over a decade, our opponents have talked about how marriage equality will lead to teaching homosexuality in the schools. Rather than wasting time trying to refute their arguments, we must find a way to send the message that teaching respect for all is in everyone's best interest.

We don't have to do this directly by saying it. We can do it by showing kids getting beat up because they are perceived as different" (i.e. children who are over-weight, physically challenged, LGBTQ, have two parents of the same-sex or are raised by a grandparent, or children from a marginalized religious background or cultural background) and then have a message that shows that it's wrong to pick on people and treat them unfairly because of these differences. Debra Chasnoffs' "Let's Get Real"[54] video about bullying in the schools is a great example of showing our shared concern about preventing kids from

---

54 *"Let's Get Real" Video http://www.groundspark.org/press/letsgetreal*

being bullied for their individual differences in race, religion, sexual orientation, socioeconomic status, ethnicity, and physical ability.

And we need to better confront fundamentalist religious legal organizations intimidating schools with lawsuits for teaching tolerance and about LGBT people in diversity curriculums.

26. CREATE ADS THAT ADDRESS ANTI-GAY VIOLENCE AND TALK ABOUT HOW CAMPAIGNS TO TAKE AWAY GAY PEOPLE'S RIGHTS INCREASES HATE CRIMES.

The 1,200 people who reported to Marriage Equality USA that they personally experienced "homophobia, hate speech, or threats of violence" during the Prop 8 campaign were not confined to rural areas or to gay people. 35% of respondents from the Bay Area and 38% of the respondents from Los Angeles also reported being verbally harassed and threatened by Yes on 8 supporters and 42% of the respondents that experienced hate speech were LGBT and 27% were heterosexual, the rest did not identify their sexual orientation.

During the 2004 election, 14 states amended their constitutions to deny same-sex couples the right to marry. States continue to amend their constitutions to deny same-sex couples the right to marry and the rate of hate crimes against LGBT people continues to grow. FBI statistics show that hate crimes against gays and lesbians account for the third largest number of bias crimes in the country with anti-gay hate crimes growing since 2005. According to the FBI Hate Crimes Statistics Report in 2005, 14.2% of hate crimes nationwide were based on sexual orientation bias. That number rose to 15.5% in 2006, and to 16.6% in 2007. A Hate Violence Summary from Communities United Against Violence (CUAV) in 2007 also showed a 6% increase in anti-LGBT hate crimes in California's San Francisco Bay Area. In the Bay Area alone, there was a 7% increase in victims, a 282% increase rape in 2007 (11 to 42), and 5 murders in 2007.

In 2008, the FBI reported that 16.7% of hate crimes nation-wide were based on sexual orientation bias. While the percentage of hate crimes because of sexual orientation rose only .1%, the actual number of hate crimes related to the sexual orientation of the victim rose to 11% (1,617 offenses).

Three weeks after Proposition 8 passed, a lesbian was violently gang-raped by five men, two of them teenagers, who repeatedly called her derogatory anti-gay names. She was abducted in front of her home that she shares with her partner and son.

And, it's not just gay people who are the victims of anti-gay violence. Many straight people campaigning for No on 8 were also harassed. One Sacramento woman reported, *"I, a straight female, was called a faggot and a slut countless times. 'Yes on 8' was painted all over my windshield so I was unable to drive a way."* Only weeks after the gang rape of the lesbian, two brothers in Brooklyn, were perceived to be a gay couple. They were brutally beaten with baseball bats and beer bottles, kicked repeatedly, and called anti-gay names by their attackers. They had gone to a church party, then out to a bar to drink and were leaning on each other as they walked home. One brother, Jose Sucuzhanay, 31, died from severe head injuries a week later.

There are a plethora of real life stories that show how marriage discrimination breeds hatred and violence. Bear in mind that these figures account for only hate crimes reported. The actual number is greater.

27. Learn from mistakes

The marriage equality movement can apply the lessons learned from California's No on Prop 8 Campaign to prevent the same mistakes from being repeated in future campaigns. Just as football teams watch prior games they lost, we must review our current playbook, as well as analyze the opposition's in order to move forward successfully.

The mistakes made by our friends and colleagues in the marriage equality movement have been highlighted in this chapter not to pin failure on them, but to urge all of us to take a new look at our political models. Each of the leaders mentioned by name in this chapter is a committed activist and their tireless work should be applauded. However, it's time to produce an effective strategy before gay marriage is outlawed in another state.

CHAPTER NINETEEN:
CALLING ALL LOVE WARRIORS!

It's a terrible mistake thinking of anti-gay organizers as phony or that they're just doing it for money. They use the gay issue because it creates fear and mobilizes volunteers, but they really believe this stuff they're saying and it's much more difficult to deal with a true believer than it is with somebody who's a phony. To laugh them off is the worst, most dangerous, long-range decision we could make. They are more mobilized than the liberal community. Progressives kind of wait and hope things will blow over, but the religious right were organized since the 1970's to create fear and bring people together, whatever their religious beliefs. The religious right has reached out to a sectarian crowd because people there are also afraid of this phony gay threat.

—Mel White, Founder of Soulforce and Author of
"Stranger at the Gate"

COME OUT, COME OUT WHOEVER YOU ARE!

Folks, we are in campaign mode until we have global marriage equality. Therefore, if we are going to get marriage equality around the world, same-sex couples and their families must be visible! LGBT people need to come out to everyone. Same-sex couples need to come out to everyone. Non-gay friends and family members, you need to put up pictures and start talking about your lesbian sister and her wife, your gay son and his husband/partner, your transgender nephew and his girlfriend, your MTF transgender father or mother, and your bisexual friend and his/her same-sex spouse.

TELL YOUR STORY!

There is no underestimating the power of the personal story to open hearts and minds. We all have a story to tell about why marriage equality is important to us, regardless of our sexual orientation. We have to start telling our truths! Gay or straight, you have a story about why marriage discrimination is wrong and hurts people. Now, go and tell it straight from the heart. No holds barred. We need to stop being polite and asking nicely for our rights and speak up. We must speak up for ourselves and for the others who can no longer speak or who are too afraid.

Will you speak out for Fred Martinez, a young Native American who was killed because he was transgender and for Mathew Sheppard who was murdered because he was gay? Will you speak out for Joanne, who has AIDS because she used drugs and alcohol to fight off the pain and shame of being rejected by her family? Will you speak out for Guadalupe, who committed a crime to go back to prison where she can be openly gay, rather than live a life of fear and hiding because her family did not accept her? Will you speak out for Regina in Italy who will marry a man in the Catholic Church, but have secret affairs with her true love, Anna Maria, because she doesn't want to disappoint her mother and the church keeps telling her that being gay is a sin? Will you speak out for those who cannot speak out for themselves, because they are too afraid or dead? Our stories must be told.

And we must all share our why-I-give-a-damn-about-gay-marriage stories on our Facebook page, in our tweets and blogs, in school newspapers and editorials, in term papers and class presentations, in our faith communities, at parties, on radio and TV talk shows, in the songs and stories we write, and by simply sharing when the opportunity arises.

When same-sex couples started to marry in California, Marriage Equality USA initiated a project called "Couples Across California" and collected personal stories of couples who got married from across the state. MEUSA encouraged these couples to submit local wedding announcements and send messages to families, friends and neighbors.

In Connecticut, Love Makes a Family, assembled photos and personal stories from LGBT people, their families, and straight allies in support of marriage equality. They created a binder with all the images and gave one to each of their state legislators.

Stories should be the centerpiece of all future campaigns for marriage equality, especially on TV commercials and radio ads.

- Stories from same-sex couples about why they need marriage equality.
- Stories from LGBT youth who dream about getting married someday.
- Stories from children of same-sex parents who need their parents to be married.
- Stories from friends and allies and parents of LGBT people about why they want their friends and family members to be able to be legally married.
- Stories from people of diverse racial, political, spiritual, and ethnic backgrounds sharing the impact of marriage equality on their communities and society-at-large.
- Stories from community leaders and politicians about why marriage equality is a human rights issue that calls us to take a stand for others and tear down this wall of discrimination.
- Stories from clergy and people of faith bringing forth the moral arguments for equality for all.
- Stories from our supportive bosses and co-workers about how gay people deserve the same rights as married people

when it comes to health and pension benefits, sick and family leave, etc.

WORDS CAN HURT YOU

As we tell our stories we must ensure that our language is working for us, not against us. As discussed we must carefully examine our language. Is the language of affirmation of negation? Is it of abundance or scarcity? Are we reaffirming the struggle by talking about the "fight" for marriage equality or affirming our "right" to marriage equality? If you say we are "married in our hearts" does that send the message that we don't need to be married legally by our government? Do you say, "I don't care what they call it?" Or "I'd be happy with civil unions." Look to see if the way you talk about this issue suggests that marriage doesn't matter to you.

BECOME A LEADER

As mentioned previously, beginning in 2001, on Freedom to Marry Day (2/12) or Valentine's Day, Molly and I would go to the marriage license counter in San Francisco and ask for a marriage license. On February 12, 2004, we got one. Sadly, our first marriage license was invalidated by the court. But four years after that, the court struck down the marriage ban and we were legally married! And on February 12, 2009, eight years after we started the annual tradition of asking for marriage licenses, same-sex couples in 62 cities around the United States followed in our footsteps by asking for a marriage license at their County Clerk's Office.

THE CALL TO EQUALITY! EMPOWER YOURSELF AND OTHERS

Winning marriage equality requires empowering individuals to become leaders and employing a grassroots approach. For over a decade, Molly and I have worked as community leaders for equal marriage rights. We believe that our best investment towards marriage equality and equal rights for LGBT people is by empowering individuals to actively participate in their own liberation and become leaders in their local community.

In 2001, we joined Marriage Equality USA, since then, we have worked to create a grassroots infrastructure that empowers individual volunteers in their local communities to eliminate marriage discrimination against LGBT people. We provided people access to web and educational tools, talking points, marriage equality educational materials, and media and leadership training. This allows them to return to their communities and educate people about the need for marriage equality and creates a self-replicating structure for the cycle of empowerment to continue and expand. Some people we met were already leaders in their local community and together we've used our collective wisdom to determine what would and wouldn't work in their community to garner support for marriage equality.

Marriage Equality USA has had leaders as young as 18, seniors, straight men and women, single lesbians, single gay men, transgender men and women, same-sex couples, black, white, Indian, Latino, Native American, and Asian. Our leaders are teachers, stay-at-home moms, attorneys, realtors, electricians, construction workers, social workers, psychologists, clergy, accountants, students, among others. Some MEUSA leaders went on to start LGBT centers in their rural communities, a few became guest writers or speakers for local newspapers and television shows, and some were inspired to become lawyers or politicians after working for years as activists. All have stretched themselves out of their original comfort zones and stepped up as public speakers, leaders, organizers, mentors, and role models and will have treasured memories of the contributions they made to righting this wrong.

We have found repeatedly that having local people speak out in their community, opening their hearts, and coming out of the closet helps people get to know them and their families, and has earned our community long-lasting support. For example, Jamila lives in rural Eureka, California with her wife, Michelle, and their young daughter, Abigail. The family has shared their story with the local newspaper, the Eureka City Council, and the Humboldt County Human Rights Commission. They have spoken about why their family needs marriage equality at community forums, churches, and colleges, so that people can see who LGBT people are and the impact marriage equality has on our lives. Jamila and her family have changed the hearts and minds of politicians, policy makers, and local citizens, by getting resolutions in support of marriage equality passed at the city and county level, and getting their assemblymember to vote in support of the statewide marriage equality bill. Their openness is even more powerful and more personal than any commercial, especially in a very conservative, rural area.

CREATE AN INFRASTRUCTURE THAT WILL ALLOW YOU TO ENLIGHTEN AND ELEVATE YOUR LOCAL COMMUNITY!

Do you know who the LGBT leaders and straight allies are in your local area, college, religious group, etc.? Could you bring a few people together who aren't yet leaders but want to work for marriage equality and together nurture your and their leadership skills, round up resources, and empower yourselves to make a difference? You can meet over coffee, in a library or at a gay-friendly church.

In our early marriage equality activist days, a handful of us met in the back room of World Grounds, a gay-friendly café in Oakland. Sometimes it was hard to hear over the Poetry Slam in the front room, but it was a safe public space. Remember in 2001, marriage equality was a radical pursuit even in the gay community. Some chapters held their meetings over dinner or had potlucks. Nowadays, people can meet on conference calls and never even have to leave their homes. Find out what works for you and your community.

If you could get a handful of people together, those individuals could reach out to a handful of people who can reach out to a handful of people and before you know it, you have a powerful network for equality or a weird spin off on an old shampoo commercial. But I'm sure you get it, your strength will come in numbers and connection. This is a movement about connection bringing people together, uplifting people, and if you grow yourselves in this way, you will be a strong coalition.

Rather than re-invent the wheel, contact Marriage Equality USA www.marriageequality.org, and find out how you can start a chapter in your area. They can set you up with a webpage, T-shirts, brochures, and other educational materials to help you get started. Once you have a handful of people, you could start with telling your stories to your city council and ask them to pass a resolution supporting marriage equality. See the sample non-binding city council resolution in the Chapter entitled "Get Engaged: Marriage Equality Interactive Resources."

MAKING AN IMPACT

Others of you will be called to create something new and different, like college friends Amy Balliett and Willow Witte, who after e-mailing about their shock at the passage of California's Proposition 8 decided to use their advanced knowledge of computer networking to create a very successful netroots approach to LGBT activism, known as Join the Impact (JTI). JTI allowed people across the globe to sign on and begin creating meet ups and connecting with others who wanted to take a stand against Prop 8. The result—300 rallies with thousands of people gathering across the country on November 15, 2008 to protest Prop 8's passage. Or like, Kip Williams, another young person who wanted to make a difference in the LGBT community. Kip formed One Struggle, One Fight and marched across California speaking out about marriage equality which led to his working with Cleve Jones on the 2008 National Equality March in DC. Since Proposition 8's passage, more people than ever before have heard the call to equality. I hope you will hear it too and join me in creating equality for LGBT people across the globe.

Take Action Now

Go to Marriage Equality USA's website at www.marriage-equality.org and become a Marriage Equality USA member. Or better yet, find out how you can become a Marriage Equality USA chapter leader and support marriage equality in your town.

Go to the Love Warriors International website at www.love-warriors.org and become an International Love Warrior™ and find out how you can advance equality for LGBT people around the world.

Chapter Twenty:
Targeting Marriage Equality:
Reaching the Movable Middle

Marriage Equality Supporters Come On Out!

We can't win our equality from the closet. LGBT people, you need to bust down that closet door and keep busting it down every day, by telling the truth of who you are and who you love! Straight allies don't keep your beliefs to yourself, let everyone know about your gay neighbors, friends, co-workers and family members and that you support their right to marry and be treated equally under all laws. Only roughly 10% of the population is gay. If we are ever going to make marriage equality a reality it's going to be because heterosexuals are standing with LGBT people and tipping the scales in favor of equality. Do what my wife, Molly, says and "make every moment a marriage equality moment."

"Our enemy is untruth." —Ghandi

A heart change is more powerful than a mind change. We must appeal to emotion, not logic. We must show positive images of gay people. We must show love. We must show family.

In May 2009, Goodwin Simon Victoria Research and David Binder Research released a statewide "Survey on Marriage Equality in California" that reported that "The most effective messages focused on gay and lesbian couples having the same hopes and dreams as everyone else, and it being unfair to deny them and their children of the dignity, responsibility, and security of marriage." I have summarized the survey's[55] findings below.

---

55 Goodwin Simon Victoria Research and David Binder's Research as conveyed during the Get Engaged Tours 2009, following the loss of Prop 8.

Characteristics of Marriage Equality Supporters
- Under 45 years old
- Not religious
- Rarely/Never attend church, but if they do, are likely Jewish, progressive Christian or—Buddhist
- Know LGBT people
- Have a friend or family member who is LGBT

Characteristics of Conflicted Voters
- Politically moderate
- 45-64 years old
- Non-evangelical
- Attend church monthly
- Have a co-worker or acquaintance who is LGBT

These voters are conflicted because they don't want to harm anyone, but are uncomfortable with the idea of marriage for same-sex couples largely because they forget about the civil institution of marriage and focus only on religious marriage. Emphasizing that same-sex couples are seeking civil marriage, which will not affect marriage in the church, is an important persuasion point for this group. Additionally, helping these voters understand that same-sex couples seek to join the existing civil institution of marriage because we seek the stability and family protections that marriage provides.

Characteristics of Voters who Oppose Marriage Equality
- Politically conservative
- Over 65 years old
- Evangelical or "born again"
- Attend church once a week or more
- Don't know LGBT people or at least don't think they know LGBT people.

The majority of those who oppose marriage equality do so because of their religious beliefs. They view marriage as a religious covenant. They do not see the civil distinction. Their hearts and minds are unlikely to change if they are not able to see that same-sex couples simply want the same rights and protections that other families have and that they are seeking these rights and protections from the government which will not affect the church. Without adequate information about the civil and religious marriage distinction, they will be more likely to vote against marriage equality motivated by the rhetoric that the churches will be forced to marry gay people and that first graders will be taught about gay sex. These voters would also benefit from hearing about the harms caused to same-sex couples and their families.

However, the majority of opponents of marriage equality still see one's sexual orientation as a choice and homosexuality as a sinful choice, instead of something biological and more akin to left-handedness. And they believe bisexual people should "choose" only to be with the opposite sex. As long as these beliefs are held, it will be very difficult to get these voters to support equal rights for gay people.

Messengers are as important as the message. To speak to this group, it behooves the marriage equality movement to educate people about sexual orientation, especially showing gay people and their families from religious households. People of faith with gay family members, in my opinion, are the best messengers for this group. Finding opportunities to introduce people who still view homosexuality as a sin to the messages in the compelling documentary *Anyone and Everyone*, the docudrama *Prayers for Bobby*, and the *Unlearning Homophobia Series: All God's Children, Straight from the Heart, and De Colores* would be a very effective place to start.

These films have been shown in college classrooms, church discussion groups, and educational forums, as well as on PBS and mainstream media channels.

Target population

According to the research the most movable population that we need to target, referred to as "the movable middle," are people who are politically moderate, between the ages of 40-65, who attend church less than monthly within the African-American, Latino, Asian or Pacific Islander communities. We need to engage people in the movable middle to see the difference and inherent inequality of domestic partnerships and civil unions and why anything less than marriage, is less than equal.

Who supports marriage equality?

The California findings were very similar to the national findings of a Gallup Poll on American's views of marriage equality also published in May 2009. The "Survey on Marriage Equality in California" summary found that 47% of Californians polled support marriage equality for same-sex couples, compared to 40% of Americans according to the Gallup Poll.

Supporters of marriage equality by political party:

Californians	Americans
Simon & Binder's Findings	Gallup Poll Findings
May 2009	May 2009
57% of Democrats	55% of Democrats
49% of Independents	45% of Independents
14% of Republicans	14% of Republicans

Supporters of marriage equality by political ideology:

Californians	Americans
Simon & Binder's	Gallup Poll
Findings May 2009	Findings May 2009
69% Liberal and 80% Very Liberal	75% Liberal

41% Moderate   50% Moderate

14% Conservative and

5% Very Conservative   19% Conservative

In 1997, a year after Clinton signed DOMA, Gallup Polls reported that only 27% of Americans supported marriage equality. This still exceeded the percentage of Americans that supported interracial marriage a full year after it was legal in the United States. (Only 20% of Americans supported interracial marriage in 1968).[56] However, unlike interracial marriage which continued to see an increase in support in the Gallup polls, support of marriage equality began fluctuating after 2004.

Gallup Poll Findings of Percentage of Americans who support equal marriage rights for same-sex couples over the past 13 years.

1997	2004	2006	2007	2008	2009	2010
27%	42%	37%	46%	40%	40%	44%

Most Americans report their religious beliefs as the number one reason they do not support civil marriage for same-sex couples and the Catholic, Mormon and Evangelical Christian churches have made fighting "gay marriage" their top priority and use church services as a bully pulpit to stop marriage equality from expanding.

IMPORTANT FINDINGS-IT'S ONLY A MATTER OF TIME

- **6 out of 10 young Americans support marriage equality.** Young people get marriage equality! Like young people who grew up after integration and didn't see what big deal was with interracial marriage, today's youth don't see what the big deal is with gay people getting married. According

---

56 Go to www.gallup.com to see the polls on interracial marriage and same-sex marriage.

to a May 2009 Gallup Poll, young Americans between the ages of 18-29 supported marriage equality 19% percent more than 30-49 year olds and 19% more than the average American, (only 40% of Americans supported marriage equality in 2009). Here's the overall breakdown of Americans in support of marriage equality (Gallup Poll 2009):

59% of 18-29 year olds
40% of 30-45 year olds
37% of 50-64 year olds
32% of 65 and up

- **Support for marriage equality doubles for those who know an LGBT person compared to those who don't.** Again come out people! You know who you are! Your living in the closet is hurting everyone. Be brave! Get counseling or coaching if you need help coming out. Hire me as your coach or come to one of my coming out workshops. I'll help you tear down that closet door and you'll never look back. Living out loud is an incredible experience. It beats lurking in the shadows.

- **Frequency of worship is a greater predictor of one's view on marriage equality than race or ethnicity.** In other words, more frequent church attendance means you are more likely to be against marriage equality regardless of your race. In Simon and Binder's 2009 survey: only 20% of Whites, 19% of Blacks, 23% of Latinos, and 18% of Asians and Pacific Islanders who *attended church once a month or more* and supported equal marriage for same-sex couples, compared to 58 % of Whites, 44% of African Americans, 51% of Latinos, and 47% of Asian and Pacific Islanders who *attended church less than once a month* and supported equal marriage for same-sex couples

Race/Ethnicity	Attends church **more than** once a month and supports marriage equality	Attends church **less than** once a month and supports marriage equality
White	20%	58%
Black	19%	44%
Latino/a	23%	51%
Asian and Pacific Islander	18%	47%

- **Eleven per cent of the people who voted to take away marriage rights for same-sex couples in California, were not clear on the difference between civil and religious marriage.** Let's do the math! 48% + 11% = 59% which means we could have defeated Proposition 8 if we had only educated people about civil and religious marriage. Ahhh!!! We've got to *get this book* circulating so everyone can be totally clear that there is a HUGE difference between civil and religious marriage!

Civil Marriage ≠ Religious Marriage

Civil Marriage	Religious Marriage
Performed by judge or commissioner, or by clergy member because they are DEPUTIZED BY THE STATE and granted the privilege of signing a CIVIL marriage license.	Performed by clergy
Government Sanctioned. Government sets the rules and terms of marriage contract, differs by states.	Church or temple sanctioned, and recognized by the state ONLY because clergy member is DEPUTIZED BY THE STATE and granted the privilege of signing a CIVIL marriage license. Clergy have the option to refuse to marry anyone they don't want to marry, regardless of who the state allows to marry.
Civil Ceremony	Holy Union
Marriage restrictions determined by civil law only.

For example, even Satan-worshippers on their third marriage can marry as long as they and their partner meet age requirements and are not closely related blood relatives. | Marriage restrictions determined by civil marriage laws and religious doctrine.

For example, the couple must meet age requirements and not be closely related blood relatives, plus -of the same faith, not previously married, belong to that church or synagogue, etc.) |

Our Strongest Messages Are:

- Same-sex couples seek civil, not religious, marriage. Separation of church and state allows religious organizations to choose who they wish to marry, but prohibits the government from discriminating.
- Marriage discrimination hurts children of LGBT people.
- Marriage discrimination is unfair towards LGBT people.
- Fairness is a faith issue.
- Marriage equality hurts no religious groups, but denying marriage equality hurts or impinges on religious freedom of spiritual communities who want to recognize and perform same-sex marriages and the individuals who would like to be married in supportive spiritual environments.
- Our personal stories, especially stories from communities of color and communities of faith are very powerful!

Voters need to be clear on the following points:

1. Churches will not be forced to marry gay couples, or for that matter, interfaith couples, atheists, or divorced people, if they don't want to.
2. This is not gay marriage versus religious freedom.
3. It is civil marriage rights versus anti-gay bigotry (wolf) disguised in sheep clothing (religious freedom).

SECTION SIX:
COMMUNITY VOICES AND ALLIES

Chapter Twenty-One:
People of Faith Speak Out
for Marriage Equality

"Marriage equality is important to me because of my faith. I believe our country, and some of our faith traditions, have been co-opted by fear and people are convinced that anything outside the current status quo is dangerous. But, if love is the predominant tenet of most faith traditions, and if we recognize a deity with an infinite capacity for love, why would we try to limit who and how love can best be expressed?"

—Lynn Fallon, I'm For Iowa, straight, Christian, ally

Conscious or unconscious bias?

The repeated media bias giving air time only to anti-gay church leaders has led to the belief that faith leaders are uniform in their opposition to equal marriage rights for same-sex couples. Newscasts frequently juxtapose a gay rights activist with a right-wing clergy member. Rather than interviewing pro-equality clergy or congregational members, the media frames the issue as if it is a debate of gay people versus religious people.

In the San Francisco Bay Area, many reporters covering same-sex marriage repeatedly go to the gay Castro District, find a vacationing white gay man, and ask him questions about how he feels about current marriage equality litigation, legislation, or ballot results and then drive out to a conservative church in suburban Contra Costa County, across the Bay, to interview a minister or congregational member of color.

This same media bias can be noted with regard to showing gay people of color. During the time same-sex couples were marrying in San Francisco in February 2004, sometimes called the Winter of Love, the media failed repeatedly to interview and show images of the large percentage of couples of color or interracial couples who were marrying, reaffirming the myth, either unconsciously or intentionally, that being gay is a "white thing."

Newscasters should work to eliminate bias. If they interview clergy, they should interview a clergy member in support of marriage equality and one against. They should interview people from the same county. Rather than going to "gay ghettos" or known conservative locations, ask the average person on the street. Find one person who is in support of marriage equality and one who is not.

Ministers like Rev. Amos Brown, of the Third Baptist Church of San Francisco, have been at the forefront of the campaign to show that religious leaders do support equal civil rights for same-sex couples. Following the passage of Proposition 8, 300 cities across the nation held rallies protesting this human rights violation. Rev. Brown was one of the many ministers who came out to condemn the injustice of Proposition 8 passing. He said, "I am heterosexual and in my faith tradition we do not perform same-sex marriages, but I say to you, though I am a Baptist, I refuse to be a bigot. In the bill of rights, we are accorded freedom of religion and freedom from religion and no religion tells the state what to do."

Former Speaker of the California Assembly and former Mayor of San Francisco, Willie Brown, also a longtime civil rights and marriage equality advocate, believes that marriage equality is a spiritual issue and denying LGBT people equality is discrimination. He says, "My vision of the supreme-being is a God who loves all his children. My God would not separate one segment of the population and subject it to discrimination, ridicule or unequal status; that's something human beings do, not the good Lord."

PICK AND CHOOSE

Other clergy challenge faith communities to view how they use some Biblical passages as weapons against LGBT people and ignore passages that encourage love and the Golden Rule. Rev. Roland Stringfellow, Baptist Minister and Coordinator of the Coalition of Welcoming Congregations at the Center for Lesbian and Gay Studies in Religion and Sexuality at the Pacific School of Religion, reminds us of "Matthew 22: 37 - 40: 'Love the Lord, your God, with all your heart and with all your soul and with all your mind.'" This, Rev. Stringfellow says, is "the first and greatest commandment. The second is 'Love your neighbor as yourself. All the Law and the Prophets hang on these two commandments.' To love, protect and care for another human being is the highest form of discipleship a person can exhibit."

Rev. Stringfellow encourages people of faith to apply these commandments to gay people. He says, "Marriage between same-gender loving individuals is a commitment to the love both partners feel and a testament of the gift that only God can provide," and therefore, "should be honored."

Rabbi Lisa Edwards of Beth Chayim Chadashim in Los Angeles agrees. She believes that gay people deserve to be married and to "seek God's blessings," and to "state publicly that this is the relationship that they are committed to for life." She asserts the importance of having "the community be supportive and celebrate the primacy of that relationship."

SACRED RIGHT TO SACRED RITES: BLESSING SAME-SEX UNIONS

Beginning in the 1960s, a handful of courageous ministers—some with church support, others without—led the way in blessing same-sex unions.

Unitarian Universalist Church ministers began blessing same-sex couples' unions and advocating for equal marriage rights in the late 1960s. On June 29, 1984, the Unitarian

Universalist Church became the first major church to approve of same-sex blessings as an official denomination-wide spiritual practice. On May 17, 2004, the very first legal same-sex marriage in the United States was performed in a Unitiarian Universalist Church in Boston for Robert Compton and David Wilson.

In 1963, Rev. Cecil Williams became the minister at San Francisco's Glide Memorial Methodist Church, and within six months he began blessing same-sex unions. "Everyone should have the same legal right to get married," Rev. Williams says. "I had a choice and I want my brothers and sisters to have a choice for full marriage, complete marriage, whatever it takes." He argues that by denying same sex couples full equality America fails to follow its own credo of equality and justice. Rev. Williams is therefore committed "to make sure that this nation will live its righteous declaration of independence where all of us are free to be ourselves. We are going to make sure that people aren't left out and get what they need. Marriage, anything less is less than equal. I will not accept anything that is less than equal."

In response to many churches anti-gay teachings and the practice of removing gays from their parishes, Rev. Troy Perry created the first openly gay church in the United States, called the Metropolitan Community Church (MCC)in 1968. Rev. Perry himself had been a Pentecostal minister and was defrocked because he was gay. According to MCC's website, the church now counts 43,000 people as members in their almost 300 MCC congregations around the world. Rev. Perry performed his first same-sex wedding in 1970. Since then, MCC ministers have been performing same-sex blessings and continue to be at the forefront of the marriage equality movement.

ANSWERING TO A HIGHER CALLING

Rev. Jimmy Creech began performing blessings of same-sex unions in 1990. He believed he was answering to a higher calling by supporting and affirming the love of same-sex couples. Although this was at odds with the politics of the United States Methodist Church he continued to bless same-sex couples' unions even after he was told by Methodist church officials to stop. Soon he was told he was "no longer welcome to serve churches in North Carolina." However, in 1996, he was invited to serve as the senior pastor at the First United Methodist Church in Omaha, Nebraska.

In 1997, Rev. Creech blessed the union of a lesbian couple who attended that church. When church administrators heard of the news they brought charges against him. Luckily Rev. Creech was acquitted since, at that time, there was no clear law prohibiting ministers from celebrating same-sex holy unions. Rev. Creech was willing to sacrifice his career in order to stand as a straight ally and religious voice to end discrimination. By the time he blessed the union of two men in April 1999, the Methodist Church officially prohibited gay unions and Rev. Creech was defrocked.

He responded by saying that "it's just clear evidence of the heterosexism and prejudice within the church, that even the highest court of the church would decide that one little sentence out of a whole document of material would be law when every-thing else is guidance. The church wants to use its power and all of its resources to persecute gay people and to deny them full equality."

In 1999, Rev. Creech had his credentials of ordination re-moved and is no longer a clergy member in the United Methodist Church. Since then, he has made equality for LGBT people his life's work. He believes LGBT people deserve the same mar-riage rights, and Rev. Creech and his wife speak out for marriage equality across the country.

He believes that "[marriage equality] is a justice struggle for gay, lesbian, bisexual, and transgender people and also a struggle for the church's integrity. The Christian church has compromised its ability to really communicate or talk about God being love when it teaches and preaches hate against LGBT people, and denies them the right to love and couple with whomever they choose. To regain its integrity,[the church] must fully welcome, accept and affirm [LGBT] people, and honor their loving relationships... this movement is not just a movement for gay people. The misguided notion that non-gay people are morally superior to gay people really harms non-gay people. It gives them a sense of superiority the same way the idea that white is superior to black or male is superior to female. That kind of distorted understanding is very harmful and produces consequences that are damaging to society the way it did with slavery and the patriarchal structures that oppress women."

He is not the only Methodist minister who holds this belief and is willing to stand up to injustice. In January 1999, in an act of solidarity and to protest the Methodist Church's new anti-gay policy, 69 Methodist ministers in Sacramento co-officiated at a holy union ceremony for two lesbians. Charges were filed against all of the ministers.

Two months later, Rev. Gregory Dell also violated Methodist law in response to a higher calling when he performed a ceremony between two gay parishioners. He was given the choice of signing a pledge vowing that he would no longer perform same-sex marriage ceremonies or be defrocked. Dell declined to sign and was barred from the ministry.

Rather than risk losing their credentials by marrying same-sex couples, some clergy who want to register their support for civil marriage equality are coming together in coalition to support civil marriage, advocating for a change in the denomination's position, but refraining from performing marriages for same-sex couples. Minister Rev. Phil Campbell, senior pastor of Park Hill United Church of Christ in Denver founded Colorado Clergy for

Equality in Marriage (CCEM). Campbell says he founded CCEM because "Gay men and lesbians are entitled to the same right to marry—in a marriage of love, mutuality and respect—that is available to my wife and me as a heterosexual couple."

> **"** *Marriage is a civil right.* **"**
> —Rev. William Sinkford, President
> of the Unitarian Universalist Association.

Many clergy see the discrimination gay people face today as similar to civil rights abuses of the past and feel a spiritual calling to be a part of the change. Rev. Gilbert Caldwell, a retired United Methodist minister and CCEM member, told *Rocky Mountain News* reporters in 2003 that he believes history "will view legislation against same-sex marriage as being insensitive, invalid and illogical, as was the legislation that prohibited interracial marriage." Anglican Archbishop of Central Africa, Khotso Makhulu, likened the discrimination against gays to discrimination against blacks under apartheid. "The notion of exclusivity is abhorrent, and it is a heresy in the same way as apartheid was described as a heresy."[57]

STANDING UP FOR MARRIAGE EQUALITY

In Connecticut and Massachusetts in 2003, a group of ministers from the Universal Unitarians, Presbyterians, Reform Rabbis, the United Church of Christ, and other denominations within the Religious Coalition for the Freedom to Marry, followed the leadership of Rev. Kathleen McTigue, senior minister at the Unitarian Society of New Haven, and decided to refuse to sign marriage licenses for heterosexuals since they could not sign

---

57 *2003 New York Times article.*

them for same-sex couples. Today, some clergy members, will do spiritual blessings of heterosexual couples' unions, but will not sign marriage licenses until they can also sign marriage licenses for same-sex couples as well.

In 2005 the California Assembly introduced "The Religious Freedom and Civil Marriage Protection Act" AB 849 which would have allowed same-sex couples the right to marry and a case was filed challenging marriage denial in the California state court. Hundreds of Californian clergy and people of faith said they felt "called to support marriage equality and one way they did this was by signing on to an amicus brief that challenged the state's denial of marriage to same-sex couples.

This coalition of clergy and people of faith is now called California Faith for Equality. California Faith for Equality was created "to heal the rift between faith communities and lesbian gay, bisexual and transgender people...by engag(ing) congregations and people of faith in the movement for LGBT equality and to safeguard religious freedom." California Faith for Equality has created several resources, including a list of prayers and sermons on marriage equality that you can find on their website: http://www.cafaithforequality.org/reflect.html. Similar interfaith coalitions of clergy have formed in other states and act as powerful voices of faith in support of marriage equality. See the Resources list at the back of the book or contact California Faith for Equality to find the coalition in your area.

JEWS FOR MARRIAGE EQUALITY

"The essence of being a Jew is to seek to heal the world, to achieve social justice for all. Jews for Marriage Equality fight for legalization of same-sex marriage to seek social justice for gay, lesbian, bisexual and transgender people."

—Steve Krantz, Ph.D., straight ally and founder
of Jews for Marriage Equality

Jewish Americans have played an important role in the marriage equality movement. Jewish people have long known what it is like to stigmatized, denied equal treatment under the law, and worse have been the victims of organized, state-sanctioned violence. Having been scapegoats and victims of discrimination around the world, many heterosexual Jews are more sensitive to the plight of gay people and are actively involved in the fight for marriage equality.

As early as 1981, Rabbi Denise Egger, an open lesbian, who now leads a Reform Congregation in Los Angeles called Kol Ami, was advocating for marriage equality. She was part of an organization called the Union for Reform Judaism[58] that in 1993 advocated for the Reform Jewish Movement to support relationship recognition and benefits for same-sex couples. In April 1996, the Central Conference of American Rabbis (CCAR) adopted a resolution supporting the right of gay and lesbian couples to share fully and equally in the benefits of civil marriage.

No Laws Were Ever Broken

On June 27, 2009, at a Pink Triangle Memorial, that recalled the anti-Semitic and anti-gay violence in Nazi Germany, California State Senator Mark Leno reminded the audience that the atrocities committed at the concentration camps and throughout Germany and Europe were committed without a single law being broken.

"Every year the California Senate honors survivors of the Holocaust, and I remind my colleagues that no laws were broken in the Holocaust. First, the Nazis passed laws making it illegal for Jews to marry, then it was illegal for Jews to own property, then to own businesses, and soon they had outlawed an entire group of people, and once that was done we know what the next chapter was."

---

58 *Then known as UAHC*

Leno likened the passage of Proposition 8, where constitutional rights of LGBT people were stripped away by a popular vote, to the Racial Laws in Germany that preceded the Holocaust. "It's happening here in California as we speak," he said. "California is amending its state constitution to outlaw a group of law-abiding, tax paying, loving citizens and denying them their fundamental right to marry the person that he or she loves. We are fighting wars around the world, spending billions of dollars, to make sure that no one interpretation of any one holy book is put into state law. It's what we're doing in Afghanistan and Pakistan, but it's happening here in California when one group of people think their interpretation of their holy book gets to be state law."[59]

END SPIRITUAL VIOLENCE

"Spiritual violence is the misuse of religion to sanction the condemnation of any of God's children. It leads to intolerance and discrimination."

—Soulforce website

For centuries, religious doctrine has been used as a weapon against minority faith groups, "non-believers," gays, and women. Today, the majority of funding to take away state-sanctioned civil rights for gay people has come from church groups and right-wing religious groups, which is why Mel White founded Soulforce and "started mobilizing against the teachings of many denominations, including the Catholic Church, to resist the fundamentalist takeover of the country using gay issues falsely to divide and conquer."

Rev. Mel White was a ghost writer for Billy Graham and the Evangelical church movement for more than thirty years.

---

59 *The following day the pink triangle was set on fire by an arsonist.*

He was raised in a home that he describes as "predominantly Evangelical religious." The church was his life. As a youth, he "started the Bible club at Santa Cruz High and went to all the youth camps. I went to church on Sunday morning, Sunday night, and Wednesday night, Thursday night was choir practice. Billy Graham was my hero."

White said he knew he was romantically attracted to men when he married his wife at the age of 22, but that he followed the Evangelical mandate to cure himself of his homosexuality. He prayed and tried numerous aversive "reparative therapies" including shock therapy and exorcism,[60] a still widely practiced, though debunked, Evangelical Christian approach to homosexuality, but nothing changed the way he felt.

After a failed suicide attempt in 1994, he told his wife he was gay and came out of the closet. He was 54 years old. White then took a stand against the spiritual violence LGBT people are subjected to as a result of the Evangelical church's archaic understanding of LGBT people and started an organization called Soul Force.

White says that he was particularly drawn to the non-violent teachings of Ghandi and Dr. Martin Luther King, Jr. and started teaching others their principles of non-violence. He describes Soulforce as a group of people around the country working towards ending "spiritual violence that flows out of religious teachings against LGBT people. As the Catholics say, we are intrinsically evil and deplorably dangerous, or as the Methodists say, we're irreconcilable with Christian teachings, or as the Baptists say, we're sick and sinful and a threat to the nation and the nation's values." White emphasizes that using these religious teachings as a weapon against LGBT people leads to "suffering, intolerance, discrimination and death."

---

60 In June 2009, a video was released showing a young gay African-American male having his "homosexual demon" exorcised from him from screaming church-goers at a Connecticut Church called Manifested Glory Ministries. See the youtube video. Type in "gay exorcism."

FREEDOM FROM RELIGION-YOUR DOGMA ATE MY MARRIAGE LICENSE

Within days of the California State Supreme Court granting same-sex couples the legal right to marry, leaders in the Catholic, Mormon, and Evangelical churches in combination with right-wing organizations worked together to put a ballot initiative on the November 2008 election to outlaw same-sex civil marriage.

> "*How tragic that the Church be so concerned with this issue {same-sex marriage} when God's children all over the world over are suffering.*"
>
> —Desmond Tutu, Nobel Peace Prize Laureate and Anglican Archbishop of South Africa.

According to a January 2009, *San Francisco Chronicle* article, the Yes on 8 Campaign reported $190,000 in previously unreported contributions from the Mormon Church which included paying for the travel and accommodations of high-ranking members of the Mormon Church. As well as $20,575 for the use of church facilities and equipment at the Salt Lake City headquarters and an additional $96,849 to pay the wages of church employees for working on the Yes on Prop 8 Campaign.

Mormon contributions were not confined to California. A *Gay and Lesbian Times* article noted that Mormons raised $3 million of the $8 million spent on the "Yes on 102" Campaign which took away the right to marry from same-sex couples in Arizona in 2008.

But the Mormons were not the only religious organization that played a key role in funding initiatives to take away LGBT people's constitutional rights. Catholic Bishop Salvatore Cordilieone helped raise 40 million dollars for the Yes on 8 campaign. How many poor people could have been fed with all that money? How many job skills programs, educational, health and wellness programs could have been funded with the millions that were used to strip gay families of legal protections and dignity? "Bishop Sal," as he is called by his parish, bragged about the Catholic Church's involvement in the success of the Yes on 8 Campaign.

Similarly, Rick Warren's fundamentalist Christian Saddleback Church, assembled thousands of people in San Diego's Qualcomm Stadium to pray for passage of Proposition 8. Couldn't good people of faith find a better use of their time and prayers by helping people in need?

Is this doing God's work?

Using church funds to take away gay civil rights is nothing new. In 1998, the Mormon and Catholic Churches worked in tandem to change the Hawaii Constitution so that it expressly outlawed same-sex couples from marrying after the Hawaii State Court said it was unconstitutional to continue to deny same-sex couples the right to marry.

I encourage you to examine carefully where your tithing goes. Personally, I am drawn to spiritual leaders and faith communities that uplift the human spirit and put their money towards making a positive difference in other people's lives. Open and affirming congregations and temples that invest in their community and use congregational members' money to educate, counsel, and serve people in need are the one's who are really doing God's work.

The Call Gets Louder-More People of Faith Coming Out for Equality

> *Everyone has a right to believe what they want to believe, but everyone has a right to have civil rights."*
>
> — singer Marie Osmond.

Singer Marie Osmond, who is Mormon and the mother of a lesbian daughter, does not agree with the Mormon Church advocating to take away civil rights for LGBT people. In an interview with L.A. radio station KOST, she said she thinks "it's important to live the commandment love they neighbor as thyself...each of us has the right to choose who makes that medical decision for us. I think everybody should have the right to share homes and finances with somebody that they care about. You know on those types of things I'm very supportive. When it comes to marriage, I think that civil rights need to be for all."

She went on to say, "I do believe in the Bible...And, God said to be married and be productive with your children and replenish the earth or whatever...One of the things we have to be careful of is that we don't create hate...Everyone has a right to believe what they want to believe, but everyone has a right to have civil rights."

There are a growing number of communities that recognize that marriage equality is a spiritual and moral issue, as well as a civil rights issue (e.g. the Quakers, United Church of Christ, United Centers for Spiritual Living, and Reform, Renewal, and Reconstruction Jewish faith communities).

Rev. Dr. Michael Beckwith, Founder and Spiritual Director of Agape International Spiritual Center in Los Angeles and author of *Spiritual Liberation,* agrees. He sees marriage equality as similar to other civil rights issues that have played an integral part in our global, spiritual and moral evolution. Beckwith says that "visionary, progressive spiritual leaders have always spoken and continue to speak to more than what are traditionally political issues. They were abolitionists. They spoke for women's rights. They spoke for the African Americans and other minorities. They are now speaking for gay marriage, reforming our prison systems, and stopping torture." For Beckwith, "a genuine spiritual leader holds and conveys a vision of the highest possibilities for humankind, that he or she keeps high ideals at the forefront so that individuals remain encouraged that we live in a friendly universe that is constantly conspiring on our behalf, that cherishes humanity, and is constantly providing inspiration that speaks to our next stage of evolution. The role of a spiritual teacher is to consistently point to the limitless possibilities available to us. And if it rattles some people's chains so be it."[61]

On May 26, 2009, after the California State Supreme Court upheld Proposition 8, a group of forty visionary faith leaders, including Buddhist monks and nuns, Rabbis, ministers from the UU church, MCC, United Methodist, Lutheran, Episcopalian, and Baptist church sat down in the middle of the street outside of San Francisco City Hall. Showing their solidarity for equality for LGBT people they refused to leave and all were arrested along with 100 demonstrators in a non-violent, peaceful protest organized by One Struggle, One Fight.

Rev. William Sinkford, President of the Unitarian Universalist Association, issued this statement in response to the Prop 8 ruling: "In spite of the setbacks, we are making progress, one state at a time. Justice is knocking and our work is helping to open a very heavy door. Our patience, passion, and determination will carry us through the disappointments. We will continue to stand on the side of love. And we will win, because love will win."

Today, groups like California Faith for Equality, a statewide network of over 6000 clergy, lay leaders and congregations from diverse faith traditions are coming together monthly to "ensure that faith is a force that propels LGBT people toward full equality under the law." LGBT people need the voices of our progressive faith communities to become louder and more unified in their messages of equality. Open and affirming congregations where LGBT people were welcomed and accepted was the first step, but now the loud voice of unequivocal justice is needed

---

61 *Getting Spiritual With Michael Beckwith Article, Balanced Living Magazine September 2009 Issue*

from our spiritual communities to correct the erroneous belief that all religious people are against marriage equality.

For a list of supportive denominations and religious organizations working to secure marriage equality go to Marriage Equality USA's "Community Voices of Faith" at www.marriageequality.org.

Chapter Twenty-Two:
"Gay, straight, black, white, marriage is a civil right!"

"When an individual is protesting society's refusal to acknowledge his dignity as a human being, his very act of protest confers dignity on him."

—Bayard Rustin, organizer of the 1963 National Civil Rights March of Washington, gay African-American

"I still hear people say that I should not be talking about the rights of lesbian and gay people . . . But I hasten to remind them that Martin Luther King Jr. said, 'Injustice anywhere is a threat to justice everywhere.' I appeal to everyone who believes in Martin Luther King Jr.'s dream to make room at the table of brother and sisterhood for lesbian and gay people."

—Quote from Coretta Scott King, widow of Dr. Martin Luther King, Jr., 1998.

In their attempt to make marriage equality a wedge issue, the media and anti-gay leaders have perpetuated the myth that African Americans are more anti-gay than whites. The fact is, that African American leaders, many of them Christians, have always been at the forefront of the marriage equality movement, as have Latino and Asian and Pacific Islander civil rights leaders.

The Black Community and Marriage Equality

For decades African American Christian and Civil Rights leaders have taken a stand for gay rights. People like Coretta

Scott King, Martin Luther King Jr.'s widow; John Lewis, Democratic congressman from Georgia, who marched with Dr. King at the Edmond Petus Bridge in Alabama and was one of the coordinators of the 1963 March on Washington; Rev. Cecil Williams of Glide Memorial Church; Rev. Eric P. Lee of the Southern Christian Leadership Conference; Rev. Dr. Amos Brown, minister of the Third Baptist Church, the oldest African American church west of the Mississippi; Julian Bond and Alice Huffman of the NAACP; Reverend William Sinkford, President of the Unitarian Universalist Church; Eva Paterson of the Equal Justice Society; Mildred Loving, plaintiff whose case brought down the existing bans against interracial marriage; Former Speaker of the California Assembly and Mayor of San Francisco, Willie Brown; Oakland Mayor and former Congressman Ron Dellums; Congresswoman Barbara Lee; Rev. Eric Michael Dyson; Rev. Peter Gomes of Harvard University; Ambassador Carol Moseley Braun; Henry Louis Gates, Jr.; Dr. Joycelyn Elders former U.S. Surgeon General; Rev. James Forbes formerly of Riverside Church in Harlem; Whoopi Goldberg, actor/producer; Ron Oden, Mayor of Palm Springs, CA, and the list could go on.

"At a Crossroads on Gay Unions" by Congressman John Lewis[62]

"From time to time, America comes to a crossroads. With confusion and controversy, it's hard to spot that moment. We need cool heads, warm hearts, and America's core principles to cleanse away the distractions.

We are now at such a crossroads over same-sex couples' freedom to marry. It is time to say forthrightly that the government's exclusion of our gay and lesbian brothers and sisters from civil marriage officially degrades them and their families. It denies them the basic human right to marry the person they love. It denies them numerous legal protections for their families.

This discrimination is wrong. We cannot keep turning our backs on gay and lesbian Americans. I have fought too hard and too long against discrimination based on race and color not to stand up against discrimination based on sexual orientation. I've heard the reasons for opposing civil marriage for same-sex couples. Cut through the distractions, and they stink of the same fear, hatred, and intolerance I have known in racism and in bigotry.

Some say let's choose another route and give gay folks some legal rights but call it something other than marriage. We have been down that road before in this country. Separate is not equal. The rights to liberty and happiness belong to each of us and on the same terms, without regard to either skin color or sexual orientation.

Some say they are uncomfortable with the thought of gays and lesbians marrying. But our rights as Americans do not depend on the approval of others. Our rights depend on us being Americans.

---

62 *Printed in the Boston Globe, Oct. 25, 2003 and reposted on Lewis's Website*

Sometimes it takes courts to remind us of these basic principles. In 1948, when I was 8 years old, 30 states had bans on interracial marriage, courts had upheld the bans many times, and 90 percent of the public disapproved of those marriages, saying they were against the definition of marriage, against God's law. But that year, the California Supreme Court became the first court in America to strike down such a ban. Thank goodness some court finally had the courage to say that equal means equal, and others rightly followed, including the US Supreme Court 19 years later.

Some stand on the ground of religion, either demonizing gay people or suggesting that civil marriage is beyond the Constitution. But religious rites and civil rights are two separate entities. What's at stake here is legal marriage, not the freedom of every religion to decide on its own religious views and ceremonies.

We hurt our fellow citizens and our community when we deny gay people civil marriage and its protections and responsibilities. Rather than divide and discriminate, let us come together and create one nation. We are all one people. We all live in the American house. We are all the American family. Let us recognize that the gay people living in our house share the same hopes, troubles, and dreams. It's time we treated them as equals, as family."

Dr. Sylvia Rhue, Director of Religious Affairs of the National Black Justice Coalition and co-producer of *All God's Children*, a documentary film that looks at sexual orientation within the context of traditional African-American values of freedom, inclusion, and Christian ethics, agrees with Congressman Lewis. She says that many African-Americans have "come to see that LGBT rights and marriage equality are the next phase of civil rights. In fact, we believe that challenging homophobia is part of the unfinished business of the Civil Rights Movement."

That not all people agree frustrates Dr. Rhue. "It's so basic. Two consenting adults love each other and want to make a commitment to each other that is public and acknowledge that to the state. To me, it is just like when white people made laws that whites and blacks couldn't marry and these are recent laws, miscegenation laws. I see no difference! There was a time when blacks weren't considered to be equal people under the law, they were considered merchandise and merchandise can't get married. There's a connection. You are not human, you're not good enough, you don't measure up, you can't get married."

BLACK, CHRISTIAN, AND FOR SAME-SEX MARRIAGE

Reverend Eric P. Lee, President of the Southern Christian Leadership Council's (SCLC) Los Angeles Chapter, sees it the same way. He marched fifteen miles in the hot sun in support of marriage equality less than a week after the California State Supreme Court upheld Prop 8. Despite opposition from some within the SCLC, which in fact was instrumental in leading the Black Civil Rights movement, Rev. Lee is solidly committed to helping liberate people from the homophobic, narrow-minded views of the past. In a *New York Times* article, he said that his support for equal marriage rights for same-sex couples has "created tension in my life I had never experienced with black clergy. But it is was clear to me, that anytime you deny one group of people the same right that other groups have, that is a clear violation of civil rights and I have to speak up on that."

Change is never easy, it was not easy for white segregationists to accept black people as their equals, and it will be very hard for many straight people to accept gays as their equals too.

> *In 1955, at the age of 14, one hot summer in Mississippi, I opened a Jet magazine and I saw the mutilated body of a black boy named, Emmett Till who was beaten to a pulp by white racists. And when I saw that image I said to God, that I would never be mean to those who are different, like white folks were mean to us because our skin was different.*
>
> —Rev. Dr. Amos Brown, Minister of the Third Baptist Church at a post-Prop 8 rally in San Francisco

Contradicting media reports that black people are, as a group, more anti-marriage equality than others, a 2009 poll conducted by Goodwin Simon Victoria Research and David Binder Research found that frequency of worship is a greater predictor of one's view on marriage equality than one's race. In other words, the more frequent church attendance the more likely to be against marriage equality regardless of your race.

Many African American leaders are speaking out about white conservatives who are spending time courting black church goers for votes and that churches that are so focused on gay people that they are failing to help communities in need and address the real issues harming African-Americans today.

In response to the passage of Proposition 8, Rev. Al Sharpton said, "It amazes me when I looked at California and saw churches that had nothing to say about police brutality, nothing to say when a young black boy was shot while he was wearing police handcuffs, nothing to say when the they overturned affirmative action, nothing to say when people were being delegated into poverty, yet they were organizing and mobilizing to stop consenting adults from choosing their life partners. There is something immoral and sick about using all of that power to not end brutality and poverty, but to break into people's bedrooms and claim that God sent you."

MARRIAGE EQUALITY IS A BLACK ISSUE!

H. Alexander Robinson, former Executive Director of the National Black Justice Coalition (NBJC), a civil rights organization dedicated to empowering Black LGBT people and ending racism and homophobia, acknowledges the anti-gay religious right's efficacy "at conflating the issues of religious sacraments and civil marriage." Jasmyne Cannick, Board Member of NBJC, emphasizes that marriage equality is a black issue. She says, "When African Americans vote against marriage equality, they are also voting against other African Americans."

According to a report by the National Gay and Lesbian Task Force Policy Institute and the National Black Justice Coalition entitled *Black Same-Sex Households in the United States Report (October 6, 2004),*[63] "Black gay and lesbian couples have more to gain from the ability to marry and more to lose if marriage and other forms of partner recognition are banned." This is because black same-sex couples:

1. Earn less money than black heterosexual married couples.
2. Are less likely to own the home that they live in.
3. Black lesbians are raising children with almost the same frequency as their heterosexual counterparts (61% of black lesbians compared to 69% of black heterosexuals). Forty-six per cent of black gay male couples are also raising children and cannot access the benefits and protections of marriage for their families.
4. Black lesbians are four times as likely to have served in the military and will not get any of the substantial spousal benefits for veterans and active duty service members until "Don't Ask, Don't Tell" and DOMA are repealed.

63 *Black Same-Sex Households in the United States Report* www.thetaskforce.org/reslibrary/list.cfm?pubTypeID=2

Mandy Carter, Executive Director of Southerners on New Ground says that black gay people must educate about "the unrelenting attack by the predominately white radical right trying to do outreach to conservative Black churches to bring that wedge down between our Black community and our gay community." Carter says that Black gay people need "to be out and organized in our communities. We are Black and we are gay. Trying to compartmentalize these two identities is not healthy."

Rev. Ken Samuel pastor of the Victory Church in Georgia blames the high rate of HIV/AIDS in the black community on religious conservatives who stir up homophobia in the churches which results in the closeted phenomenon known as "the down low." Rev. Samuel says that "due to fear of being ridiculed, isolated, and ostracized in religious communities" black gay men often marry women, but continue to have "down low" encounters which may include anonymous or unsafe sexual encounters.

It's clear, as Rev. Al Sharpton says, that gay marriage is being used as distraction from the real issues that are hurting black communities today like poverty, unemployment, and racism. It's also clear that homophobia is creating increased hardships for the black gay community, including a continued rise in HIV infection rates that affects the entire black community.

CHAPTER TWENTY-THREE:
ASIAN AMERICANS FOR MARRIAGE EQUALITY

Asian Americans and Pacific Islanders have played an integral leadership role in the marriage equality movement. In 1993, Native Hawaiian Genora Dancel and Nina Baehr filed the first successful lawsuit challenging the constitutionality of being denied a marriage license because of their gender and sexual orientation. The Japanese American Citizens League (JACL) was one of the strongest and earliest allies working to keep marriage wins in Hawaii and to prevent the passage of the anti-gay Proposition 22 in 2000 in California. Additionally, straight Japanese-Americans, like Al and Jane Nakatani, parents of two gay sons, traveled throughout the country speaking out against racism and homophobia and in support of marriage equality. Their book *Honor Thy Children* talks about their coming out journey as a family to accept their gay sons.

Margaret Cho,[64] a Korean American comedian, a vocal proponent of marriage equality has spoken at dozens of marriage equality rallies and fundraisers. Cho jokes that, "Same-sex marriage is good for the economy....just the ice sculptures alone could curb the national deficit!" Asian Americans, including Mabel Teng, San Francisco City and County Recorder and Minna Tao, Deputy City and County Recorder were central in helping same-sex couples get marriage licenses in 2004. As is the current San Francisco, City and County Recorder, Phil Ting and his wife, Susan. Both are strong marriage equality advocates. In 2007, while the California State Court was weighing the evidence in

---

64 Cho created a website loveisloveislove.org which provides marriage equality resources. Cho can also be seen telling great jokes about the absurdity of marriage equality denial in the documentary film Freedom to Marry. (www.freedomtomarry.tv) and in the outtakes of her film Cho Revolution, 2004.

support or against marriage equality, several Asian American Bar Associations and over 60 Asian Pacific American civil rights organizations; including the Japanese American Citizens League, National Korean American Service and Education Consortium, and the Asian American Legal Defense and Education Fund signed on to a historic and influential amicus brief stating their support of marriage equality.

The brief stated that Asian Pacific American organizations "are familiar with the history of discrimination, especially California's history of exclusionary efforts targeted at Asian immigrants which made it difficult to marry, establish families, have children, build communities and integrate into the larger American society. We see important parallels between the contemporary exclusion of lesbians and gay men from marriage in California."

Kevin Fong, former president of the Asian Pacific Bar of California, who co-authored the APA amici brief, stated that the brief was intended to, "bring to light some of the historical examples of California's exclusionary laws to remind the Court of the negative and real harms that these unfair laws have had on the impacted communities." Fong said that "The Asian Pacific American communities suffered from the legalization of popular prejudices of yesterday that can clearly be seen as Constitutionally unconscionable today. The Court must ensure that popular prejudice does not cloud Constitutional principles that apply equally to all people."

The brief states that "Laws limiting the ability to marry can limit the growth of a community and impede integration into society," and Fong emphasizes that marriage specifically is "an important necessary step for an excluded group to integrate fully into society," and "is essential for an excluded group to achieve security within the larger society."

Fong references the Chinese Exclusion Act of 1882, a federal law aimed at restricting virtually every aspect of life including immigration, naturalization, taxation, employment and education, and argues that laws created that have treated gay and Asian people differently, when compared to heterosexual and white society, have increased the general public's perceptions of differences between these groups and has perpetuated their marginalization.

He also references the California Legislature enactment in the 1880s of "anti-miscegenation" laws, which prohibited certain racial categories from marrying "white persons" and forming families together. Interracial marriages were considered "illegal and void," in fact, white American women were stripped of their U.S. citizenship for marrying a "foreigner" until that law was repealed in 1931 (but only so far as to allow white women to marry white "foreigners.")

As a result, Chinese immigrant men were restricted from marrying white American women, and because of extremely restrictive immigration laws that did not allow them to become citizens, they could not leave the country and return. Therefore, Chinese men were unable to go to China and bring their Chinese wives to the United States or sponsor them for immigration. Additionally, according to Eithne Luibheid, Author of "Entry Denied: Controlling Sexuality at the Border," the Page Act of 1875, denied immigration to women who might become prostitutes, and because white culture perceived that Chinese women "caused disease and immorality among white men," they effectively denied Chinese women entrance into the United States.

After participating in some of the most physically arduous work that was crucial to the success of the American West, Chinese men were faced with the choice of abandoning the U.S. or living alone in bachelor societies without the hope of ever having families. Thus, restrictions of marriage laws were an integral part of excluding, isolating and limiting the participation of the Chinese from benefiting from the fruits of their labors in securing California's early prosperity. For more specific information, I refer you to the Page Act of 1875 and the Chinese Exclusion Act of 1882.

Fong argues that when the government creates laws that treat one group as less deserving of marriage rights, it stigmatizes that group which emboldens both public and private discrimination, which he says can be seen repeating throughout history with Asians and gays and lesbians.

For Japanese Americans, immigration was restricted in stages such that Japanese men initially had more opportunity to bring Japanese brides to America. However, as Japanese Americans made inroads into farming and began developing economic power, they were seen as a threat to whites. Then in 1924, the Johnson-Reed Act passed which severely restricted immigration. Anti-immigrant laws, coupled with anti-miscegenation laws, created an environment of social isolation and lack of integration for Japanese Americans where fear and intolerance against them flourished and eventually resulted in the travesty of the internment of Japanese Americans during World War II.

Filipino Americans were initially not subject to exclusion laws because the U.S. annexed the Philippines and considered its residents "U.S. nationals." However, in 1932, when a Filipino male and white female were denied a marriage license and appealed to the California Supreme Court, rather than striking down the anti-miscegenation laws, the court instead ruled that this couple could marry because Filipinos were part of the Malay, not Mongolian, race and therefore not listed as one of the categories precluded from marrying a white person.

In response to the court ruling, the California Legislature immediately passed a law adding Malay to the categories of races that could not marry a white person and expressly invalidated their marriage and all marriages between Filipino and white Californians in 1933.

Punjabi Indian men, an ethnic group from the state of Punjab in India and the Pakistan province of Punjab, were also precluded from marrying white women under the anti-miscegenation statute. As was the case for Chinese women, immigration restrictions on Punjabi Indian women were severe. The laws did not preclude Punjabi men from marrying Mexican American women, and therefore, there became a sizable community of mixed-ethnic Punjabi-Mexican Californian families formed, illustrating how the state's restrictive marriage laws have played a role in the particular multi-ethnic composition of many Californians alive today.

Racially-motivated laws were not repealed until 1943 for the Chinese community, 1946 for the Filipino and South Asian (Indian) community, and 1952 for the Japanese and Korean communities. In 1948, the California State Supreme Court ruled in a 4 to 3 decision that denying interracial couples the right to marry was unconstitutional. The case, entitled Perez v. Sharp, struck down all of California's anti-miscegenation laws.

According to the Asian Pacific American amicus brief filed in support of marriage equality for same-sex couples, similar rhetoric was used by opponents of interracial marriage that are being used today to deny same-sex couples the right to marry. For example, opponents argued that interracial marriage would destroy American culture because white people "would be overwhelmed by the habits of people thought to be sexually promiscuous, perverse, lascivious and immoral." Therefore laws were retained "that not only impeded full integration [of Asian Americans] into society, but promoted segregated communities and institutions."

Stuart Gaffney, a 48 year old, plaintiff for the California State Marriage Case, *In re Marriage Cases* (2008), is the child of parents from different racial backgrounds. His parents met at the University of California at Berkeley and were legally married in

California in 1952, but their marriage was not valid in many states.

Gaffney, who also volunteers as the Asian Pacific Islander (API) liaison for Marriage Equality USA, says, "My mother, who is Chinese American, was only able to marry my father, who is English and Irish, because the California Supreme Court 60 years ago became the first state supreme court in the nation to overturn a ban on interracial couples marrying. My mother still remembers the day when one of her friends in the Chinese Students Club at U.C. Berkeley had to leave the state to marry her white fiancé a few years before the Court's decision. My mom's friend literally had to run from the law to marry the person she loved, simply because they were of different races. My parents married in the International House at Berkeley, the very same place they'd met. But as they moved to other states, they found that each state's laws treated their marriage differently simply because of their races."

While looking for a house in Missouri, Stuart's parents learned that Missouri law prohibited marriage between whites and "negroes" or "Mongolians," the term then used for most Asian Americans, and considered their California marriage license "null and void."

One generation later, Gaffney and his partner of 20 plus years, John, successfully challenged the exclusionary law prohibiting them from marrying and were one of the first couples to marry in California on June 17, 2009 with both of Stuart's parents in attendance.

"We shared our family's personal story to raise awareness of our state's history of exclusion and to encourage our society to continue to challenge unjust laws and embrace the American tradition of fairness and equality for all," said Gaffney. "Exchanging vows surrounded by our family and friends was one of the happiest moments of our lives. Having my parents witness a second generation in our family attain the freedom to marry was especially meaningful, because of their experiences as an interracial couple. It took 19 years for the U.S. Supreme Court to follow suit in the landmark Loving v. Virgina decision of 1967, when the high court declared marriage is one of the "basic rights of man" and overturned all remaining state laws banning marriages between people of different races. Today it would be unthinkable to ask interracial couples like my own Mom and Dad to settle for an 'interracial partnership' or 'interracial civil union' instead of marriage, and we look forward to the day when it is unthinkable that we had to wait 21 years for our wedding day."

> "*The exclusion of gay couples from marriage pushes them outside of the common framework and vocabulary of family and civic life; it forces them to be outsiders.*"
> —Asian Pacific American amicus brief

MARRIAGE IS ABOUT THE JOINING OF TWO FAMILIES

As journalist Helen Zia recalled in a declaration filed with the state court in the case *In re Marriage Cases* (2008), becoming registered domestic partners with her life-partner, Lia Shigemura, was not meaningful to them or their families.

"To both of our families, my Chinese American family, and Lia's Japanese American family, the bonds of family are critically important. [Marriage] is a bonding of two families, the family of each person in the couple. My mother's inability to say that we are married prevents her from sharing with many of her friends the pride and joy and sense of connection that she would have if our union were recognized as a marriage by society."

In 2008, Zia married Shigemura during the brief period when it was legal for same-sex couples to marry. Two years later, Zia testified as a witness in a federal court case challenging Proposition 8. In her testimony, she described the impact legal marriage had on her and Shigemura's friends and family. "Before we were married, we would tell people we were partners. 'Partner, partner in what business?' they'd ask. We'd say, 'we are partners in life.' And get used to seeing this look on their face. 'What does life mean? Do you mean life insurance?'"

Zia said that "Marriage also made a difference on Lia's parents and family. It's a matter of how our families relate to people. We show up to every family event and they ask 'who is that?' 'This is Helen's friend.' Now with marriage, they are able to say 'Helen is my daughter-in-law.'"

Since she and Shigemura were married, Zia testified that she and her wife's family "relate to each other differently. My brother lived near my father-in-law for years, but they never communicated. After we were married, Lia's father started stopping by my brother's house to visit and drop food off. When he introduced his children, he said 'These are my daughters and this is my favorite daughter-in-law,' referring to me." Zia also spoke about how when her wife's father died she was a part of the memorial and listed in the obituary. "Marriage defines who family is, who is in the circle."

Zia's sentiments are emphasized in the American Pacific Asian brief which notes that by "taking a lesson from Asian American history, there is ample reason to believe that allowing lesbian and gay couples to enjoy their fundamental interest in marriage will permit normalization and incorporation of these couples within the fabric of California society and support stability of the family unit." We have a wonderful opportunity here to learn from our past mistakes and correct current injustices.

Chapter Twenty-Four:
Marriage Equality
"Si se puede!"

"Once social change begins, it cannot be reversed. You cannot uneducate the person who has learned to read. You cannot humiliate the person who feels pride. You cannot oppress the people who are not afraid anymore. We have seen the future, and the future is ours."

—Cesar E. Chavez, Latino Civil Rights Leader
and Co-founder of the United Farm Workers

Si se puede!

Two of the most well-known, loved, and respected American civil rights leaders from the Latino community are Cesar Chavez and Dolores Huerta. Together they co-founded the United Farm Worker's Union (UFW) and literally, through boycotts and masterful community organizing, transformed our nation's consciousness around the dismal treatment of farm workers that led to the change for better working conditions and social justice for the broader Latino community. These civil rights leaders understood the interconnectedness of all struggles for equality and social justice and both have been pioneering straight allies for LGBT equality.

Though Cesar Chavez died in 1993, his granddaughter, Christine Chavez-Delgado, carries on his legacy and mission. Christine remembers going to Gay Pride Marches in California in the 1970s where she rode on the shoulders of her grandfather. Christine says, "Before there was widespread public acceptance of gay people especially among Latinos, my grandfather spoke out strongly for gay rights, attended gay rights rallies and marches, and brought the UFW's black-eagle flags and farm workers who wished to participate." She emphasizes that Latinos are about strengthening families and "one of the ways to do that is through supporting marriage equality." Christine believes that if "my grandfather were alive today he would support and advocate for marriage equality."

Christine learned important lessons from her grandfather, including that "you can't champion equality for your own people when you tolerate discrimination against any people because of who they are. Leadership isn't about following the crowd. It's about getting out in front and leading people in the right direction." Christine feels that because farm workers and Latinos have "so often been the victims of discrimination" that they have "a strong affinity for equal rights and opportunities." She asserts that "Freedom is indivisible. You cannot grant it to some and deny it to others. It is either for everybody or it is for nobody."

These lessons launched Christine into the marriage equality movement in 2003 when she stepped into the role of public wedding celebrant and conducted marriage ceremonies for same-sex couples on the steps of the California State Capitol to show her support for marriage equality. In 2005, she took a leave of absence as UFW Political Director to work for Equality California, an LGBT rights lobbying organization, and helped successfully help lobby for and pass AB 849: the California Religious Freedom and Civil Marriage Protection Act.

Christine, and her husband, Oscar, personally responded when some members of the UFW were upset by her support of AB 849. Through mutual support of each movement's struggles (EQCA endorsed the successful Gallo wine boycott and UFW endorsed AB 849), both communities were able to hold a glass of Gallo wine at the end of the season and celebrate our victories at a joint press conference. "I know my grandfather would be proud of my decision to take a temporary leave from UFW to join EQCA to engage in a joint project to expand organizing and education efforts in the Latino community on the issue of marriage rights. Securing equality for all families is a shared goal of both organizations."

Latino legislators played a key role in passing AB 849 – the first marriage equality bill to pass through a State Legislature. The bill, co-authored by California Assembly Speaker Fabian Núñez, was supported by fifteen Latino Assemblymembers, and approved only after Latino Assembly members, Gloria Negrete-McLeod (D-Chino) and Simon Salinas (D-Salinas), changed their minds after having abstained on a similar proposal that failed earlier in that same legislative session.

Negrete-McLeod later said that she thought long and hard about the words of the Pledge of Alliance that the Assembly took each day and that the phrase "with liberty and justice for all" kept running through her mind, compelling her to vote for marriage equality. Her fellow Assemblymember Joe Baca, did not vote for the bill and in a subsequent election race with her for the State Senate seat, tried to use her marriage equality vote against her in the District with a large Latino population. Negrete-McLeod soundly defeated him and continues to work to secure LGBT equality as State Senator.

The day of the vote, Marina Gatto, a Latina teenager with two moms, firmly took Simon Salinas' hand and told him, "When you vote on the marriage bill today, please see my face and think of my family." Later that day, with the bill one vote short of passing, Salinas sprung from his chair and voted "Yes." The entire chambers erupted in cheers.

Despite Governor Schwarzenegger receiving a letter of support from Lt. Governor Cruz Bustamante, the state's highest ranking Latino elected official, he vetoed the bill in 2005 and again in 2007.

Chavez-Delgado reflecting on her experience said that regardless of Governor Schwarzenegger's vetoes, "Educating key elected officials and local communities about the importance of LGBT rights has been truly one of the most rewarding and heart-felt experiences in my life."

LA PASIONARIA! (THE PASSIONATE ONE)

Co-founder of UFW, Dolores Huerta, has been a tireless advocate for the rights of laborers for fifty-five years and now, at 80 years old, is also a tireless advocate for marriage equality. I met Dolores when she was lobbying the California Assembly to pass the California Religious Freedom and Civil Marriage Protection Act in 2005. She was in Sacramento again two years later, lending her name and support to the 2007 marriage equality bill, and urging Governor Schwarzenegger to reconsider his position.

During the summer of 2008, she was featured in an Equality Campaign internet PSA where she encouraged Latino voters, in English and Spanish, to vote for equality by voting no on Prop 8. Unfortunately, these PSAs were never shown on TV.[65]

In February 2009, Huerta, stood on steps of the state capitol and spoke passionately about the injustice of Proposition 8 and continues to speak out across the United States about marriage equality. "Equality in marriage is a human rights issue. We have to be leaders. We need to go out and educate people."

Alicia Huerta, Dolores's daughter, describes her mother as "a living hero and true American. She has the vision and heart to care and the faith for positive change in all communities. My mom is selfless." Alicia is the President of the Dolores Huerta Foundation and works to support Huerta in her advocacy for

---

65 *Robin Tyler, Executive Director of the Equality Campaign, worked with Power Up and several television celebrities to co-produce Huerta's PSA and several other PSAs with special outreach to people of color, including several in Spanish. She submitted 17 PSAs to the official No on 8 campaign, but none of them were ever aired on TV. Tyler said the campaign sent her an e-mail thanking her for submitting the PSAs, but advised her that "we already have what we plan to air."*

equality for all. "Mom says, there is much work ahead of us and we must educate and help people understand to not discriminate. Now is the time to be active and better your community."

MARRIAGE EQUALITY IS A LATINO ISSUE

"There is a large overlap between the LGBT and Latino communities that is being harmed by marriage discrimination. As gay Latinos, we've experienced a culture clash having grown up fighting for civil rights and then seeing them be taken away at the ballot box. We hope that our fellow Latinos recognize that we are fighting for a common cause – civil rights."

—Ari Gutierrez, Co-Chair of the Latino Equality Alliance and HONOR PAC Executive Vice President

Latino culture places a high importance on family and community and many straight Latinos see marriage equality as an expression of individual freedom and liberty, as well as a universal human right to love and create family. Anthony Villaraigosa, Mayor of Los Angeles and another straight, Latino ally for marriage equality, stated at a rally the night before the California Supreme Court ruling upholding Prop 8, "I believe in marriage equality and I hold this belief, as someone who believes in God. We are taking about families. We are talking about people's lives. We have a right to love, we have a right to have children and…marriage is a fundamental right!"

Mauricio Perez is a Mexican American gay man who married the love of his life Ryan James, at Oakland City Hall, the first day it was legal to marry in California. Mauricio feels that respect for diversity, including the diversity of families, is an important value instilled in him by his Latino culture. He says, "My culture prides itself on family and community. Many children in my neighborhood were raised by grandparents, sisters, uncles and aunts—sometimes without a mother or father in the home. It didn't matter. We were a community. Families varied, but they were always made up of people who loved you just as you were and wanted the best for you. Why should that be any different with same-sex marriage?"

According to a 2006 Zogby poll of New Jersey voters, 81% of Latinos across the state support marriage equality. Rev. Anahi Galante, cochair of Garden State Equality's Latino and Latina Caucus, testified before the New Jersey Civil Union Review Commission in favor of marriage equality. Rev. Galante reported that gay couples in which both partners are Latino or Latina on average earn at least $25,000 less annually compared to white/Latino(a) same-sex couple households. She says that "fifty-four percent of Latina same-sex couples, where both partners are women, have at least one child," and that "given the income disparities between Latino and Latina same-sex couples and much of the rest of society" LGBT Latinos in New Jersey who are denied marriage protections and benefits are "being hurt most by our state's continued denial of marriage equality."

The anti-miscegenation laws of the past hurt Latinos too and kept them from creating families. The first successful legal challenge in the nation to laws banning couples of different races from marrying was led by a Mexican-America woman in California in 1948.

Andrea Perez, met her future-husband, Sylvester Davis while working in the defense industry in Los Angeles. Despite laws denying interracial couples from marrying, he was black, the couple applied for a marriage license with the County Clerk of Los Angeles. The marriage license application form asked applicants to list their race. Davis was African-American and identified himself as "negro," and Perez identified herself as white, since California law, viewed individuals of Mexican ancestry as white, as the U.S. Census does today. W.G. Sharp, the L.A. County Clerk, refused to give them a license because interracial marriage had been banned in the state since 1850 and the California Civil Code stated that "All marriages of white persons with Negroes, Mongolians, members of the Malay race, or mulattoes are illegal and void."

Perez and Davis petitioned the California Supreme Court to obtain a marriage license. Like many plaintiffs in the same-sex marriage cases, Perez and Davis were both people of faith whose church was willing to marry them. One of the primary arguments in Perez, was that the state's anti-miscegenation law infringed on their right to participate fully in the sacraments of their religion, including the sacrament of matrimony.[66]

In a 4-3 decision, the court ruled that marriage is a fundamental right and that laws restricting that right must not be based solely on prejudice. The court held that restrictions due to discrimination violated the constitutional requirements of due process and equal protection of the laws. The opinion voided the California statute and Perez and Davis were finally able to marry.

The power of the 1948 Perez v. Sharp decision was cited in the U.S. Supreme Court's *Loving v. Virginia* (1963) decision, which struck down the thirteen states remaining bans preventing interracial couples from marrying in the remaining states. Sixty years later, the California Supreme Court in *re: Marriage Cases*, also based much of its decision to allow same-sex couples to marry on the Perez decision.

In its legal briefs filed in support of marriage equality litigation across the country. The Mexican American Legal Defense and Educational Fund (MALDEF), the leading national civil rights organization for Latinos in the United States cited the Perez v. Sharp decision along with the historical role that Latinos have played in confronting marriage discrimination MALDEF

---

66 *Rachel F. Moran, Loving and the Legacy of Unintended Consequences, 2007 Wis. L. Rev. 239, 268.*

affirms that their "primary goal is defending the right of all Latino families to equal treatment under law, including those headed by lesbian or gay Latinos who wish the equal right to marry and in which Latino children are disadvantaged because their same-sex parents are denied civil marriage."

With such a strong cultural and historical commitment to family and equality, perhaps it's not surprising that a Latino was the only dissenting voice on the California State Supreme Court when Proposition 8 was declared constitutional. In his dissenting opinion, Justice Carlos R. Moreno asserted that Prop 8 violates the equal protection clause of the California Constitution protecting fundamental minority group rights from the will of the majority. He wrote, "Discrimination against a minority group on the basis of a suspect classification strikes at the core of the promise of equality that underlies our California Constitution."

The vision and tenacity of the Latino community to advocate for equal treatment for all people and the value of family life has had a profound impact on the freedom to marry movement. Latinos have and will continue to play a key role in equality for same-sex couples and their families. As Prop 8 makes its way to the U.S. Supreme Court Justice, we can only hope that Justice Sonia Sotomayer, will continue the civil rights legacy of Latino Americans have put forth when she casts her vote on the historical marriage lawsuit that will eventually decide the fate of marriage equality in this generation.

CHAPTER TWENTY-FIVE: MARRIAGE EQUALITY IS AN INDIGENOUS VALUE

"Being able to marry, Diane, after 10 years together, was an important part of receiving community acknowledgement and respect of our commitment. Equality for all people to choose who they will marry was a Native American traditional value before colonization."

—Ruth Villasenor, Native American Outreach Coordinator, Marriage Equality USA, Chiricuhua Apache & Mexican American

STOP COLONIZING HEARTS AND MINDS

"No matter what the white people say, no matter what they tell us their God says, what this is really about is: assimilation, guilt and indoctrination. Diversity and tolerance are integral to all of our cultures. Don't let them die too."

—Gabriel Duncan, a California Paiute, and founder of Bay Area American Indian Two-Spirits Youth Circle, a Bay Area organization for LGBT Native American Youth

Before contact with Europeans, many Native American tribes recognized four genders: masculine male, masculine female, feminine male, and feminine female. Feminine males had special names and roles, for example the Wingkte in the Dakota tribe and the Nádleeh in the Navajo (Dine) tribe. These feminine males were able to marry masculine men or masculine women and were considered sacred by the people because they carried both masculine and feminine energies.[67]

---

67 See the book *Two-Spirit People: Native American Gender Identity, Sexuality, and Spirituality* for more information.

According to Gabriel Duncan, a young California Paiute Native American, "If a man chose the basket instead of the bow, his tribe would socialize him with the women. Two-Spirits like myself, the modern term for gay, lesbian, bi and trans Native Americans, were hailed as medicine men." "We were depended on to heal, keep the history of our people, and care for the children. Two-Spirited people were often 'cookers,' though they could also be warriors – gender roles didn't really matter." Duncan says if you look at the diaries of Spanish conquistadors you will find reports of the occasional female warrior who took a wife, like her male counterparts.

In the documentary *Anyone and Everyone*, Cherokee Calvin Rock, parent of a gay son, explains "If you go back in Native society, you'll find [gay] people were honored because they were different from the others. Some were medicine men. Some would give names to the children. The things that turned tribes [against gays/two-spirits] was the early churches that come in and said 'that's wrong.' I appreciate my son, because he's another voice in the village."

Brian Gilley, a University of Vermont anthropology professor, also affirms the respected role of Native gay people in his book, *Becoming Two-Spirit: Gay Identity and Social Acceptance in Indian Country.* He writes that Native American tradtionally accepted same-sex relations," before European contact.

Randy Burns, a Northern Pauite and co-founder of the Gay American Indian Organization (GAI), agrees. In *Living the Spirit, A Gay American Indian Anthology,* includes a resource section listing over 135 North American tribes' words for gay Indians, he says that "for centuries before and after the arrival of Europeans, gay and lesbian American Indians were recognized and valued members of tribal communities."

REDEFINING MARRIAGE

Despite gender and sexuality being more fluid in the Native tradition than the Western tradition, colonization and Christianity has led to a more narrow definition of marriage. Mirroring the efforts in many states, and at the federal level, to keep marriage from gay people, several tribal governments followed in their footsteps and passed initiatives banning same-sex marriage on tribal land. In 2006, the Navajo Nation, the largest recognized Native American tribe, and the Cherokee Nation's Tribal Councils, voted to pass their own DOMAs.

Joe Shirley, President of the Navajo Nation, a reservation that covers four states (Arizona, Colorado, New Mexico, and Utah), vetoed against a bill by the Navajo National Council to ban same-sex marriages on the Navajo Nation. He says, "Driving under the influence is really killing a lot of people; bootlegging; domestic violence; gangs. These are just some of the issues that we really need to be working on," he says, "not banning same sex marriage. I believe that is a real basic right, and in this case, what 67 people are trying to be is discriminatory, you know, trying to take away a real basic human right. I don't think that's right." Unfortunately, Shirley's veto was over-ridden, and same-sex marriage is outlawed on the Navajo Nation.

Dawn McKinley and Kathy Reynolds of the Cherokee Nation received a marriage certificate from their tribal government. This triggered a lawsuit challenging same-sex marriage on the Cherokee Nation and they were stopped from recording their license. McKinley and Reynolds, along with their attorney, Todd Hembree, appealed to the tribal court arguing that the Cherokee words for husband and wife are gender-neutral therefore the couple should be able to be legally married. Still, this law was upheld and they were unable to be legally married.

WALKING IN ANOTHER'S SHOES

On May 24, 2009, the Coquille Indian Tribe off the southern Oregon coast passed a law allowing same-sex couples to marry, provided at least one of the spouses is a Coquille tribal member. Ashland's Ken Tanner, Chief of the Coquille Indian Tribe said "Native Americans are sensitive to discrimination of any kind. For our tribe, we want people to walk in the shoes of other people and learn to respect differences. Through that, we think we build a stronger community." According to Coquille committee chairman, Jack Lenox, in the past "same-sex domestic relations were accepted with no exclusions from tribal citizenship, the community auspices or spiritual activities." The tribe wants to go back to their traditional ways of acceptance and inclusion.

Within a week of the Coquille passage of the law, Kitzen Branting, a lesbian Coquille Indian Tribe Member, and her wife, Jeni Branting, were legally married in the Plankhouse on the tribe's reservation in Coos Bay, Oregon by Chief Ken Tanner. Banting says, "I wanted my tribal family to say, 'Yes, we recognize that you are equal to any other tribal member, and you are just as important, and your spouse should have the same rights as any other spouse.'"

The tribe was able to marry the couple and to perform same-sex marriages, because tribes are supposed to be recognized as sovereign nations with tribal governments determining laws and policy, therefore they are not required to follow Oregon's constitution. However, because of anti-gay marriage initiatives passed in Oregon and Washington, the couple's marriage will only be recognized by the tribe on tribal land and in other states that allow same-sex couples to marry.

The marriage entitles Jeni Branting to health care, housing, and other tribal benefits because the tribe is a sovereign nation. Jeni should also be entitled to federal recognition of her marriage under law for other tribal rights (e.g. under Title 25 there are certain rights related to treatises, "descent and distribution rights for Indians' property, laws pertaining to health care eligibility for Indians and spouses and reimbursement of travel expenses of spouses and candidates seeking positions in the Indian Health Service"). However, the Defense of Marriage Act may trump tribal sovereignty in this case and keep Jeni from being recognized as a legal spouse. Despite these limitations and some opposition, Chief Tanner believes that allowing same-sex marriage is going to "have a very positive impact" on the Coquille tribe.

WELCOMING TWO-SPIRITS BACK TO THE TRIBE

On April 15-18, 2009, the Seventy-Fourth Annual Tribal Assembly of the Central Council of Tlingit and Haida Indian Tribes of Alaska, met in Juneau, Alaska. During the assembly, the council passed a resolution in support of Two-Spirit Native people in an attempt to begin healing and restore the place of the two-spirit in tribal community. The resolution declared that there are "more than 26,000 tribal citizens; and WHEREAS, many of the sons and daughters of our own Tlingit people who are two-spirited (gay, lesbian, bi-sexual, and transgender) have left their homes and communities to live among strangers because of the prejudice, homophobia, harassment, and rejection they experience, often from even their own families; and WHEREAS, even in terminal illness, many of our own Native people have been denied their wishes to come home and die in their own homes and communities because of non-acceptance of them as the beloved human beings they once were considered; and WHEREAS, suicides among teenage youth have been attributed to their fears and anxieties of facing life in this atmosphere. BE IT RESOLVED, that the Seventy-Fourth Tribal Assembly of Central Council of Tlingit and Haida Indian Tribes of Alaska convened in Juneau, Alaska on April 15-18, 2009, and that we as a tribe offer our support and caring for all two-spirit sons and daughters in every way, as well as all the beloved children of this nation, and wish to open communication and support groups to have better understanding."

TWO-SPIRIT WARRIORS

A higher percentage of Native American men and women serve in the United States Military than any other racial group. Because of this, LGBT Native American soldiers suffer in greater proportion from the Don't Ask, Don't Tell Policy and the Defense of Marriage Act laws denying LGBT servicemen/servicewoman and veterans spousal rights and privileges. How can we create more hardship for people who've been disenfranchised, discriminated against and had their language and culture stolen from them when they have served and protected us and our country? If it were not for the Navajo, Cherokee, Choctaw and Comanche Code Talkers who during World War II created a code from their native languages to communicate tactical maneuvers on the front lines, the United States may have never defeated the enemy and won the war.

STOP TAKING AWAY CONSTITUTIONAL RIGHTS FROM MINORITIES.

Native Americans have suffered what many call the "American Holocaust," at the hands of genocidal polices of the United States which stripped them of their land, their customs, their spiritual traditions, their language and their lives. Many were denied citizenship until 1924. Furthermore, under the guise of helping Native Americans, religious leaders and white settlers made it a crime for them to practice their religious traditions. Their children were taken from them and placed in boarding schools where they were beaten for speaking their language, and practicing their spiritual ways which were likened to devil worship.

It wasn't until Native Americans had been fully acculturated under the premise "Kill the Indian, save the man," (which to me sounds a lot like "Love the sinner, hate the sin,") that Native

Americans were seen as "acceptable." Forcing Native Americans to "be white," sounds a lot like forcing gays to be straight.

J. Miko Thomas of the Chickasaw Nation co-chairs the Bay Area American Indian Two-Spirits organization. He is also a Veteran of the US Navy Desert Shield/Desert Storm, USS F lint AE-32. He sees the strong connection between the oppression of Native Americans and the injustices facing LGBT people today. Thomas says, "In 1924, U.S. citizenship was finally bestowed on Native Americans. It wasn't until 1948, that Native people could vote. In 1978, the American Indian Religious Freedom Act went into effect and we were finally able to practice our traditional ways without government interference, as many of our practices were outlawed and perceived as witchcraft."

Thomas reminds fellow Native Americans of the need to protect all Native American rights, including the right of two-spirit people to marry. "As Native people we must continue to fight for our rights – from hunting and fishing, to self governance, which is why I am asking you today to support marriage equality rights for two spirit Native Americans."

WE ARE ALL RELATED.

The Lakota have a sacred prayer, Mitakuye Oyasin, which means, "we are all related," or "to all my relations." The prayer is said on behalf of all people and acknowledges the sacredness of the universal oneness of all people. What is done to one of us, is done to all of us, therefore when we lift our neighbor, we lift ourselves. As Thomas has asked his Native American brothers and sisters to take a stand for the rights of LGBT people, I ask my LGBT and allied community, especially the mainstream gay rights organizations, to reach out and support the rights of Native Americans, as well as other communities of color. Working together for each other's equality we create stronger coalitions and a more just world for all of us.

SECTION SEVEN:
INTERSECTIONS OF MARRIAGE DISCRIMINATION

CHAPTER TWENTY-SIX:
MARRIAGE INEQUALITIES FOR TRANSGENDER AND INTERSEXED PEOPLE

Transgender is an umbrella term for people whose gender identity and/or gender expression differs from the sex they were assigned at birth. Some transgender people use the terms female-to-male (FTM) or male-to-female (MTF) as a means of identifying their transition. Transgender people may or may not choose to alter their bodies hormonally and/or surgically.

Transsexual refers to people who desire to have, or who have had, sex reassignment surgery, to achieve a different physical sex from their physical sex at birth. Pre-operative (pre-op) means that no sex reassignment surgery (SRS) has been completed and post-operative (post-op) means that top surgery (breast reduction or implantation), bottom surgery (reconstruction of sexual organs) or both have been completed.

TRANSGENDER MARRIAGE RIGHTS

"Marriage equality will benefit everyone, not just the LGBT community, because at its heart, it means the removal of institutionalized discrimination and takes us one step closer to fulfilling the American promise of life, liberty, and justice for all."

Transgender activist and President of San Francisco Pride, Mikayla Connell.[68]

LIVING OUTSIDE THE BOX

"My partner is transgendered, she has not had sex re-assignment surgery because of a medical condition, but

---

68 Connell is featured in two Discovery Channel documentaries: *Changing Sexes-Male to Female* and *Switching Sexes-The aftermath.*

has changed her name and identity for over twenty years. I
don't think she can marry anyone legally.

—Maryann Smith, Marriage Equality
Activist and partner of a transgender woman.

Transgender people live at varying levels of physical transition. Some people do not opt for full surgery because of the expense, health concerns, or other personal reasons. Top surgery is more often completed, while because of physical complications and financial cost, bottom surgery is not. Because of marriage discrimination, the degree to which people are able to afford these surgeries can effect whether and whom they are able to marry. The law often only recognizes those who have had full sex reassignment surgery as person eligible for the rights of marriage pertaining to of their self-identified sex.

According to transgender activist Owen Wolf, "Whether one can change one's sex–surgery or not–depends on which state the transgender person lives in. Birth certificates can be changed in California with one surgery, in some states with 'all' possible surgeries for the appropriate sex being assumed, and can not be changed in some other states regardless of surgery. No state allows a transgender person to declare themselves to be of the other sex without surgery, even if surgery is not needed to present as the preferred gender (in the case of an FTM with minimal breasts) or if surgery is ill-advised due to other health issues such as heart condition or diabetes."

According to Shannon Minter, attorney for the National Center for Lesbian Rights (NCLR) "the legal validity of marriage involving a transsexual spouse is not yet firmly established in most states. Some states, may allow FTM/MTF transsexuals to marry their now opposite-sex spouses, but the legality of the marriages may be contested later in court," as it was in the Kantaras v. Kantaras case (2000).

According to NCLR, this case was "the first in the country to determine whether a transgender man has the right to marry and be a parent." Michael Kantaras had been born female, but had a sex change in 1987. He met his wife, Linda, two years later, and told her he was a transsexual before she married him. They were married for nine years and raised two children together. Although Linda had always known Michael was a transsexual, during the divorce proceedings she still asked the court to invalidate their marriage and to deny Michael any parental rights solely because he was not a "real man." Ouch! Luckily, the court ruled that Michael was the better parent and should have primary custody.

When it comes to marriage rights, transsexual men and women in this country have an even more complicated road to traverse. Whether or not a marriage is legal for a transgender person depends on three things:

1. The state they live in.
2. Whether they have surgically transitioned their genitalia.
3. The gender of their spouse.

For example, in California, surgically transitioned Female to Male (FTM) or Male to Female (MTF) people are able to legally marry partners of the opposite-sex only. So, depending on your sexual orientation and the gender of your preferred spouse, you may find that you could marry pre-operative and be barred from marrying that same person post-operative and vice versa. Post-surgical MTF's can only legally marry males and post-surgical FTMS can only marry females. Pre-surgery MTF's can only legally marry females and pre-surgery FTM's can only marry males, again. So, at least in California, a male transitioning to female who is attracted to females (MTF lesbian) would do well to marry her female partner before her gender re-assignment surgery. After her surgery, she would only be able to marry a man, at least until California overturns Proposition 8 and then she could marry her female partner either before or after her surgery.

A male transitioning to female who is attracted to males (MTF heterosexual) is denied the right to marry, but allowed to a register as a same-sex domestic partner in California. Then, once she has transitioned, she is eligible for a legal marriage license—and no longer eligible to enter into a domestic partnership. Therefore one advantage of going through hormone therapy and sex re-assignment is that if pre-op you are considered 'homosexual' and denied the right to enter into a marriage with the person of your choice, once you transition, you will be able to enter into a heterosexual marriage with that same partner. Does that straighten things out? Pun intended!

In either case, the validity of these marriages can still be potentially challenged at probate, in the courts by trans-phobic (and greedy) next of kin, and in federal courts. In states where marriage is gender-neutral, transgender people can marry the person they love regardless of their pre or post-op sex.

LEGAL GAY MARRIAGE IN TEXAS AND KANSAS

Unlike California which recognizes the right to change one's gender legally, states like Kansas and Texas don't. Lawsuits contesting the validity of a marriage between a transgender woman and a man, in Texas and in Kansas both ruled that those states will not recognize sex changes and will only recognize an individual's birth sex for the purposes of eligibility and validity of a marriage.

A Texas appellate court invalidated the seven year marriage of Christine Littelton (MTF), and her deceased husband. The same thing happened to J'Noel Gardiner (FTM) in Kansas when the court ruled for the deceased's contesting child, on the grounds that "a person's legal sex is genetically fixed at birth." These rulings barred both Littelton and Gardiner from having access to marriage protections that included rights as widows to Social Security benefits, inheriting without a will, the right to sue for wrongful death, the right to retirement benefits, other survivorship benefits, and the dignity and respect normally afforded other grieving widows.

Rulings that state "a person's legal sex is genetically fixed at birth," result in post-operative transsexual men only being able to legally marry males and post-operative transsexual women only being able to legally marry women. No matter how much is spent on surgery, name changes, and so on, transsexual men and women in Texas and Kansas cannot marry people of their previous gender. In other words, a transsexual gay man or lesbian *can* legally marry his or her partner; but a transsexual heterosexual man or woman cannot. And so, Kansas and Texas actually allow a form of same-sex marriage.

Following the Littleton ruling in Texas, two women, one of them an MTF, applied for, and obtained, a marriage license in San Antonio. In an article entitled "Lesbian Wedding Allowed in Texas by Gender Loophole," Jessica and Robin Wicks discuss picking up their license. "We know we love each other, and in a real sense we're already married in our hearts, but there's something about the piece of paper that says this is the way it should be." According to the article, Republican Texas Representative, Arlene Wohlgemuth, stated, "We don't object to a marriage license being issued, since we do favor a marriage between a man and woman and this fits the legal definition of gender." Huh? The couples' attorney Phyllis Randolph Frye welcomes other transsexual gay couples to travel to San Antonio and get hitched.

Welcome to legal limbo land!

Only New Jersey, California and Florida have established case law recognizing and affirming the marriage of a transgender person as valid when contested in court. Because of this, legal advocates urge couples where one or both partners are transgender to create written documentation that includes wills of both partners, financial and medical powers of attorney, a written personal relationship agreement including a detailed account of each spouse's rights and responsibilities with regard to finances, property, support, children, and other issues that are important to the couple and contain an acknowledgement that the non-transsexual partner is aware that his or her spouse is transsexual. Using an attorney to do the above is advised. Can you imagine what it must be like to be legally married in New Jersey, but unable to move to Utah because your marriage may be contested or rendered null and void? So much for the equal protection clause!

The adoption of full marriage equality would create gender-neutral marriage laws and provide all transgender people, regardless of sexual orientation and regardless of level of transition and socio-economic class—equal participation in the institution of marriage without the fear of a future court case contesting the validity of that marriage.

INTERSEX MARRIAGE RIGHTS

"Not everyone is born with a set of chromosomes, XX or XY, that clearly defines gender. Hermaphrodite and other cases of confused genetics could pose problems."

–Jack Sampson, University of Texas Law
Professor in reference to the Littleton Case

"The Law, by clinging to a binary system that blindly denies the existence of intersexuals and the importance of self-identity, reinforces the perception that intersexuality is unacceptable."

—Julie Greenberg,, Esq. Professor of Law,
Thomas Jefferson School of Law.

Intersex is an umbrella term for variations in sexual anatomy, sex chromosomes, and/or mixed genital and reproductive anatomy. According to the Intersex Society of North America (ISNA), "a person might be born appearing to be female on the outside, but having mostly male-typical anatomy on the inside. Or a person may be born with genitals that seem to be in-between the usual male and female types—for example, a girl may be born with a noticeably large clitoris, or lacking a vaginal opening, or a boy may be born with a notably small penis, or with a scrotum that is divided so that it has formed more like labia. Or a person may be born with mosaic genetics, so that some of her cells have XX chromosomes and some of them have XY chromosomes." Approximately, one in 1,500 children are born intersex, although, this condition may not be identified until puberty or post-mortem during an autopsy.

For the most part, intersex individuals are just people with some degree of genital or chromosomal anatomical variation–just like hair and skin color. However, some intersex individuals may have health complications such as a serious endocrine condition or other medical condition that requires treatment. According to intersex educator, David Cameron, "Because many of us don't fit into the social definition constructed within our society's two sex - two gender binary system, intersex children and adolescents are being surgically or hormonal 'fixed' and 'cured' of their variations so they 'fit visually' into that system. Cameron notes that *"approximately 65,000 intersex people are born worldwide every year and in the USA, on average, five surgeries a day are performed on children that appear sexually different."*

As Cameron says the reality of intersex people has thrown a "monkey wrench" into marriage laws that define marriage as one man and one woman. Intersex people do not neatly fit into either the category of man or woman. Some are both physically male and female, and don't clearly identify as just a man or just a woman. Some intersex people are attracted only to males, some only to females, some to both males and females, and some intersex people are asexual. Existing marriage laws force intersex people to deny the complexity of their physical sex and gender and compromise their free will to marry the person of their choice.

According to Julie Greenberg, there are few known marriage cases where intersex people have challenged the courts for the right to marry based on chromosomal status. She was aware if at least one case in Australia in the 1970s, where the courts ruled that an "intersex husband was neither a male nor a female for purposes of marriage."

National Center for Lesbian Rights attorney, Karen Doering, noted that the courts in the Littleton and Gardiner cases in Texas and Kansas presumed that the women were both chromosomally (XY), however, to her knowledge, genetic testing was not done.

What determines sex or gender is more complicated than our binary system allows. Intersex individuals are forced into boxes they don't fit into. Shouldn't a person with an XXY make up be able to legally marry either sex because they are chromosomally both? Some cultures have recognized more than just two sexes and genders and have embraced and revered such "two-spirited" people. Science has confirmed the natural diversity of gender and sexuality. Why don't we return to the wisdom of the past and end the suffering for those who don't fit neatly into these constructed binary boxes.

Chapter Twenty-Seven:
Marriage Inequalities in the Military: Denying LGBT Soldiers the Right to Serve Openly and Marry the One They Love.

Don't Ask, Don't Tell

"*The time for hiding, lying and shame is over. We will not hide anymore and we will not lie anymore and the discriminatory laws of Don't Ask Don't Tell that take away the soldier's rights to be who they are need to be repealed, right now, today! No more waiting. Our soldiers who are gay and lesbian go overseas and they fight terror, but they come back home and they are terrorized to tell the truth about who they are. They sign up because they are told 'be all you can be,' and they come back home and they can't even be who they are. They fight so that we can be protected at home, so our neighbors can have the protection to love and marry. But we come home and we are not allowed to love and we are not allowed to marry. We do what we are told, but the laws say we can't tell, and we do what we are asked, but the laws say 'don't ask.' Well, Don't Ask, Don't Tell is over! It's time to tell, it's time to demand. We are not asking anymore, we are telling, we are telling, we are telling and we will never stop telling.*"

—Lt. Daniel Choi, United States Army Iraq
Veteran and West Point Graduate

According to a May 2010 Gallup Poll, 70% of Americans are in favor of gay men and lesbians being able to serve openly in the military. However, the Department of Defense's "Don't Ask, Don't Tell" policy keeps LGBT people from serving openly in the military.

ACCORDING TO THE SERVICEMEMBERS LEGAL DEFENSE NETWORK (SLDN):

- During President Obama's first year in office approximately 651 soldiers were discharged under "Don't Ask, Don't Tell."
- Over 12,000 soldiers have been kicked out of the military since the implementation of Don't Ask Don't Tell in 1993.
- It has cost more than $200 million to replace service members fired under "Don't Ask, Don't Tell." (GAO report)
- An estimated 65,000 gay Americans serve in the military now.
- The U.S. is home to more than 1,000,000 gay veterans.

When I contacted a Northern California Army Recruiting Office and asked about the "Don't Ask, Don't Tell" Policy, the Sergeant who answered the phone down played the discrimination involved. He said, "As long as someone doesn't come right out and say it, we don't care." This is not correct, that is only one aspect of the "Don't Ask Don't Tell" policy. In addition to denying LGBT Americans the right to serve openly with dignity, under the "Don't Ask, Don't Tell" Policy, U.S. servicemembers may be investigated and administratively discharged if they:

1). Make a statement that they are lesbian, gay or bisexual
2). Engage in physical contact with someone of the same-sex for the purposes of sexual gratification; or
3) Marry or attempt to marry, someone of the same-sex.
[Dept. of Defense Directive No. 1332.14]

The "Don't Ask Don't Tell" policy means that gay Americans will be kicked out of the military for dating, falling in love, expressing affection for, committing to, living with and/or marrying a member of the same-sex. We ask these same men and women to die for our freedoms, yet we deny them the freedom to love and to have adult relationships.

The "Don't Ask, Don't Tell" policy is a discriminatory policy that punishes our LGBT soldiers for being honest about who they are and having integrity. It supports lies, blackmail, deception, and promotes shame and bigotry. It also keeps gay Americans from being able to take care of their families. As fair-minded American citizens we must encourage our leaders to end this shameful policy now.

The military claims it must spend millions in advertising to recruit new members, yet we waste millions of dollars kicking hundreds of those recruits out of the military every year, not because they are doing an inadequate job, but simply because of their sexual orientation.

Our U.S. troops are currently serving without incident, alongside troops from Great Britain, Israel, Canada, Czech Republic, Sweden and other countries who allow LGBT people to serve their countries openly. In fact, 67 countries allow gays to serve openly including Albania, Austria, Bosnia, Bulgaria, Columbia, Croatia, Hungary, Lithuania, Maldova, the Philippines, Poland, Russia, Slovakia, South Africa, and the Ukraine to name just a few.

BE ALL YOU CAN BE WITHOUT LOVE OR EQUALITY

Gay and lesbian servicemembers are fighting for freedoms for others overseas, but do not have the freedom at home to be who they are, to be open about the person they love, and to marry and form family. Despite the fact that same-sex marriage is legal in several states, "Don't Ask, Don't Tell," keeps gay and lesbian soldiers from marrying the person they love. What's worse is that they while they are "liberating Iraq and Afghanistan," and fighting for other's freedoms, they run the risk of being expelled if they turn to their fellow soldier if shot and said, "Please call my partner and let him know I'm okay." Or of they carry a same-sex partner's picture in their wallet, make phone calls home to their loved one, or tell their fellow soldiers and officers anything about their lives.

THE COST OF TELLING THE TRUTH

A few days before Air Force Captain Monica Hill was scheduled to report to Andrews Air Force base she learned that her partner of 14 years, Terri, was dying of brain cancer. Monica requested a deferment to care for Terri from her commanding officers. When pressed for a reason for the request, Monica had to choose between lying or telling them the truth about Terri.

Monica told the truth.

Her commanding officer immediately initiated discharge proceedings.

Less than two months after Terri's death, Monica was interviewed as part of the discharge proceedings. Despite the evidence of Terri's death certificate and proof that they had signed a rental contract to live together in an apartment outside of the Andrews Air Force base, the interviewing officer insinuated that, in revealing her sexual orientation, Monica was only trying to get out of completing her service commitment. The Air Force "honorably discharged" Hill on October 2, 2002 and then demanded that she pay the Air Force back for her medical school tuition.

According to the Service Members Legal Defense Network's Survival Guide, if a service member discloses their sexual orientation to a superior regardless of circumstances, they will be required to pay back scholarships, bonuses or special pay, because the military views these disclosures as voluntary.

Lieutenant Colonel Victor J. Fehrenbach followed in the footsteps of his parents. His father was an Air Force lieutenant colonel, his mother was an Air Force nurse and captain. In the eighteen years he has served his country as a F-15E pilot, also known as a fighter weapons systems officer, Lt. Col. Fehrenbach has received nine air medals. He is a war hero who has flown numerous missions against Taliban and al-Qaida targets, including the longest combat mission in his squadron's history.

With only two years left until his retirement, Lt. Col. Fehrenbach is being thrown out of the Air Force because of the Don't Ask, Don't Tell Policy. Being discharged after eighteen years of faithful service by his country is dishonorable enough, but he is losing a $46,000 a year retirement pension which would otherwise be paid to him for the remainder of his life, and all of his military benefits, including health insurance, because he is a gay man.

When Lt. Daniel Choi, a translator, fluent in Korean, Arabic, and Farsi, spoke the three English words "I am gay," on the Rachel Maddow Show, despite his being a West Point Graduate and having an exemplary record as a First Lieutenant who served as a combat veteran in the Iraq war, the military started his discharge proceedings.

Even though a petition signed by 162,000 people was submitted to the National Guard Bureau on his behalf, on June 30, 2009, a panel of New York National Guard officers recommended Lt. Choi's discharge.

Since his disclosure on the Rachel Maddow Show, Lt. Choi has helped lead the charge to overturn "Don't Ask, Don't Tell." He's working with Knights Out, an organization of LGBT West Point Graduates who are all coming out and speaking out against the military's "Don't Ask Don't Tell" Policy. On March 18, 2010 Lt. Choi chained himself to the White House fence to protest the unfairness of the "Don't Ask, Don't Tell Policy." Only a

few months later, Lt. Choi was discharged under the"Don't Ask,
Don't Tell" policy.

MILITARY READINESS ENHANCEMENT ACT (H.R. 1283).

On March 3, 2009, Rep. Ellen Tauscher (D-CA) introduced
the Military Readiness Enhancement Act (H.R. 1283). The bill
has 148 bipartisan cosponsors and according to SLDN would
replace the existing ban on letting gay people serve with "new
provisions prohibiting discrimination based on sexual orientation in the armed forces." HR 1283 would allow people to
serve in the military regardless of their sexual orientation and
allow former military personnel discharged under "Don't Ask,
Don't Tell" to re-enlist. Finally, HR 1283 would prevent any
future limitations on the right of gays and lesbians to serve in
the military.

> **"***To amend title 10, United States Code, to enhance the
> readiness of the Armed Forces by replacing the current
> policy concerning homosexuality in the Armed Forces,
> referred to as "Don't Ask, Don't Tell", with a policy of
> nondiscrimination on the basis of sexual orientation.***"**

REPEAL DOMA FOR GAY VETS

Additionally, DOMA keeps active military personnel and
veterans from accessing the family benefits that their fellow heterosexual comrades receive. There is no justice in second-class
citizenship. Why should Dale, a Vietnam Vet, not be able to
share his pension and health benefits with his loving partner
Jake? Why should Elida, a Vietnam veteran nurse exposed to
Agent Orange, not be able to share her benefits with her partner
of 20 years? Gay veterans should not be denied the rights and
benefits their heterosexual servicemembers get.

"NO COMMISSARY FOR YOU!"

270 of the 1,138 federal rights associated with marriage have to do with Federal Civilian and Military Service Benefits. Spouses of military servicemembers are granted numerous privileges not afforded civilians. Privileges like the right to shop at the tax-free commissary and buy gas on the base at a significantly reduced rate. Such benefits provide considerable financial savings to military families.

By not being able to serve openly and be legally married, the partners of gay servicemembers and veterans are denied access to counseling, educational, and financial benefits including; commissary benefits, death benefits, medical benefits, and veteran's preferences, student loans, housing loans, and many of the other rights afforded spouses of veterans.

Additionally, deployed married servicemembers are allowed special phone privileges not granted unmarried service members. Spouses of those deployed overseas are also afforded special housing. Further, married couples jointly serving in the military are given additional privileges like the right to be live together and be transferred together. Needless to say, gay and lesbians in the armed forces and their partners automatically forfeit all of these benefits.

"There are two basic tenants of citizenship throughout history— the right to marry and the right to serve proudly in the military. Until Washington wakes up and repeals DADT and DOMA we are all still second class citizens in this country."

—Senator Mark Leno, (D) California

Take Action Now

Call the Department of Defense 703-545-6700 and ask them to stop discharging LGBT soldiers. Write letters to your Congressmember and the President.

Sample Letter to Congress to Pass the Military Readiness Enhancement Act (H.R. 1283)

Congresswoman Mary Bono Mack
104 Cannon House Office Bldg
Washington, D.C. 20515

RE: SUPPORT for Military Readiness Enhancement Act (H.R. 1283

Dear Congresswoman Bono Mack:

I am writing to urge you to support the **Military Readiness Enhancement Act (H.R. 1283** and all efforts to **repeal the Don't Ask Don't Tell Policy** which has cost taxpayers more than $200 million to replace service members fired under **"Don't Ask, Don't Tell."** Seventy-five percent of Americans support allowing gays to serve openly in our nation's military.

Further there are already more than 65,000 gay Americans now serving in the military with the U.S. home to more than 1,000,000 gay veterans. The Military claims it must spend millions in advertising to recruit new members and yet wastes millions of dollars kicking hundreds of those recruits out of the military every year, not because they are doing an inadequate job, but simply because of their sexual orientation. This is unacceptable!

Our U.S. troops have served without incident, alongside troops from Great Britain, Israel, Canada, Czech Republic, Sweden and other countries, who allow LGBT people to serve their countries openly. Gay and lesbian servicemembers are fighting for freedoms for others overseas, but do not have the freedom at home to be who they are. What's worse is that while they are "liberating Iraq and Afghanistan," they can't even carry a same-sex partner's picture in their wallet, make phone calls home to their loved one, or tell their fellow soldiers and officers anything about their lives.

Gay, lesbian, and bisexual soldiers are fighting for their country, yet they cannot enjoy the rights of family and freedom that their heterosexual colleagues do. I urge you to support equal employment opportunities in the military for gay, lesbian, and bisexual recruits and soldiers.

Sincerely,

Sample Letter to President Obama to Repeal Don't Ask Don't Tell

The Honorable Barack H. Obama
President of the United States
The White House
Washington, D.C. 20500

RE: REPEAL DON'T ASK, DON'T TELL

Dear President Obama:

I am writing to urge you to follow up on your campaign promise and repeal the Don't Ask Don't Tell Policy by executive order.

According to the Servicemembers Legal Defense Network, tax-payers have paid more than $230 million to facilitate this federal policy of job discrimination since the policy's implementation in 1993. The military claims it must spend millions in advertising to recruit new members and yet we waste millions of dollars kicking hundreds of those recruits out of the military every year, not because they are doing an inadequate job, but simply because of their sexual orientation. This is unacceptable!

This reality is even more disturbing considering that our U.S. troops have served without incident, alongside troops from Great Britain, Israel, Canada, Czech Republic, Sweden and other countries, who allow LGBT people to serve their countries openly. Yet the U.S. does nothing, despite your campaign promise, to right this wrong.

Gay and lesbian soldiers are fighting for their country, yet they cannot enjoy the rights of family and freedom that their heterosexual colleagues do. Is this the best we can due for the men and women who put their lives on the line to defend our country? I think not. Please act, Mr. President, your pen is truly mightier than the sword in protecting freedom and equality. Repeal Don't Ask, Don't Tell.

Sincerely,

SECTION EIGHT:
REPEALING DOMA AND PROP 8

Chapter Twenty-Eight:
Repeal Public Law No. 104-199, 110 Statute 2419, AKA the Defense of Marriage Act (DOMA)

"Massachusetts has a single category of married persons, and we view all married persons equally and identically. {The federal Defense of Marriage Act} divides that category into two distinct and unequal classes of marriage."

—Massachusetts Attorney General, Martha Coakley quoted by CNN July 8, 2009

DOMA—The Federal 'Denial of Marriage Act'

The so called federal "Defense of Marriage Act" aka DOMA, which I think would be better defined as the "Denial of Marriage" Act marked the first time the federal government got involved in the definition of marriage, an area that has always been reserved to the states. The purpose of DOMA was to (1) allow states to reject legal relationships between persons of the same-sex, even if the couple are legally married in another state and (2) to define marriage as a legal union exclusively between one man and one woman under federal law.

DOMA denies same-sex couples the right to have their marriages recognized as legal in all 50 states, U.S. territories, and Indian reservations, as well as access to 1,138 federal rights that marriage provides heterosexual married couples. In 1996, Congress approved DOMA by a vote of 85-14 in the Senate and a vote of 342-67 in the House of Representatives. President Bill Clinton signed DOMA into law on September 21, 1996. DOMA was a homophobic reaction to the expectation that Hawaii (and possibly other states) were going to legalize same-sex marriage and under the Full Faith and Credit Clause and Equal Protection Clause of the United States Constitution those marriages would be recognized in other states.

The DOMA legislation was an explicit homophobic act taken by the U.S. Congress to exclude gay people from the rights, benefits and portability of marriage enjoyed by all other Americans. DOMA is unfair and discriminatory. President Obama has pledged to repeal DOMA and several lawsuits are pending challenging DOMA as unconstitutional.

LEGAL CHALLENGES TO DOMA

The first serious legal challenges were filed in 2009. Two federal employees were denied the right to give their same-sex spouses access to the federal employee family health care benefits. The employees, represented by Lambda Legal and private attorneys, submitted their complaints to the Ninth Circuit Court of Appeals. Judges Stephen Reinhardt and Alex Kozinski, both ruled that the federal employees grievances were valid, and as Federal Employee Dispute Resolution officials, ordered that health benefits be provided to the employees' same-sex spouses. However, the Office of Personal Management (OPM) issued a directive to the federal government health plan to block the judges' orders which prompted Lambda Legal to file a lawsuit in federal court challenging OPM's directive.

The second legal challenge to DOMA was filed on March 3, 2009 by the Gay & Lesbian Advocates & Defenders (GLAD), a New England legal group, headquartered in Massachusetts. GLAD filed a lawsuit against OPM on behalf of married same-sex couples in Massachusetts who are denied federal marriage protections and benefits because of DOMA. The case, *Gill v. Office of Personal Management,* seeks to overturn the DOMA provision that holds that the federal government does not have to recognize the marriages of same-sex couples in Massachusetts.

A third challenge was filed on, on July 8, 2009, by the State of Massachusetts entitled *Commonwealth v. United States Department of Health and Human Services.* This lawsuit also challenges the constitutionality of DOMA and argues that Congress "overstepped its authority, undermined states' efforts to recognize marriages between same-sex couples, and codified an animus towards gay and lesbian people."[69]

In response to a fourth legal challenge to DOMA, the Obama Administration issued a legal brief on August 17, 2009, stating that DOMA is discriminatory. The brief was in response to *Smelt v. USA*, (2009) a lawsuit filed in federal court by Arthur Smelt and Christopher Hammer,[70] two gay men from Orange County California challenging DOMA and Proposition 8. The legal brief states that, "With respects to the merits, this Administration does not support DOMA as a matter of policy, believes that it is discriminatory, and supports its repeal."[71]

Perry v. Schwarzenegger, a lawsuit challenging Proposition 8, does not directly challenge DOMA. However, it could end up as the fifth federal challenge if the court finds that Proposition 8 violates the Equal Protection and Due Process clauses of the U.S. Constitution, because then the constitutionality of DOMA would be seriously called into question. This case will be discussed in greater detail in the following chapter.

INITIAL RULINGS

On July 8, 2010, Judge Joseph Tauro of the United States District Court, who was randomly assigned to hear legal arguments for *Gill v. Office of Personal Management* and *Commonwealth v.*

---

69 *Boston Globe, August 7, 2009. Article "Mass. challenges federal Defense of Marriage"*
70 *On 9-24-09 a federal judge dismissed the case on a technicality and said that the couple's lawsuit needed to be re-filed due to procedural problems..*
71 *The Washington Post, "Obama Makes Explicit His Objection to DOMA." August 17, 2009,*

United States Department of Health and Human Services, concluded that section 3 of DOMA was unconstitutional. In his ruling he stated, "As irrational prejudice plainly never constitutes a legitimate government interest, this court must hold that Section 3 of DOMA as applied to Plaintiffs violates the equal protection principles embodied in the Fifth Amendment to the United States Constitution." He also found that DOMA violated that Tenth Amendment of the Constitution which protects states' rights because it forces a state, in this challenge Massachusetts, to violate the right of equal protection to its own citizens.

These lawsuits will likely be appealed, possibly consolidated, and eventually heard by the U.S. Supreme Court. If these lawsuits are successful, it is unclear if only Massachusetts' same-sex married couples would benefit or if all legally married same-sex couples would have to access the 1,138 federal marriage rights they are currently denied.

TEAR DOWN THE WALL

Congressman Jerrold Nadler (D-New York), a long-time advocate for equality, introduced H.R. 3567 The Respect for Marriage Act (RMA) into the 111th congress on September 15, 2009. The bill has 100 co-sponsors. According to a press release from Congressman Nadler, the "Respect for Marriage Act" is supported by former President Bill Clinton who signed DOMA into law, and former Republican Congressman, Bob Barr who wrote DOMA.

The Respect for Marriage Act would repeal Section 2 and 3 of Public Law No. 104-199, 110 Statute 2419 (aka DOMA) and "restore the rights of all lawfully married couples—including same-sex couples to receive the benefits of marriage under federal law."

However this bill only provides federal recognition for married same-sex couples, not those with marriage-lite alternatives like reciprocal beneficiary, domestic partnership, and civil unions. Nadler's bill would only repeal Section 2 and Section 3 of Public Law No. 104-199, 110 Statute 2419. If Section 2 and Section 3 are repealed, same-sex couples married in states that allow same-sex marriage, including the 18,000 same-sex couples married in California in 2008, would receive access to the 1,138 federal marriage benefits, (i.e. Social Security benefits and filing joint taxes). Additionally, those married couples' marriages would still be legally recognized by the federal government when traveling to, or relocating to, one of the other states that do not recognize same-sex couples to marry, though those married couples living in states that do not allow gays to marry, would still be denied the hundreds of state marriage rights (the right to visit their spouse in the hospital, make medical and burial decisions, and inherit shared property without a will) until those individual states repealed their state constitutional amendments. Additionally, even if the RMA passes all the couples in domestic partnerships in California, Washington, Nevada, New Jersey, Maine, etc. would be denied the 1,138 federal rights and further marginalized. Repealing DOMA outright is the only way to secure full equality under the law.

DOMA REGRETS

In 1996, U.S. Senator, Ted Kennedy was one of only 14 senators,[72] all Democrats, who voted against the Defense of Marriage Act. He stated that DOMA would "make a minority of Americans permanent second-class citizens of this country.... And it would write discrimination into a document that has served as a historic guarantee of individual freedom."

As a politically expedient gesture to appeal to conservatives, former President Bill Clinton, approved DOMA and signed it

---

72 *Senators who voted no on DOMA: Daniel Akaka, Barbara Boxer, Russ Feingold, Diane Feinstein, Daniel Inouye, Ted Kennedy, Bob Kerrey, John Kerry, Carol Moseley-Braun, Patrick Moynihan, Claiborne Pell, Chuck Robb, Paul Simon, and Ron Wyden.*

into law on September 16, 1996. Thirteen years later Clinton finally came around to Kennedy's way of thinking and at a Campus Progress National Conference in June 2009, confirmed that he now supports same-sex marriage. When confronted later that summer at a Netroots Nation conference in Pittsburgh about why he signed DOMA into law in the first place, Clinton said while he regretted that action, he felt passing DOMA kept Congress from passing a more restrictive constitutional amendment. "We were attempting at the time, in a very reactionary Congress, to head off an attempt to send a constitutional amendment banning gay marriage to the states. The president doesn't even get to veto that."

Former U.S. Senator, Bob Barr, has said he has also had a change of heart. In an Op-Ed for the *Los Angeles Times* in 2009, Barr wrote "I have come to agree with [President Obama] that the law should be repealed," because "If one truly believes in federalism and the primacy of state government over the federal, DOMA is simply incompatible with those notions."

Take Action Now

You can help same-sex couples access those 1,138 federal rights currently denied by writing a letter to your elected officials and the President.

Sample Letter to Senator to Give Same-Sex Couples 1,138 Federal Rights Denied by DOMA

Congressman Earl Blumenauer (OR-3)
2267 Rayburn House Office Building
Washington, DC 20515

RE: SUPPORT for Respect for Marriage Act H.R. 3567

Dear Congressman Blumenauer:

I am writing to urge you to support the **Respect for Marriage Act H.R. 3567** which will repeal the so-called "Defense of Marriage Act," also known as "DOMA," that currently denies same-sex couples access to 1,138 federal rights.

DOMA denies gay Americans the right to "life, liberty and the pursuit of happiness," and more than one thousand benefits, protections, and responsibilities that come with civil marriage, including the right to designate a same-sex partner or spouse for health insurance, the right to file taxes jointly, the right to Social Security survivor benefits and federal employee pensions, and the right to sponsor a same-sex spouse/partner for immigration.

DOMA is a mean-spirited law that denies same-sex couples the security of the full faith and credit clause of the U.S. Constitution and principles of comity, which requires states to recognize and enforce marriages performed in other states.

Since civil marriage in the United States is a contractual arrangement with both federal and state governments, it is unfair that the federal government refuses to recognize gay American citizen's legal marriages in Massachusetts, Connecticut, Iowa, Vermont, New Hampshire, California, Canada, The Netherlands, Norway, Sweden, Spain, Belgium, and South Africa, as well as their civil unions and domestic partnerships.

Please act now in support of the **Respect for Marriage Act H.R. 3567** so we can remove this unjust federal law. Then, same-sex couples who marry or enter into civil unions and domestic partnership in one state will not become "legal strangers" after crossing state lines. Please protect all families by supporting the **Respect for Marriage Act H.R. 3567** to remove DOMA from the books.

Sincerely,

Chapter Twenty-Nine:
Proposition 8-Out
of the Darkness

"*The passage of Proposition 8 is an out-picturing of the darkness of fear and hate. Yet, in the midst of this darkness, bright possibilities exist, and light is seeking to emerge. A new way of relating for all people is ready to be birthed. We continue to plant the seeds of love, compassion, peace, harmony and freedom into the very darkness that stares us in the face. We turn on the light of our awareness, our love, our determination that all people be given the opportunity to love and be loved in the same way.*"

—Rev. Dr. Joan Steadman, Oakland Center for Spiritual Living

Despite setbacks for marriage equality in the state of California, the passage of Prop 8 has had some positive ramifications. The shock that a minority groups' civil rights can be stripped away by a popularity contest, has birthed a new generation of equality advocates and fueled a global movement for equal rights for LGBT people.

Key among the newly committed advocates, are two prominent and nationally recognized U.S. attorneys—Ted Olson and David Boies. Olson is a former U.S. Solicitor General and conservative Republican. Boies is a liberal Democrat. Olson represented George W. Bush and Boies represented Al Gore, in *Bush v. Gore,* the hotly contested and high stakes U.S. Supreme Court case over the 2000 Presidential election vote recount.

While Olson and Boies were on opposite sides of the *Bush v. Gore* case, both lawyers believe that Prop 8 is unconstitutional and should be overturned. In May 2009, the lawyers filed a federal challenge *(Perry V. Schwarzenegger)*[73] in the U.S. District Court for the Northern District of California.

PROP 8 –UNCONSTITUTIONAL

"The constitutional issue is quite simple." Boies says. "The Supreme Court repeatedly has held that the right to marry the person of your choice is a fundamental human right guaranteed by the equal-protection and due-process clauses of the Constitution."[74]

Olson agrees. "The United States Supreme Court has repeatedly held that marriage is one of the most fundamental rights that we have as Americans under our Constitution...marriage is a part of the Constitution's protections of liberty, privacy, freedom of association, and spiritual identification." He questions how the California justices could find Proposition 8 constitutional when it took away the right to marry from some Californians based solely on their sexual orientation.[75]

Even the state chose not to defend Prop 8 in court. Attorney General, Jerry Brown, whose office petitioned the California Supreme Court to declare Proposition 8 unconstitutional, has chosen not to defend Proposition 8 as valid state law in *Perry v. Schwarzenegger*, because he believes that Proposition 8 is in violation of the 14th Amendment of the U.S. Constitution. Nor has Governor Schwarzenegger taken a position or appeared in federal court to defend Prop 8 despite the express invitation to do so from Judge Vaughn R. Walker, Chief Judge of the U.S. District Court of the Northern District of California, who heard the case. The only people to argue that Proposition 8 was constitutional,

---

73 *Perry V. Schwarzenegger was poised to be the first federal trial to be televised, but the U.S. Supreme Court stepped in on a technicality and ordered the case not be televised. You can watch a re-enactment of the entire trial proceedings at www.marriagetrial.com.*
74 *Philly.com, November 1, 2009 article entitled "Yes, it is a fundamental rights under the U.S. Constitution"*
75 *Newsweek.com, January 9, 2010 article entitled "The conservative case for gay marriage."*

was the privately funded anti-gay Prop 8 proponents who put Prop 8 on the ballot in the first place.

THE CHALLENGE

The federal challenge to Prop 8 began on January 11, 2010 and lasted for three weeks with closing arguments heard on June 16, 2010. The Boies-Olson team brought eight expert witnesses to the stand who overwhelmingly proved that allowing persons to marry someone of the same-sex will not in the slightest way deter heterosexuals from getting married, staying married, or pro-creating.

In his opening arguments, Olson said, "This case is about marriage and equality. Plaintiffs are being denied the right to marry and under the law." He went on to say that "Marriage is the most important relationship in life and of fundamental importance of all individuals... central to psychological, emotional, and physical health. Marriage is the building block of family, neighborhood, and community in our society."

Olson criticized Prop 8 because "Prop 8 singles out gays alone...even convicted murders and child abusers in California enjoy the freedom to marry." The three points he argued were:

1. Marriage is vitally important in American Society.

2. Prop 8 causes grievous harm against gay and lesbian individuals and adds another chapter of discrimination and suffering.

3. Prop 8 perpetrates immeasurable harm for no good reason.

During the trial, Judge Walker heard testimony from a variety of experts on the history of marriage discrimination, the history of discrimination and violence against gay people, the financial benefits of marriage for same-sex couples, the cost of marriage discrimination, theories on sexual orientation and the impact of same-sex parenting on a child's adjustment.

Harvard University Professor, Dr. Nancy Cott, spoke on the history of marriage and marriage discrimination against unpopular minorities. She discussed that interracial marriages were considered "illegal and void," and that the government created laws to strip white American women of their U.S. citizenship if they married Chinese men or other non-white foreigners because immigrants of color were disfavored by white society.

Dr. George Chauncey, a Yale Professor, spoke about the history of discrimination against gays and lesbians. He said that gays and lesbians have been "a despised class of people, outlaws in the eyes of the law," subject to discrimination in housing, employment, and many other areas. For example, he testified that private sexual behavior between two members of the same sex was a crime punishable by jail in many states up until 2003, Hollywood censored movies and television shows removing any gay content, the federal government in the 1950s equated homosexuals with communists and fired gay people without just cause, and how it was against the law for gay people to frequent establishments where alcohol was served. He said that this law allowed police to raid clubs at will and led to bars posting signs that said "If you're gay stay away," for fear of losing their liquor license. He concluded that marriage discrimination is just one more form of the unequal treatment LGBT Americans have been subjected to.

Dr. Michael Lamb, a Professor at the University of Cambridge, former head of the National Institute of Child Health and Human Development for seventeen years, and expert in children's social and emotional development, stated that children raised by gays and lesbians are just as well-adjusted as children raised by heterosexual parents. He testified that over forty years of research on parenting and child adjustment shows that what makes "a good parent is someone who is committed to, loves the child, is engaged with the child, and provides appropriate guidance for and limits on that child." Lamb concluded that allowing same-sex couples to legally marry would enhance the emotional and social adjustment of children raised by same-sex parents.

Economists also testified about the impact of marriage discrimination on the finances of same-sex couples and their families, as well as the cost of marriage discrimination to local and state governments. According to Lee Badgett, a professor of economics at the University of Massachusetts, Amherst and Research Director of the Williams' Institute at UCLA, state and local governments are losing out on $40 million dollars annually by denying same-sex couples the right to marry (and that doesn't even include the $1 billion dollars that our federal government would save by recognizing same-sex couples marriages).

Plaintiff couples, Kristin Perry and Sandra Steir and Paul Katami and Jeffrey Zarrillo, shared personal testimony on the emotional, psychological, and social impact of being denied the right to marry. Jeffrey Zarrillo told the court that marriage would allow him "to partake in family gatherings, friends' and work functions as a married individual and have the pride of being able to be married." He added that "When someone is married, whether it's an introduction to a stranger, or someone noticing my ring, it says these individuals are serious, they are committed to another, they have taken that step to be in a relationship that one hopes will last the rest of their lives." Zarillo believes that domestic partnership, which is the only relationship status available to same-sex couples in California since the passage of Prop 8 "would relegate me to second-class citizenship. It does not give us due respect."

Kristin Perry, who had married Sandy Stier in 2004, but whose marriage was later invalidated by the California court along with the 4,000 other same-sex marriages performed in San Francisco, said "I'm a plaintiff in this case because I want to marry the woman that I love and right now we can't get married."

Perry testified that to her, "Marriage is about making a public commitment to the world, to your wife, to our friends and our family. It's the way we tell them and each other that this is a lifetime commitment. It's so different from domestic partnership."

The lawyers challenging Prop 8's constitutionality introduced into evidence Yes on Prop 8 campaign materials and depositions of leaders who worked with "Protect Marriage," the official "Yes on 8" campaign. During the testimony, it was clear that the Yes on 8 leaders intentionally misled the public. For example, William Tam from the California based Traditional Values Coalition, testified that he told people, in his official capacity at the rallies he held throughout Northern California, that the "gay agenda" was to "legalize sex with children." He also authored campaign materials that warned voters that if gay marriage continued to be legal in California "more children would become homosexuals."

Yale Professor Chauncey testified that many of the Yes on 8 campaign messages echoed the Anita Bryant's "Save Our Children" campaign in Dade County Florida in the 1970s. Bryant's most bigoted campaign quote was that gay people go after children because they "must recruit to refresh their ranks."

Defending Discrimination

During cross-examination, Prop 8 proponents tried to make the case that gays are not discriminated against. They went so far as to suggest that the success of the movie *Brokeback Mountain* proves that discrimination against gay people no longer exists. They tried to make a case that sexual orientation is a choice, and therefore, gay people have the right to marry a person of the opposite sex if they want marriage rights.

A third argument proponents of Prop 8 tried to make was that gay marriage causes heterosexual couples to stop marrying. For example, during cross-examination, the defense asked a witness if heterosexual marriages in the Netherlands had declined since 2001 when same-sex couples were able to legally marry. The witness began to answer the question, but the defense attorney insisted on a "yes" or "no" answer. The witness, under oath, answered "yes," which created the impression that gay marriage caused a decline in straight marriage. However, when the plaintiff attorney returned to re-interview the witness, he put up a slide with a chart of the number of marriages in the Netherlands dating back to the 1960s. It was clear from the chart that marriages had been consistently declining since the 1960s. There appeared to be no difference in the rate of decline before or after gay marriage became legal in the Netherlands.

Their fourth position was that same-sex marriage hurts children. Yes on Prop 8 attorneys presented no tangible evidence, but suggested that two men raising a child would be like having two Homer Simpsons as parents. No on 8 attorneys, on the other hand, cited decades of research and expert opinion that clearly refuted claims that same-sex marriage hurts children.

The attorneys advocating to uphold Proposition 8 failed to present any real evidence and had only one witness, David Blackenhorn. Blankenhorn opposes same-sex marriage, but stated that children raised by same-sex parents would benefit if their parents were able to legally marry because of the protections marriage provides. Additionally, despite Blankenhorn's support of upholding Prop 8, he said during his testimony that "we would be more American on the day we permit same-sex marriage than the day before."

Two of the witnesses they originally deposed, Paul Nathanson and Katherine Young, both professors of religious studies at McGill University, ended up testifying on behalf of repealing Prop 8. In his testimony, Professor Nathanson stated that even though some have religious objections to same-sex marriage, the research does not show that children raised by same-sex parents are any less well-adjusted than their peers who were raised by different sex parents.

Additionally, Yes on 8 proponents asserted same-sex marriage should be outlawed because marriage has only been between a man and woman for the past "5000 years."[76] Professor Young, however, said this was not true and stated that same-sex marriage was practiced by Native Americans before colonization, during the Roman Empire, and among female silk workers in China.

During closing arguments, Judge Walker inquired why proponents of Proposition 8 failed to present more witnesses. He asked Cooper, who was advocating on behalf of upholding Proposition 8. "If you've got 7 million Californians who took this position, 70 judges as you pointed out, and this long history as you described, why in this case did you present but one witness on the subject? Why only one witness and I must say his testimony was equivocal in some respects." Cooper, unable to answer the question logically, suggests that Judge Walker go back to his chambers and look up the definition of marriage in the dictionary to show him that marriage is for pro-creation only. "Unless," he retorts, "the book has been written by one of their experts (points to the plaintiff attorneys) or written in the last thirty years."

PERRY V. SCHWARZENEGGER RULING

On August 4, 2010, Judge Walker ruled that Proposition 8 was unconstitutional under the due process and equal protection clause. The court confirmed that there is no rational reason to deny same-sex couples the fundamental right of marriage.

---

76 FOX News Interview with Rev. Rick Warren, Saddleback Church

> *"Proposition 8 fails to advance any rational basis in singling out gay men and lesbians for denial of a marriage license. Indeed, the evidence shows Proposition 8 does nothing more than enshrine in the California Constitution the notion that opposite-sex couples are superior to same-sex couples. Because California has no interest in discriminating against gay men and lesbians, and because Proposition 8 prevents California from fulfilling its constitutional obligation to provide marriages on an equal basis, the court concludes that Proposition 8 is unconstitutional."*

The case is being appealed to the Ninth Circuit and will be reviewed by three judges. These judges will first decide whether or not the case can be appealed by proponents, because Republican Governor Arnold Schwarzenegger and the Democratic Attorney General, Jerry Brown, agree with Judge Walker that Prop 8 is unconstitutional and they want the state to be able to issue marriage licenses to same-sex couples again. However, if the Ninth Circuit Court of Appeals finds Prop 8 proponents have legal standing, *Perry v. Schwarzenegger* is likely to be a landmark case headed all the way to the U.S. Supreme Court.

When that day comes, and if the U.S. Supreme Court finds Prop 8 unconstitutional, it is still unclear if *Perry v. Schwarzenegger* would only strike down California's gay marriage ban to allow same-sex couples in California to begin marrying again or if finding California's Prop 8 marriage ban unconstitutional would lead the U.S. Supreme Court to strike down all same-sex marriage bans, as the Court did with all remaining interracial marriage bans in *Loving v. Virginia (1967)*.

AMERICAN FAMILY VALUES: EQUAL PROTECTION UNDER LAW

In the meantime, we must continue to advocate and educate people about the impact of marriage discrimination in the court of public opinion. Attorney Ted Olson urges Americans who "believe in the words of the Declaration of Independence, in Lincoln's Gettysburg Address, in the 14th Amendment, and in the Constitution's guarantees of equal protection and equal dignity before the law" to not "sit by while this wrong continues. This is not a conservative or liberal issue; it is an American one, and it is time that we, as Americans, embraced it."

I couldn't agree more. I look forward to the day when we can see all people's inherent dignity, worth, and equality recognized by law, a day when we can truly stand as one nation, indivisible, with liberty and justice for all.

SECTION NINE:
TAKING ACTION AND RESOURCES

CHAPTER THIRTY:
GET ENGAGED: MARRIAGE EQUALITY INTERACTIVE RESOURCES

Following are several marriage equality interactive resources including:

1. Questions for Book Club Readers-These questions are designed to stimulate thoughtful conversations and add to an educated debate on the personal as well as the political realities of marriage discrimination.

2. Resources: Educational and Organizational-This section lists educational resources, such as books, movies and other materials related to marriage equality and other LGBT people's rights and issues. It also includes a list of organizations working for LGBT people's equality, rights, and well-being.

3. Gender Neutral Marriage Ceremony-This is a template for ministers, justices of the peace, and any other marriage celebrant who want to conduct a marriage ceremony for same-sex couples or for heterosexual couples who want an egalitarian service and prefer to remove potentially sexist or gender-based language from their ceremony.

4. Example of Non-Binding Resolution in Support of Civil Marriage Equality for City Councils, Human Rights Commissions, Universities, etc.

5. Appendix A: List of links to Prop 8 commercials

Book Club Discussion Questions

1. How do non-gay people benefit from allowing gay people to marry?

2. What is the cost of keeping gay couples separate and unequal?

3. What will LGBT people have to give up for marriage equality?

4. What will straight people have to give up for LGBT people to have marriage equality?

5. Is how we win as important as winning the freedom to marry? Why?

6. How can straight allies best support the marriage equality effort?

7. How does denial of marriage equality for same-sex couples hurt transgender and intersexed people?

8. What does the research say about the effects of constitutional amendments on the psychological health of LGBT people and their families?

9. What part does religion play in the issue of marriage for same-sex couples?

10. What are your reasons for or against marriage rights for same-sex couples?

11. If research shows that marriage has positive physical and psychological benefits for heterosexual couples what would be

the outcome of extending those benefits to same-sex couples? And if the outcome research were positive for same-sex couples as it is with different-sex couples, why would people want to deny same-sex couples that benefit?

12. Do you think same-sex couples will have legal marriage in all 50 states in your lifetime? Why or why not?

Resources: Educational and Organizational

United States Government
White House Comments Line: (202) 456-1111 www.white-house.gov/CONTACT/
Switchboard: 202-456-1414

Congress Phone Number (202) 224-3121 www.house.gov

Department of Defense 703-545-6700 www.defense.gov

Organizations Fighting for Marriage Equality

Marriage Equality USA (MEUSA) www.marriageequality.org

Marriage Equality New York (MENY) www.marriageequalityny.org

Marriage Equality Ireland http://www.marriagequality.ie/

California Faith for Equality www.cafaithforequality.org

Courage Campaign California www.couragecampaign.org

Equal Love Australia www.equallove.info

Freedom to Marry Collaborative www.freedomtomarry.org

I'm for Iowa www.imforiowa.com

Jews for Marriage Equality www.jewsformarriageequality.org

Join the Impact www.jointheimpact.com

Love Exiles International   www.loveexiles.org

Love Warriors   www.lovewarriors.org

Natl. Assoc. for Advancement of Colored People www.naacp.org

National Black Justice Coalition www.nbjc.org

Native Out   www.nativeout.com

Soulforce   www.soulforce.org

Southerners on New Ground   w w w . s o u t h e r n e r s o n n e w -
ground.org

American Civil Liberties Union   www.aclu.org

Freedom to Marry Collaborative   www.freedomtomarry.org

Gay and Lesbian Advocates and Defenders   www.glad.org

Lambda Legal Defense and Education   www.lambdalegal.org

Mexican American Legal Defense   www.maldef.org
and Education Fund

National Center for Lesbian Rights   www.nclrights.org

Support Organizations
Parents, Friends, and Family of Gays and Lesbians   w w w .
pflag.org
(PFLAG)

Straight Spouse Network www.straightspouse.org

Films on Marriage Equality

Freedom to Marry: The Journey to Justice www.freedomtomarry.tv

Pursuit of Equality www.pursuitofequality.com

Freeheld-The Laurel Hester Story www.freeheld.com

The Loving Quilt

The Loving Quilt: A People's Living History of Marriage Equality and Family Justice Movements shows the diversity of LGBTI families with photos and stories about LGBTI families and allies. Visit the website: www.marriageequality.org/index. php?page=quilt

Unlearning Homophobia Series DVDs

To help family members and friends understand their LGBT loved ones, filmmakers Dr. Sylvia Rhue, Dr. Dee Mossbacher, Garrett Lenior, and Peter Barbosa, have created the Unlearning Homophobia Series which includes the documentaries *Straight From the Heart, All God's Children*, and *De Colores*. Available at www.eyebite.com/store.htm

Sample #1 Gender-Neutral Marriage Ceremony

We are gathered today here in the presence of family and friends for the purpose of uniting in marriage _____ and _____, and to share in the joy of this memorable occasion.

Marriage symbolizes the intimate sharing of two lives. It is the development of a balanced relationship that is continually growing and changing. Acceptance of each other's differences and appreciation of each other's individuality creates an atmosphere of understanding and trust where not only joys and successes but also sorrows and disappointments can be shared.

Deep knowledge of each other's feelings can only develop fully with patience, genuine caring and respect. This understanding of each other can be the greatest and most fulfilling experience of your lives.

No other human ties are more tender and no other vows more important than those you now assume. If you both keep these vows, your home will be happy and full of joy.

(Will you please join hands)

The contract of marriage is most solemn and is not to be taken into lightly, but thoughtfully and seriously, and with a deep realization of its obligations and responsibilities.

_____, do you take this person_____, to be your lawful wedded spouse? Do you promise to love and comfort him/her, to honor him/her and keep him/her in sickness and in health, in prosperity and adversity, and forsaking all others, be faithful to him/her?

_____, do you take this person_____, to be your lawful wedded spouse? Do you promise to love and comfort him/her, to honor him/her and keep him/her in sickness and in health, in prosperity and adversity, and forsaking all others, be faithful to him/her?

(Ask one party to repeat)
I,_____, take thee_____, to be my lawful wedded spouse, to have and to hold from this day forward, for better or for worse, for richer or for poorer, in sickness and in health, to love and to cherish.

(Ask next party to repeat)
"I,_____, take thee_____, to be my lawful wedded spouse, to have and to hold from this day forward, for better or for worse, for richer or for poorer, in sickness and in health, to love and to cherish."

(To first party)
Place and hold the ring on the ring finger of your partner's left hand and repeat after me.

"This ring I thee give, in token and pledge of my constant faith and enduring love. With this ring I thee wed."

(To second party)
Place and hold the ring on the ring finger of your partner's left hand and repeat after me.

"This ring I thee give, in token and pledge of my constant faith and enduring love. With this ring I thee wed."

Now that you have joined yourselves in solemn matrimony, may your strive all your lives to meet this commitment with the same love and devotion that you now possess.

BY VIRTUE OF THE AUTHORITY VESTED IN ME AS DEPUTY COMMISSIONER OF CIVIL MARRIAGES, I NOW PRONOUNCE YOU MARRIED UNDER THE LAWS OF THE STATE OF CALIFORNIA.

You may seal your vows with a kiss.

Reprinted with permission from Santa Cruz California County Clerk's Office.

Sample #2 Gender-Neutral Marriage Ceremony

We are joyfully gathered here today to witness and celebrate the joining of _____ and _____ together in marriage.

The contract of marriage is most solemn and is not to be entered into lightly, but thoughtfully and seriously with a deep realization of its obligations and responsibilities.

_____ and _____, By entering into this marriage, you are pledging yourselves to a lifetime in which each will enrich the life of the other. When two people pledge to love and care for each other in marriage, they create a unique spirit, a spirit which minds them closer than any spoken or written words.

The purpose of marriage is to create a loving partnership in which you can express your intimate thoughts and emotions. By working together and planning for the future, you can make your dreams come true.

Insert couples vows here
I understand you have written personal vows to each other.
_____, please read your vows to _____.
And _____, please read your vows to _____.

How very fortunate you are to have found one another. Help each other through all the challenges of life and encourage each other to embrace all the warmth and joys of life and of people. With patience and understanding, support each other's goals, purpose and spirit. Cherish each other and the love you share, and may your future together bring you everlasting happiness.

Please face each other and join hands.

Do you_____, take_____, to be your lawful wedded spouse? To have and to hold from this day forward, for better or for worse, for richer or for poorer, in sickness and in health, to love and to cherish as long as you both shall live?

Do you _____, take _____, to be your lawful wedded spouse? To have and to hold from this day forward, for better or for worse, for richer or for poorer, in sickness and in health, to love and to cherish as long as you both shall live?

Ring Ceremony

_____, the ring please. Place the ring on his/her left ring finger and repeat after me, "I give you this ring, in token and pledge of my constant faith and abiding love. With this ring, I thee wed."

_____, the ring please. Place the ring on his/her partner's left ring finger and repeat after me, "I give you this ring, in token and pledge of my constant faith and abiding love. With this ring, I thee wed."

You have joined yourselves in civil marriage. May you strive all your lives to meet this commitment with the same love and devotion that you now possess. Remember to treat yourselves and each other with respect, and to remind yourselves often of what brought you together today. Give the highest priority to the tenderness, gentleness and kindness that your marriage deserves. And if each of you will take responsibility for the quality of your life together, it will be marked by abundance and delight.

And now, in as much as you_____ and _____ have given and pledged your love and faithfulness, each to the other, and have declared the same by joining hands, I now pronounce you spouses for life.

Ceremony used in San Francisco 2004 when Mayor Gavin Newsom allowed same-sex couples to marry in civil ceremonies.

Sample Non-Binding Resolution for Marriage Equality

Non-binding resolutions for marriage equality are statements of support for organizations, city councils, human rights commissions, universities, etc. to endorse marriage equality. It is a political tool that sends a message in support of marriage equality even if no direct action can be taken to give same-sex couples equal rights. I am attaching the Durham North Carolina City Council's resolution passed August 17, 2009 because I think it is an eloquent example of how these resolutions can give a voice to equality and ending discrimination. In California, we worked hard to get these resolutions passed by local governments and this helped us considerably in passing legislation in support of marriage equality through the assembly and state senate. Marriage Equality could have been a reality in California in 2005 had Gov. Schwarzenegger not vetoed the legislation. Additionally, I believe it was an excellent tool to bring people together to discuss marriage equality in a community setting.

A RESOLUTION IN SUPPORT OF CIVIL MARRIAGE FOR SAME-SEX COUPLES

WHEREAS, The Election Day victories by anti-gay activists in California, Florida, Arizona and Arkansas were a painful reminder that the gay rights movement still faces many challenges; and

WHEREAS, discriminatory marriage laws in the United States deprive same-sex couples of over 1000 federal rights and benefits automatically bestowed by civil marriage including, among others, health care coverage, tax benefits, divorce, domestic violence protections, privileges under immigration and naturalization law, inheritance rights, survivor benefits and child custody; and

WHEREAS, the denial of such benefits has been demonstrated to have significant psychological and social impact on the physical, social, and economic well-being of gay and lesbian couples and their families; and

WHEREAS, the U.S. Supreme Court recognizes marriage as one of the basic civil rights fundamental to our very existence and survival and

WHEREAS, heterosexual relationships have a legal framework for their existence through civil marriage, which provides a stabilizing force. In the United States, with the exception of Massachusetts and Connecticut, same-sex couples are currently denied the important legal benefits, rights and responsibilities of civil marriage. Same-sex couples therefore experience several kinds of state sanctioned discrimination that can adversely affect the stability of their relationships and their mental health; and'

WHEREAS, the love that brings and binds two people of the same, or opposite sex, together transcends gender; and

WHEREAS, as Americans, we must remember a foundational principle of our form of government: all are created equal. Consistent with the pursuit of liberty and justice for all, same-sex couples should have full and equal access to the rights and responsibilities bestowed by civil marriage; and

NOW THEREFORE BE IT RESOLVED that civil marriage for same-sex couples must include all the benefits commonly bestowed upon opposite-sex couples, including, among other rights, healthcare coverage and related decision-making, privileges under immigration and naturalization law, survivor benefits, inheritance rights, and child custody.

BE IT FURTHER RESOLVED, that the City of Durham, endorse and support the rights of same-sex couples to share fully and equally in the rights, responsibilities and commitments of civil marriage.

Thank you, Mayor William V. Bill Bell and the members of the Durham City Council: Cora Cole-McFadden, Farad Ali, Eugene A. Brown, Diane Catotti, Howard Clement, III, and Mike Woodard, for affirming that separate is not equal and that the Bull City supports diversity.

Appendix A-No on Prop 8 Commercials

Sam and Julia Parents of Lesbian Daughter
http://www.youtube.com/watch?v=l6dBUCi32c8&feature=related

Conversation Ad
http://www.youtube.com/watch?v=vB0lZ8XbmJM

Newspaper Voice Over
http://www.youtube.com/watch?v=JHeTVAE4ZkY&feature=related

Diane Feinstein Ad
http://www.youtube.com/watch?v=U7LdC1RxvZg&feature=related

Jack O'Connell, School Superintendent Prop 8 has nothing to do with schools
http://www.youtube.com/watch?v=CIL7PUl24hE

Proponents of Prop 8 are using lies to scare (no real people, voice overs)
http://www.youtube.com/watch?v=vKAqbQlWQhc&feature=related

Discrimination (still photos voice overs)
http://www.youtube.com/watch?v=Oj-0xMrsyxE&feature=related

For Latinos Family is important
http://www.youtube.com/watch?v=I9HfNwMKZ0E&feature=related

Straight Parents
http://www.youtube.com/user/NoOnProp8dotcom

About the Author

Davina Kotulski, Ph.D., is a clinical psychologist, motivational life coach, author of *Why You Should Give A Damn About Gay Marriage* and *Love Warriors: The Rise of the Marriage Equality Movement and Why it Will Prevail.* She is the former Executive Director of Marriage Equality USA.

Davina has been a tireless LGBTQ advocate. She began organizing "Marriage License Counter" protests in 2001 with her now lawfully wedded wife, Molly McKay. On February 12, 2004, Davina and Molly were the 17th couple married in San Francisco. That year Davina organized the "Marriage Equality Express," an educational bus tour across the United States that culminated in the first national marriage equality rally in Washington, DC. She has appeared on CNN, Newsweek, Time and USA Today and in a dozen documentaries including: "Freedom to Marry," and the "Pursuit of Equality." Davina has received numerous awards for her marriage equality advocacy including the "Saints Alive Award" from the Metropolitan Community Church, the Michael Switzer Leadership Award from New Leaf Counseling Center, and she was sainted by the Sisters' of Perpetual Indulgence.

Davina has a private therapy practice in Berkeley, CA and an international coaching practice. She is leading empowerment workshops and seminars for LGBTQ people and is a highly sought after public speaker and consultant.

Websites:
www.lovewarriorsthebook.com
www.davinakotulski.com
www.fearlessqueerness.com

ACKNOWLEDGEMENTS

I want to thank my wife, Molly McKay, for her incredible support and dedication. Molly, you are a dedicated wife, an extraordinary marriage equality leader, and a tireless editor. Thank you for supporting me in living my dream, editing my book and giving me your thoughtful suggestions for additions. I love and admire you for your courage and your commitment to equality for LGBT people.

I want to thank friend/mentor Ericka Lutz for her writing tips and encouragement; Pamela Brown, Marriage Equality USA Policy Director, for her incredible Prop 8 research, helpful suggestion, dedication and friendship, and Richard W. Kotulski for his exceptional web design and technical support!!

Thanks to all the Marriage Equality USA leaders who take a licking and keep on ticking for marriage equality, especially Christine Allen, Dave and Jeff Janis-Kitzmiller, Sam and Julia Thoron, Jennifer Sookne, Marvin Burrows, Frank Howell, Fernando Lopez, John Lewis, Stuart Gaffney, Whitney and Lori Weddell, Kinna and Ashle Crocker, Carole Scagnetti, Terry Stewart, Billy Bradford, Kristin Orbin, Teresa Rowe, Jane Leyland, Terry Gibb, Peter, Geoff, David, David, Beth, Cynthia, Stephanie, Martina, Anita, Lydia, Mo, Gabby, Shelly, Ellen, Bill, Joe, Chari, Jody, Sean, Maya, Karen, Luz, and so many more please know that you are loved and appreciated even if your name is not here. Thanks to my biggest fan Teresa Rowe.

Thanks to Senator Mark Leno for his humanitarianism and leadership, and especially for marrying Molly and I twice (2004 and 2008), Anna Damiani for her never-ending support, Gavin Newsom for his courage, the contributions of Christine

Chavez-Delgado, Dolores Huerta, Sylvia Rhue, Shannon Minter, Mikayla Connell, Masen and Matt at the Transgender Law Center, Emily Doskow at Nolo, Luan Strauss at Laurel Books.

Thanks to Rev. Lindi Ramsden, Kerry Chaplain, Chris Waddling, Garrett Lenoir, Frank and Joe Capley-Alfano, Alison Little and Heidi Vance, Ryan James and Moe Perez. Terri Fabris, the editor for my first book, *Why You Should Give A Damn About Gay Marriage*.

Thanks to friends; Shefa Tsbarry, Rachel Robasciotti, Tara May, Kristen Valus, Alice Lancefield, Lisa Felice, Lisa Fowler, Stephanie Rosenbaum, Gina Meyer, Shar Rednour, Mandy Benson, Sally Steuer, Barbara Gordon, Rev. Ericka Mac, Becky Robbins, Laurie York, Carmen Goodyear, Cary Littel, Carey Shaffer, Cory Nyamora, Wade Meyer, Alison Moncrieff, Dave Nash, Chloe Atkins, Erin Flynn, Dylan Kelly, Amy Suits, Margie Gordillo, Pam Tolbert, and my spiritual leaders, Rev. Joan Steadman, Rev. Gil Olmstead, Robyn Rice-Olmstead, and Camilla Hardmeyer, and others who are in my heart, but who I may have inadvertently forgotten to thank.

Thanks to my family: my mother, Jan Duchon, my father Richard Kotulski, and my brothers Abs and Richard, my sister Kathy. Thanks to Aunt Barbara, Uncle Chuck Whitman, Aunt Vicki, Grandma Elaine, my in-laws, the McKays-Nan, Jim, John, and Heidi, and my sister-in-law Amy and her wonderful family-the Harrisons. To my nieces and nephews: Kyle, Kaylee, Chloe, J.P., Dylan, Levi, Cutter, and Davis. May you all live in a world where marriage equality for your Aunt Molly and Aunt Davina is the rule, not the exception!

Special thanks to my clients, colleagues, and students who have also contributed to my endeavors and to all the people behind the scenes who have contributed to this and other projects. Thank you!

And last but not least, with gratitude to the Great Spirit for guiding me on my path!

www.ingramcontent.com/pod-product-compliance
Lightning Source LLC
Chambersburg PA
CBHW070830310526
45788CB00017B/33